The Waiting Water

signale
modern german letters, cultures, and thought

Series Editor: Paul Fleming, Cornell University
Peter Uwe Hohendahl, Founding Editor

Signale: Modern German Letters, Cultures, and Thought publishes new English-language books in literary studies, criticism, cultural studies, and intellectual history pertaining to the German-speaking world, as well as translations of important German-language works. Signale construes "modern" in the broadest terms: the series covers topics ranging from the early modern period to the present. Signale books are published under a joint imprint of Cornell University Press and Cornell University Library in electronic and print formats. Please see http://signale.cornell.edu/.

THE WAITING WATER

Order, Sacrifice, and Submergence in German Realism

ALEXANDER SORENSON

A Signale Book

CORNELL UNIVERSITY PRESS AND CORNELL UNIVERSITY LIBRARY
ITHACA AND LONDON

Cornell University Press and Cornell University Library gratefully acknowledge the College of Arts & Sciences, Cornell University, for support of the Signale series.

Copyright © 2024 by Alexander Sorenson

All rights reserved. Except for brief quotations in a review, this book, or parts thereof, must not be reproduced in any form without permission in writing from the publisher. For information, address Cornell University Press, Sage House, 512 East State Street, Ithaca, New York 14850.

First published 2024 by Cornell University Press
and Cornell University Library

Library of Congress Cataloging-in-Publication Data

Names: Sorenson, Alexander, 1988– author.
Title: The waiting water : order, sacrifice, and submergence in German realism / Alexander Sorenson.
Description: Ithaca [New York] : Cornell University Press, 2024. | Series: Signale: modern German letters, cultures, and thought | Includes bibliographical references and index.
Identifiers: LCCN 2023054118 (print) | LCCN 2023054119 (ebook) | ISBN 9781501777097 (hardcover) | ISBN 9781501777103 (paperback) | ISBN 9781501777127 (epub) | ISBN 9781501777110 (pdf)
Subjects: LCSH: German literature—19th century—History and criticism. | Water in literature. | Drowning victims in literature. | Order in literature. | Law in literature. | Sacrifice in literature. | Realism in literature.
Classification: LCC PT345 .S67 2024 (print) | LCC PT345 (ebook) | DDC 830.9/1209034—dc23/eng/20240229
LC record available at https://lccn.loc.gov/2023054118
LC ebook record available at https://lccn.loc.gov/2023054119

For my family

How riskily we fared into the morning . . .
—Seamus Heaney, "Seeing Things (I)"

Contents

Acknowledgments ix

Note on Translations xii

Introduction: Between the Surface and the Depths 1

1. Water and Stone: The End of Life and of Sacrifice in Goethe's *Elective Affinities* and Ebner-Eschenbach's *Beyond Atonement* 37

2. The Wide Sea of Light: Hidden Law and Works of Love in Stifter's Early Writing 76

3. *Flumen Publicum*: The Imitation of Right and the Recognition of Rite in Keller's *A Village Romeo and Juliet* 121

4. A Faint Wake: Atonement and Afterward in Storm's Late Works 164

Epilogue: Ophelia and the Boatman 206

Bibliography 243

Index 261

Acknowledgments

I am humbled and very happy to find myself in the lucky position of having more people to thank than memory or space will allow me to list exhaustively here. So, let me preface by saying that I owe all of them, named and not, an unrepayable debt of gratitude.

Thanks are due first and foremost to David Wellbery and Eric Santner, both of whom set an example as scholars and dedicated educators that has been formative for me in more ways than I can say. Catriona MacLeod has likewise offered helpful guidance at numerous junctures, and I thank her for it sincerely. I am further indebted to many other teachers and friends at the University of Chicago and to the inspiring work and conversations that suffuse so many corners of that campus, particularly in the Literature and Philosophy Workshop and the weekly Fellows' colloquium of the Franke Institute for the Humanities, both of which I had the privilege of participating in.

x Acknowledgments

Beyond those walls, I have been fortunate to gain the mentorship as well as friendship of several people in the invigorating intellectual community of Ljubljana, Slovenia; I especially want to thank Mladen Dolar and Jernej Habjan for enjoyable and generous conversations that inspired several important directions of this book early on. I am also grateful to Albrecht Koschorke and Juliane Vogel for facilitating a rewarding research stay at the University of Konstanz in 2016 and for graciously inviting me to sit in on their *Graduiertenkolleg*, "the Real in Modern Culture," which influenced the drafts I completed during my time there. Thomas Carlson and Andrew Norris helmed a wonderfully engaging research group at the Humanities and Social Change Center at the University of California, Santa Barbara, and the year I spent with them and my fellow postdocs was generative both for the later stages of working on this book and for the early stages of a second one. I would also like to acknowledge several other colleagues, interlocutors, and friends I've met at different conferences and symposia over the years, all of whom have positively informed numerous aspects of this book: Paul Irving Anderson, Tove Holmes, John Lyon, Petra McGillen, Peter Pfeiffer, Judith Ryan, Rochelle Tobias, Brian Tucker, Andrew Webber, and Erica Weitzman. At Binghamton University, I've been lucky to experience the kindness and support of colleagues in several departments, and particularly wish to thank Luiza Moreira, Sidney Dement, Carl Gelderloos, and Jeroen Gerrits. I'd also like to thank the Binghamton students from my spring 2023 course about the cultural history of rivers; the energy and insight that they brought to each class session was not only inspiring but also hugely helpful for me as I was putting the finishing touches on the manuscript.

My gratitude also goes to Robert MacFarlane for his kind correspondence and help in accessing Roger Deakin's unpublished writings in the archives at the University of East Anglia. I am likewise grateful to Emily Baumgaertner of the *New York Times* for her fine reporting about the increasing counts of water deaths amid global warming and for connecting me with Deborah Girasek (Uniformed Services University of the Health Sciences), who kindly pointed me toward relevant research on this correlation. My sincere thanks as well to Signale's editorial board and Paul Fleming for taking on this book, to the anonymous reviewers for their insightful and productive feedback on the manuscript, to Wendy Nelson for her attentive copyediting, and to Kizer Walker and Mahinder Kingra for their patience and expert guidance at every turn.

I want to reserve a special place for mentioning teachers who, in addition to innumerable impacts on my learning, have also had a decisive influence on the course of my life at different stages. These include (working backward in chronology) Jost Eickmeyer, Lawrence Wheeler, Kathleen Merrow, John Ott, John Albertson, David Sikking, Orestes Yambouranis, and Ruby Zigon. However, two people need to be singled out as mentors who have shaped me and determined my path the most: to Steven Fuller and Susan Schlesinger I extend *herzlichen Dank* beyond measure.

Finally, the pages that follow could not have been written without the unwavering love and support of my family across time and space, especially Paul, Carmen, Hannah, Norma, Fred, Elin, Greg, Jillayne, and Bob. Family harbors our past and our future, and it is also true that, as Galway Kinnell observes in a poem of his, "around us the meantime is already overflowing" ("A Milk Bottle," line 43); it is with gratitude for that fullness that I dedicate this book, in fullness of love, to Katie, Eamon, and Svea, without whom nothing on earth would be what it is.

Note on Translations

Throughout what follows I have aimed, whenever possible, to use previously published translations of all quoted non-English works and have cited them accordingly in the notes and bibliography. Wherever there is no such citation, the English translation is my own.

The Waiting Water

Introduction

Between the Surface and the Depths

> And everything except the river holds its breath.
> —Elizabeth Bishop, "In the Village"

Evening is falling on a young woman sitting at home, thinking about her family: her mother, her brother, but especially her father. She thinks about her mother's death, brought on by the shock of learning that her son was wanted by the police for theft; the young woman then thinks of how her father had turned to her and sworn that if she should bring any further shame upon the family, he would take his own life. She also thinks of the oath that she swore to him in return, vowing to keep the family's honor intact, and thereby to safeguard his life. But then she thinks about the child that she is bearing in secret, the child she had conceived with the man to whom she had been betrothed, but who, after learning of the scandal caused in town by her brother's crime and arrest, has broken their engagement. She thinks of this, and again of her father, and then of the well that stands near the house; she thinks about how easily one might accidentally slip while drawing water, especially in the dark. She thinks about the moonlight outside, the night around it, and her father's words. Then she rises, takes a pitcher to fill with water from the well, as she often does, and exits the stage. She does not reenter.

So ends Friedrich Hebbel's domestic tragedy *Maria Magdalena*, which appeared in the year 1844 and simultaneously drew to a close the *bürgerliches Trauerspiel* (bourgeois mourning-play) form and heralded the emergence of a new literary and aesthetic movement: German or "Poetic" Realism. The leitmotif that forms the joint of these two generic trajectories—that of a death in water just beyond the borders of vision—is remarkable not only for its chilling starkness but also for its ubiquity in the prose narratives of German Realism. Indeed, of the many motifs that pervade nineteenth-century German fiction, few are more recurrent—or troubling—than drowning. Throughout these stories, characters consistently find themselves before water, presented with the familiar, visible realm above the surface, and in the same moment confront the unobservable, uncanny domain beneath it. Then, with somber regularity, they disappear into the depths. This presents us with the task of determining how to understand this imagery of drowning, with its haunting invocation of solitary death on the societal periphery, alongside the aesthetic and cultural program of a genre like realism—what role do these hidden, individual deaths play within a literary movement that often understood itself to be engaged precisely in *showing* certain truths and realities about the lives we live in the midst of others? Moreover, what might water (and submergence, more specifically) reveal about certain dynamics of the human relationship to natural environments in light of drowning's status as a phenomenon and a topos?

In this book I take such questions as my point of departure, along with the observation that the very fact that these questions might naturally occur to a reader of German Realist texts suggests a need to revise the traditional notion of realist aesthetics as a programmatic effort to make visible the simple contours of everyday life. Focusing upon both canonical and lesser-known texts by Adalbert

Stifter, Gottfried Keller, Theodor Storm, and Marie von Ebner-Eschenbach, in the following chapters I will explore how the theme of drowning becomes host to two concepts fundamental to the epistemology of realist literature: order and sacrifice. I will consider how the narrative logic of drowning stages a conflict between the "surface" domain of lawful order (whether natural, societal, religious, or similar) and the hidden "depths" of subjective interiority. In each of my chosen texts, the resolution of this tension takes the form of an act of sacrifice that either surrenders some part of the self for the sake of order or offers up a form of order for the sake of the self. Consequently, one of my overarching claims in this book is that the space between these spheres—the locus of drowning—is also a space of ethical reflection.

In this introductory chapter I focus primarily on outlining the epistemological as well as conceptual backdrops against which the symbolism of drowning operates in German Realism. Before turning to this, however, it will be necessary to look more closely at the historical and aesthetic context of this particular literary movement.

I.

Instances and images of drowning appear now and again in the prose literature and lyric poetry of Romanticism and the Biedermeier period, but they veritably explode in German Realism—also referred to, in terminology commonly attributed to Otto Ludwig, as Poetic Realism.[1] In this book my core concern and focus in this

---

Epigraph: Elizabeth Bishop, "In the Village (1953)," in *Prose*, ed. Lloyd Schwartz (New York: Farrar, Straus and Giroux, 2011), 78.

1. For example, Novalis's *Heinrich von Ofterdingen* (1802), Droste-Hülshoff's *Ledwina* (1819/1824), and Goethe's *Die Wahlverwandtschaften* (1809) and *Wilhelm Meisters Wanderjahre* (1821/1829), all of which (save for the latter) I consider in more detail elsewhere in this book. Regarding the term "Poetic Realism," see Clifford A. Bernd, *German Poetic Realism* (Boston: Twayne, 1981), 102. Bernd points out elsewhere that this term was not new, as it had in fact been inherited from Scandinavia (specifically Denmark and Sweden), where *poetisk Realisme* had existed since the 1820s. Bernd, *Poetic Realism in Scandinavia and Central Europe, 1820–1895* (Columbia, SC: Camden House, 1995), 2–4, 17, 64.

regard is motivic rather than generic, but it will be helpful nevertheless to approach the question of how to understand the function of water deaths in German Realism via an adjacent and rather overgrown path, one that concerns the long-standing and vexed question of how exactly to characterize this literary movement in the first place.[2] For instance, Marxian critics following the itinerary of Georg Lukács have tended to prefer the qualifier "bourgeois" to "Poetic," while others are happier to oscillate between the two, and all for very specific and ably defended reasons. This seemingly cosmetic quarrel over nomenclature is set against the even larger (and mostly unanimous) agreement to disagree about how "realism" itself should be defined (a state of affairs that Roman Jakobson seems to have felt it necessary to address, with some exasperation, as early as 1921).[3]

Generally speaking, it is often easier to point to clear distinctions between German and other traditions of European realism than it is to articulate a satisfactory definition of one versus the other. In contrast to French Realism, for example, German writers opted not to focus as intently upon the minutiae of daily experience in a newly mass society, nor to investigate the "decentered" zone of this experience that emerged with industrialized capitalism's replacement of older hierarchies and social structures.[4] Instead, they train their gaze upon small, fleeting insights contained within the simplicity of

---

2. For precise as well as broad delineations of German Realism as an epoch and a movement, see the introductory chapters of the following excellent studies: Eric Downing, *Double Exposures: Repetition and Realism in Nineteenth-Century German Fiction* (Stanford, CA: Stanford University Press, 2000); Robert C. Holub, *Reflections of Realism: Paradox, Norm, and Ideology in Nineteenth-Century German Prose* (Detroit: Wayne State University Press, 1991); Claudia Stockinger, *Das 19. Jahrhundert: Zeitalter des Realismus* (Berlin: Akademie, 2010). Compare René Wellek, "The Concept of Realism in Literary Scholarship," *Neophilologus* 45 (1961): 1–20.

3. "By failing to distinguish among the variety of concepts latent in the term 'realism,' theoreticians and historians of art—in particular, of literature—are acting as if the term were a bottomless sack into which everything and anything could be conveniently hidden away." Roman Jakobson, "On Realism in Art," in *Readings in Russian Poetics: Formalist and Structuralist Views*, ed. Ladislav Matejka and Krystyna Pomorska (Normal, IL: Dalkey Archive Press, 2002), 45.

4. Fredric Jameson, "The Realist Floor Plan," in *On Signs*, ed. Marshall Blonksy (Baltimore: Johns Hopkins University Press, 1985), 373–384.

intimate communities and subjective impressions—or, as the German, "Poetic" Realists would put it, upon instances of "the true" that one finds in the interstitial spaces between material reality (*Realität*) and lived reality (*Wirklichkeit*).

"More True than All Reality": The Program of Poetic Realism

Even though some of the better-known practitioners of German Realism generally refrained from weighing in on polemical questions of what "realism" should or should not be understood to mean, a comparable number of theoreticians tried to sketch out a programmatic template. Most prominent among this latter group were Gustav Freytag and Julian Schmidt, whose periodical *Die Grenzboten* (est. 1841) provided a platform for aesthetic debates and formulations of the literary movement they were seeking to codify. Their project seems to have taken form gradually in response to a collective disenchantment with both the speculative acrobatics of Romanticism and the dour materialism of the post-1848 discursive landscape. Accordingly, it was from the hope to find a bridge between the ideal and the real that the synthetic program of Poetic Realism was first enunciated. Schmidt writes, "The belief of the past age was that the ideal is the enemy of reality and does away with it [*hebe sie auf*]; our belief, by contrast, is that the idea *realizes* itself within reality, and we hold this belief to be the principle of the future."[5]

It is worth pausing briefly to remark that although the key issues of interest to German Realists (truth, reality, experience) were located at the fulcrum of divisions within contemporary philosophical debates, only a relatively small group of these authors—Gottfried Keller in particular—are known to have engaged closely with the philosophical thought of the day. This is, of course, not to say that the movement's programmatic theorists, above all Julian Schmidt and Otto Ludwig, in any way refrained from grappling

---

5. Julian Schmidt, "Die neue Generation," in *Bilder aus dem geistigen Leben unserer Zeit* (Leipzig: Duncker und Humblot, 1870), 34 (emphasis added).

with epistemic questions related to their aesthetic project.[6] As a matter of fact, many of the issues and themes that occupied late nineteenth-century philosophers in the German sphere make important appearances in Realist fiction, such as materialism (Keller), philosophies of scientific and historical knowledge (Adalbert Stifter and Conrad Ferdinand Meyer), and postrevolutionary pessimism (Ferdinand von Saar, Theodor Fontane, and Wilhelm Raabe).[7]

In spite of these more abstract contexts, German Realists tended to focus their (and our) attention upon the seemingly mundane patterns of pastoral and domestic life. This was not, however, to cross the threshold into blithely idyllic praise of the simple and pure. Serene, quotidian, and even beautiful things were not to be depicted for their own sake; instead, the truths prone to hide behind and within them were to be *realized*, made "real" on the page, for the sake of a deeper good that might ramify out of their representation and into the minds, the homes, and (ideally) the communities of readers. Theodor Fontane speaks to this very distinction in an 1853 essay on the burgeoning movement, emphasizing that realism is not merely "the naked reproduction of everyday life." Rather, "the real" is the "stuff" (*Stoff*) of realist art, much as the marble block does not constitute the sculpture, but simply the material for it. He continues:

> [Realism] is the reflection of all real life, of all true forces and interests within the element of art. . . . It encompasses all of life in its richness, the greatest as well as the smallest things . . . it includes the highest thoughts and the deepest feeling within its purview . . . for all of this is *real*. Realism does not want the merely sensory, material world [*Sinnenwelt*] and

---

6. John B. Lyon suggests that "Realists . . . represented a unique confluence of materialism and idealism." Ulf Eisele argues that German Realism, despite being a postrevolutionary literary movement, was determined not so much by a social problematic as by a philosophical and epistemological one; in other words, by an engagement not with liberalism but with idealism, and specifically with questions of *Wirklichkeit* versus *Realität* versus *das Wahre*. Lyon, *Out of Place: German Realism, Displacement, and Modernity* (New York: Bloomsbury, 2013), 15; Eisele, "Realismus-Theorie," in *Deutsche Literatur: Eine Sozialgeschichte*, vol. 7, *Vom Nachmärz zur Gründerzeit: Realismus, 1848–1880*, ed. Horst Albert Glaser (Reinbek bei Hamburg: Rowohlt, 1982), 39.

7. See Frederick C. Beiser, *After Hegel: German Philosophy, 1840–1900* (Princeton, NJ: Princeton University Press, 2014).

nothing but this; and it wants least of all the merely tangible [*Handgreifliche*]; but it does want the *true*.[8]

Here Fontane articulates a commitment to "the true"—as opposed to pure imagination or stringent mimesis—which scholars such as Wolfgang Preisendanz have seen the qualification of "Poetic" Realism to reflect.[9] This position raised a predictably complex methodological problem for those writing Poetic Realist theory and narrative: How does one go about capturing and conveying those higher truths immanent to experienced reality without favoring a pursuit of either the ideal or the objective?[10] Schmidt broaches precisely this dilemma in his "warning" that the "new realism" must not be confused with what was previously referred to as "objectivity": "This warning is necessary since in an Idealist like Schiller one finds the opposite of both the principle of objectivity and of realism. Formerly, when one desired that poets be objective this simply meant that they should not impose their person upon the work. . . . At issue in this new principle is no longer inner but external truth, no longer consonance with oneself but consonance with what is commonly called reality."[11]

Schmidt's interest in disambiguating objectivity, truth, realism, and reality has left a lasting impression in secondary scholarship.

---

8. Theodor Fontane, "Unsere lyrische und epische Poesie seit 1848," in *Sämtliche Werke*, vol. 21, pt. 1, ed. Kurt Schreinert (Munich: Nymphenburger, 1963), 12–13 (emphases in the original).

9. Wolfgang Preisendanz, "Voraussetzungen des poetischen Realismus in der deutschen Erzählkunst des 19. Jahrhunderts," in *Wege des Realismus: Zur Poetik und Erzählkunst im 19. Jahrhundert* (Munich: Wilhelm Fink, 1977), 68–91.

10. Compare Hans Blumenberg's genealogy of the *Wirklichkeitsbegriff* vis-à-vis this question; like the Poetic Realists, Blumenberg does not think that literature's inability to mimetically capture reality deprives it of aesthetic potency. However, unlike Schmidt or Fontane, he regards this potency to be poetological rather than methodological in nature—suggesting, for instance, that the underlying theme of the novel-form per se is "its own possibility, not as a fiction of realities, but as a *fiction of the reality of realities*." Blumenberg, "Wirklichkeitsbegriff und Möglichkeit des Romans," in *Nachahmung und Illusion: Kolloquium Gießen Juni 1963; Vorlagen und Verhandlungen*, ed. Hans Robert Jauß (Munich: Eidos, 1964), 27 (emphasis in the original).

11. Julian Schmidt, "Der neueste englische Roman und das Princip des Realismus (1856)," in *Realismus und Gründerzeit: Manifeste und Dokumente zur deutschen Literatur, 1848–1880*, vol. 2, ed. Max Bucher et al. (Stuttgart: J. B. Metzler, 1975), 90.

For instance, Richard Brinkmann's classic 1957 study *Wirklichkeit und Illusion* (Reality and illusion) begins from this very question of how much realism actually has to do with objectivity, shifting attention from realism as a genre of exterior depiction and social criticism in order to focus instead on its proto-phenomenological definition of reality as a category subject as much to the Subject (that is, to the relativity of human perception) as to supposedly stable, a posteriori observation.[12] One year after Brinkmann's monograph appeared, Hannah Arendt, while analyzing the concepts of the public and private spheres, succinctly parsed the understanding of "reality" that Germanists of her day were beginning to identify as one of the *casus adversi* that had spurred the program of Poetic Realism. "The subjectivity of privacy," Arendt writes, ". . . can never replace the reality rising out of the sum total of aspects presented by one object to a multitude of spectators. Only where things can be seen by many in a variety of aspects without changing their identity, so that those who are gathered around them know they see sameness in utter diversity, can worldly reality truly and reliably appear."[13] German Realism presses itself up against an ancient epistemic *donnée*—namely, that reality and objectivity are linked by a shared dependency upon the event of external observation traditionally associated with reason (the Greek word *theoria* being rooted in the act of observation and even spectatorship, hence the etymological kinship of terms such as "theory" and "theater"). Precisely the German Realists' emphasis upon "the true" rather than upon "the merely tangible," as Fontane put it, suggests a desire to break from the scientific rationalism that was exercising such influence within European culture of the late nineteenth century. However, this break would resemble more of a "flickering gaze" playing between the methodical perception of empirical reality and a personalized, Schopenhauerian *Anschauung* (perceptual intuition) of nonempirical but nevertheless universal truths of human experience.

---

12. Richard Brinkmann, *Wirklichkeit und Illusion: Studien über Gehalt und Grenzen des Begriffs Realismus für die erzählende Dichtung des 19. Jahrhunderts* (Tübingen: Niemeyer, 1957).

13. Hannah Arendt, *The Human Condition* (Chicago: University of Chicago Press, 1998), 57.

Following this thread, Preisendanz argues that German Realists (Otto Ludwig in particular) regarded their literary project as one of transfiguration (*Verklärung*), not mimetic accuracy. For Preisendanz, the very phrase "Poetic Realism" reflects the movement's frank acknowledgment that art can never honestly purport to capture reality. The modifier "poetic" acknowledges this gap between mimesis and reality, but simultaneously designates it as a site in which the true can be manifested through a transfigurative process.

This invites us to think back to Schmidt, who stressed that even though realist literature should not necessarily pursue the strict objectivity that idealist writers such as Friedrich Schiller were thought to lack, it nevertheless should strive to convey a certain degree of what he calls "external truth." Ironically enough, in a short text by Schiller himself we can find a striking anticipation of what Schmidt seems to be after in a realism that is not reducible to pure mimesis but that reflects reality nonetheless. In his brief but rich essay "Über den Gebrauch des Chors in der Tragödie" (On the use of the chorus in tragedy), which was published as a foreword to his 1803 drama *Die Braut von Messina* (*The Bride of Messina*), Schiller assigns both structural and aesthetic importance to the modern tragic chorus as a kind of foreign body that, far from upholding classicism's obsession with verisimilitude, constitutes an "Außending" (outside thing) within the economy of the tragedy.[14] By drawing attention to its own artificiality as something "inserted" into the drama, the chorus makes an incision of sorts into the mimetic tissue of the play, interrupting the illusory spell of the onstage narrative. This is important for Schiller because, in his view, poetic art cannot—and should not attempt to—*replicate* empirical reality or experience. Instead, he argues, it more properly functions as a vehicle of higher truth—not merely of "the semblance of truth" that is achieved by an artwork's generic pursuit of "the real," but instead of "truth itself, resting on the sure and deep ground of nature."[15]

---

14. Friedrich Schiller, "Über den Gebrauch des Chors in der Tragödie," in *Sämtliche Werke: Historisch-kritische Ausgabe in zwanzig Bänden*, vol. 20, ed. Otto Güntter and Georg Witkowski (Leipzig: Hesse und Becker, 1910), 251.
15. Schiller, "Über den Gebrauch des Chors," 257–258.

According to Schiller, in a modern tragedy the chorus's primary function as the *Außending* is first to open up and subsequently to illuminate a divide between the sensible and the ideal, which he identifies as the two principal elements of poetry (*Poesie*). It is only within this gap between mimesis and poiesis that an artwork can become "more true ... than all reality and more real than all experience."[16] While such language could easily lend itself to an aesthetic or possibly even a metaphysical mantra such as those for which Schiller and his milieu were well known, one might also read it in a different mode. More precisely, one might interpret the gap that is prized open by an *Außending* as a poetological acknowledgment that a truly mimetic realism is just as implausible as a wholly ideal realism, and therefore as a precursor to the acknowledgment (or is it more a declaration?) implicit in Ludwig's synthetic locution of *Poetic Realism*—a crystalline instance of "both/and" usurping "either/or."

Drowning and the Narrative Landscape

Let me now take back up my original subject of drowning-as-leitmotif by posing the following question: Might water perform some variation of the function that Schiller ascribes to the *Außending*? To be sure, its narrative operation is less extreme than Schiller's idea of a medial break in verisimilitude itself; drowning does not take us, as readers, "out" of a text in the same way that an unexpected choral ode might shake transfixed *spectateurs idéaux* from their convinced state. But it does tug at a certain corner of the diegetic fabric, drawing our attention to a vanishing point of our readerly perception that has suddenly revealed itself in a place we would not necessarily have expected. After all, water is internal to the narrated world, as it is to the real world—it is everywhere, a ubiquitous and typically innocuous part of any German Realist landscape—and yet, when it transforms into a site of death and, most significantly, of disappearance, its homeliness becomes at once *unheimlich*. Just as actual water (at least in our usual experience of it) is constituted as much by its surface as its depths, so too do the waterways of this literature seem, strangely,

---

16. Schiller, "Über den Gebrauch des Chors," 256, 253.

to form both an inside and an outside of the narrative stage, residing in the background all along and yet in critical instants seeming suddenly to invade the flow of the drama almost from within.

How does this stand in relation with German Realism's desired aesthetics? We might recall Fontane's 1853 essay, in which he claims that realism "does not want the merely sensory, material world and nothing but this; and it wants least of all the merely tangible; but it does want the *true*." Particularly crucial for our purposes, however, is Fontane's next assertion: "Realism excludes nothing except that which is false, forced, nebulous, died off.... Once again: it lets the dead, or at least deadness as such, rest [*er läßt die Toten oder doch wenigstens das Tote ruhen*]."[17] If this is indeed so, then we must once again ask: Why is there so much drowning in this epoch?

A perceptive essay by Marianne Wünsch gestures in a helpful direction. She first notes that death plays not only a quantitatively more prominent role in German Realism than it had in immediately preceding literary movements, but also a qualitatively different role: whereas death had been a "functional repository for other problems" in the *Goethezeit*, in realism *it* is the problem to be confronted. In Wünsch's view this is because by the middle of the nineteenth century there is no longer a common "system of sensemaking" like the one that had perdured in the Enlightenment, Romantic, and Biedermeier epochs (that is, either a Judeo-Christian or a vaguely Platonic notion of an afterlife). Death in realism instead emblematizes the human experience of reality itself "as a temporal process, as something in transformation."[18] This harmonizes in several respects with the view presented by Joachim Pfeiffer, who remarks that the nineteenth and twentieth centuries bear witness to the generalized phenomenon of "repression of one's own death" that would attract Freud's and Heidegger's attention (along with that of numerous Expressionist artists) in the years following the Great War. According to Pfeiffer, the "aporetic or antinomian structure" of this unconscious-consciousness of finitude becomes both a point of fascination within,

---

17. Fontane, "Lyrische und epische Poesie," 13–14.
18. Marianne Wünsch, "'Tod' in der Erzählliteratur des deutschen Realismus," *Jahrbuch der Raabe-Gesellschaft* 40 (1999): 1, 7.

and a motor for, literary production during the long, increasingly disenchanted nineteenth century famously described by Max Weber, thus leading literature to step into a role that in prior centuries was performed alternately by religion and myth.[19] Wünsch, for her part, notes that the German Realists typically present death as an ontological transition, and then she remarks how "truly and shockingly often one finds death by drowning. . . . The sphere of death lies either under or outside normal reality, concealed beneath the surface."[20]

Wünsch's and Pfeiffer's observations sound a commanding keynote; after all, what we have seen emerge from the programmatic formulations of Poetic Realism is a project not of fixation upon the world's objective exteriors, nor of communion with the transcendent *I* of Romantic art and philosophy, but instead of what Preisendanz calls *Verklärung*—of truth's transfigurative mediation via the poetically real, actual, and true rather than either the speculatively ideal or scientifically empirical. It would therefore seem, at least at this initial stage, that the recurrence of drowning in German Realist literature does not so much contradict as recast Fontane's insistence that realism should let "the dead, or at least deadness as such, rest"—for the prevalence of death in these texts certainly suggests it to be a truth of substantial importance for those who wrote them. If this is the case, what is poetically significant about drowning may not so much be its removal of death from view as its emphasis of death's embeddedness within reality—within the literal as well as psychic landscapes of human experience.

The question of what exactly might be embedded within these narrative "landscapes" of German Realism invites a brief comparison with those of its most significant predecessor, Romanticism. In a valuable study, Kate Rigby shows how Romanticism, in broad re-

---

19. Joachim Pfeiffer, *Tod und Erzählen: Wege der literarischen Moderne um 1900* (Tübingen: Max Niemeyer, 1997), 4–6. Relatedly, Pfeiffer suggests, because the modern age fails to articulate a consistent or "homogonous image of death" to replace that of bygone ones, the problem of mortality lends itself especially well to literary experimentation, and indeed, even takes on a certain narrative impetus in its own right (8).

20. Wünsch, "'Tod' in der Erzählliteratur," 9.

action against Cartesian, Newtonian, and Enlightenment accounts of the natural world, sought to revitalize cultural understandings of nature by portraying it as animate, sacred, and, ultimately, inherently poetic.[21] According to Rigby, German as well as English Romantic treatments of the natural landscape, whether literary, philosophical, or artistic, all shared in an underlying sense of that landscape's essential coherence with the *Geist* of the human subject perceiving it. Pierre Hadot sums up this idealist grounding of the Romantic outlook on the natural world as a realization "that Nature is nothing other than Spirit unaware of itself, that the Non-Ego known as Nature is ultimately identical to the Ego, and that Nature is the genesis of the Spirit."[22]

Similarly, as Joseph Leo Koerner has elegantly demonstrated, the actual aesthetic praxis of certain Romantic artists and writers expanded upon these broader theories about nature's animate qualities. Caspar David Friedrich's paintings, for instance, frequently toy with the aforementioned questions of whether nature is theophanic, divine, or perhaps neither, but ultimately joins the work of other Romantic artists and thinkers whose representations of the natural world extend beyond matters of sacrality and emotional response, "distinguish[ing] themselves by their unique fusion of nature and consciousness, a fusion which occurs not only in the landscapes they represent (as when the poet's perceiving mind seems to merge with the scene perceived), but as well, and more radically, in the way these landscapes address their readers or viewers."[23] In Friedrich's case, Koerner argues, this address consists in making the very subjectivity of the viewer—as well as that of Friedrich himself and even the artist as such—the "subject" of the landscape in a doubled sense,

---

21. Kate Rigby, *Topographies of the Sacred: The Poetics of Place in European Romanticism* (Charlottesville: University of Virginia Press, 2004), 53.

22. Pierre Hadot, *The Veil of Isis: An Essay on the History of the Idea of Nature*, trans. Michael Chase (Cambridge, MA: Harvard University Press, 2006), 273. Also see Isaiah Berlin, *The Roots of Romanticism*, ed. Henry Hardy (Princeton, NJ: Princeton University Press, 1999), esp. 107–136.

23. Joseph Leo Koerner, *Caspar David Friedrich and the Subject of Landscape* (London: Reaktion, 2009), 22, 113.

insofar as the depicted environment of the painting both elicits *and* reflects the experience of viewing it, thereby revealing this very experience as what was in fact being represented and viewed all along.

A decade or two after the dissipation of Romanticism as an agentive movement, the role of the landscape was inherited in many respects from the Romantics by the German Realists while also undergoing a notable shift: On the one hand, in realist narratives the natural environment continues to serve as a reflective surface for the human interior, but now it does so by giving external form to that which is hidden, unseen, and unacknowledged rather than that which more readily lends itself to epistemic and aesthetic presentation (such as beauty, reason, organic processes). As such, the function of nature in German Realism anticipates a recognizably modern paradigm in which what would come to be called the unconscious quietly emerges into view via everyday spaces and landscapes (especially watery ones), yet this very mechanism of emergence also recalls the Romantic paradigm of animated, or even sacred, topographies. In the literature under consideration in this book, the thematic vessels of such emergence are neither Spirit nor the psyche, however, but sociopoetic structures of law and sacrifice. We must therefore establish the basic parameters for what law and sacrifice entail in the context of German Realist aesthetics, and our first step will be to outline some of the primary qualities of order and offering that have been articulated at various points in European cultural and intellectual history. Doing so will allow us to then take note of how the German tradition received them into the nineteenth century.

II.

Legacies of Law

A good place to look first—for conceptual rather than chronological reasons—is Thomas Aquinas's hypothesis that the very word for law in Latin (*lex*) derived from the verb "to bind" (*ligare*), "because law obliges persons to act," a dynamic that signals human reason's innate attunement to external—and ultimately, for Aquinas, divine—

ordinance.[24] More particularly, though, it is the ties linking the external world and human understanding that, in the eighteenth century, Giambattista Vico would identify as the shared root of both law and the composition and comprehension of written language (*legere*). Vico suggests that law originated from an elemental human impulse to gather and bind together certain things that otherwise would have remained dissolute, uncontained, and inconsistent. As Aquinas had done five centuries before him, Vico grounds his hypothesis in the philology of law itself. While discussing the "rustic or sylvan origins" of the Latin language, he chooses *lex* as an example:

> First it must have meant a collection of acorns. Thence we believe is derived . . . *illex*, the oak, . . . for the oak produces the acorns by which the swine are drawn together. *Lex* was next a collection of vegetables, from which the latter were called *legumina*. Later on, at a time when the vulgar letters had not yet been invented for writing down the laws, *lex* by necessity of civil nature must have meant a collection of citizens . . . so that the presence of the people was the *lex*, or "law." . . . Finally, collecting letters, and making, as it were, a sheaf of them for each word, was called *legere*, reading. (§240)[25]

Vico understands law primarily in terms of its capacity for spatial, conceptual, or temporal longevity, which results from placing distinct elements in relation to one another. If, as he proposes, the essence of law—like reading—is enmeshed with the act of gathering

---

24. Thomas Aquinas, *On Law, Morality, and Politics*, trans. Richard J. Regan (Indianapolis: Hackett, 2002), 11 [*Summa Theologiae*, Q. 90, A. 1, Obj. 3], 18 [*ST*, Q. 91, A. 2, *ad*. 3]. Medieval theologians, including Aquinas himself, commonly cite book 1 of Augustine's *De libero arbitrio* (395 CE) as the *locus classicus* for this idea.

25. Giambattista Vico, *The New Science (Third Edition of 1744)*, trans. Thomas Bergin and Max Fisch (Ithaca, NY: Cornell University Press, 1984), 78. Heidegger, while tracing the significance of the Greek verb *legein* and its derivative *logos* in his 1935 lectures on metaphysics, highlights the same etymology of "gathering" as Vico does with respect to *legere*. However, while Vico suggests that the primordial logic of gathering lies at the root of positive law, Heidegger more dramatically locates the "gathering gatheredness" (*sammelnde Gesamtheit*) of *logos* at the core of Being's very essence. (Interestingly, he goes on to link this essence with *physis*, which since Aristotle had designated "natural law" vis-à-vis positive law and custom [*nomos*]). Martin Heidegger, *Einführung in die Metaphysik* (Tübingen: Niemeyer, 1987), 94–100.

together separate things in order to comprehend them in their new jointure, then it is also enmeshed with the human activity of bringing consciousness into contact with nature, of *linking* the interior to the exterior. Here, law and literature, *lex* and *legere* align in their shared orientation toward reality.

Vico provides an important precedent for nineteenth-century German thought on law by emphasizing the elemental, innately human interest in forging a meaningful link between the particular and the universal, and in encapsulating within language a distinct observation or judgment about reality that can apply—that is, that can *bind*—as true across different times, places, and communities. These themes retained a central place in the established institution of German legal philosophy (embodied by figures such as Friedrich Karl von Savigny) as well as in new campaigns (such as that of his student Jacob Grimm) to restore law to its "proper" role as a fixture of national culture and poetic heritage.[26] Given this network of subjects—reality, language, community—it is unsurprising that law would eventually become a topic of interest for a literary movement such as German Realism. However, this relevance is more complicated than first glance might suggest, for although law was traditionally associated with the action of gathering and linking together, within German Realist narratives law is more often the backdrop—if not the catalyst—of characters' removal *from* order and boundedness. And, most paradoxically, the root cause of this removal is often the characters' desire precisely for lawfulness itself.

---

26. On the history of German legal theory in the nineteenth century—and particularly the conflicts between Savigny's "Romanism" and Grimm's Romanticism—see James Q. Whitman, *The Legacy of Roman Law in the German Romantic Era: Historical Vision and Legal Change* (Princeton, NJ: Princeton University Press, 1990), esp. x–xiv, 200–210; Theodore Ziolkowski, *The Mirror of Justice: Literary Reflections of Legal Crises* (Princeton, NJ: Princeton University Press, 1997), 188–210; Peter Stein, *Roman Law in European History* (Cambridge: Cambridge University Press, 1999), 118ff; Thomas Oliver Beebee, *Citation and Precedent: Conjunctions and Disjunctions of German Law and Literature* (New York: Continuum, 2012), esp. 45–47.

Parenthesis: *Oikonomia*

When it comes to reading and analyzing literature of the nineteenth century, which is my central aim in this book, an especially pertinent register of lawfulness to bear in mind is equally contemporary and ancient, and that is the "law of the household," the *nomos* of the *oikos*: *oikonomia*, economy. This is not merely because the plots of so many works of European realist fiction deal concretely with matters (or, better, the material conditions) of industrialized capital. The conceptual framework of economy offers a useful repertoire of interpretive tools not just for the question of a given narrative's subject matter, but perhaps much more for that of the "matter of subjects"—of human life, which, together with the significatory impetus of the natural landscape, is at the heart of German Realism. Till Breyer, invoking Koselleck, has suggested that there is a "temporalization" (*Verzeitlichung*) of the concept of capital around 1830 that coincides with its thematization in literature—specifically, "the reproduction and accumulation of capital, appearing as a liminal figure within the interstices of social reproduction."[27] Within subsequent nineteenth-century literary and economic texts alike, he notes, one finds proliferous imagery of capital's "fruitfulness" (*Fruchtbarkeit*) and "fertilization" (*Fruchtbarmachung*), including explicit comparison with natural and human processes of (re)generation, which would indicate that by the 1850s capital had come to denote not merely productive activity, wealth, or exchange, but an intrinsic dynamic of life itself.[28]

The two arenas of capital's conceptual expansion described by Breyer (objects and life processes) are also key areas of concern for realist narrative, particularly in their respective capacities to manifest the material and immaterial registers of order that are inherent not only to economy, but also to multiple figurations of law (as well

---

27. Till Breyer, *Chiffren des Sozialen: Politische Ökonomie und die Literatur des Realismus* (Göttingen: Wallstein, 2019), 141–142. He discusses Freytag's 1855 novel *Soll und Haben* as an exemplary instance of this conceptual imagery (149–154).
28. Breyer, *Chiffren des Sozialen*, 143.

as to sacrifice, as we will see shortly). Those same registers are also at the forefront of Eric Santner's theorization of "the flesh," which he defines as "a spectral carnality that forms at and as the unstable jointure of the somatic and the normative dimensions of human life."[29] According to Santner, an inaugural such instantiation of this flesh was a certain "surplus of immanence" that got redistributed from the sovereign monarch's "glorious second body" to the common body politic during the gradual transition from early modernity to modernity proper, and that has perdured into the present day as a kind of *surcharge* of political and public life.[30] Santner picks up this thread in a recent study, suggesting that one of the more vital domains of this surcharge is the same one at issue for classical Marxism, which comes into view "once the political theology of sovereignty was displaced by the political theory of popular sovereignty along with the doctrines and practices of capitalist political economy."[31] That is, the dislocated immanence of the sovereign's symbolic flesh takes up new residence among the various "laws of the household" that oversee labor's generation of surplus value, becoming the new fabric (or skin) of the modern human subject's life among, and libidinal imbrication with, objects and their exchange.[32]

Breyer's and Santner's respective approaches to the concept of economy open up a number of views onto how nineteenth-century literature might present not just law but also sacrifice as exercising a hold over the collective "flesh" of its narratives' characters. A hold, that is, over the zone of contact between the ancient Greek categories of *hyle* (matter), *soma* (body), and *nomos* (law) in which embodied selves and material objects become entangled with symbolic values and structures of meaning. In this direction, another helpful thinker to invoke in passing is Georges Bataille, whose 1949 text *La*

---

29. Eric L. Santner, *The Weight of All Flesh: On the Subject-Matter of Political Economy* (Oxford: Oxford University Press, 2015), 238.
30. Eric L. Santner, *The Royal Remains: The People's Two Bodies and the Endgames of Sovereignty* (Chicago: University of Chicago Press, 2011), e.g., 61, 82, 245–246.
31. Santner, *Weight of All Flesh*, 242.
32. Santner, *Weight of All Flesh*, 56.

Part maudite (*The Accursed Share*) develops the idea that violent sacrifice restores a "true" relationship between the human subject and the world, which the normal order of existence otherwise corrupts. Bataille argues that because sacrifice destroys its object without *utilizing* it, such rituals revive an ancient "intimacy" between humans and nature wherein things do not exist merely as objects to which use-value is ascribed. In other words, sacrifice reestablishes the distinction between objects and things. Moreover, this "profitless consumption" endows sacrifice with a rare capacity to dissolve the "surplus energy" that human existence—by means of both biological life and economic production—constantly creates but can never wholly expend.[33]

What can be gleaned from this brief parenthetical excursus, not so much on economic theory as on theories of economy? On the one hand, the kinship Breyer posits between ancient conceptions of natural and familial procreation and emerging ones of capitalistic production, reproduction, and accumulation pertains to an underlying paradigm of *life*, as teased out by Santner in turn. Yet, on the other hand, these very same themes equally imply those of dissolution, death, and loss that are inherent not only to the conceptions of sacrifice that we will now survey, but also to the proto-modernist tendencies of literature in the "long" nineteenth century underscored, as we've seen, by Joachim Pfeiffer. Whether in its religious, mythic, economic, or even political-theological valences, the pervasive function of sacrifice—like that of law—within German literature of this period will invite us to wonder, ultimately, whether it is more concerned with life or with death.

Legacies of Sacrifice

For twentieth-century thinkers and critics, sacrifice—and particularly its relation to law—fairly exploded into the foreground as a subject of study. This, of course, did not take place *ex nihilo* but arose gradually out of a common interest in sacrifice that was shared by many of the

---

33. Georges Bataille, *The Accursed Share: An Essay on General Economy*, vol. 1, trans. Robert Hurley (New York: Zone Books, 1993), 56–61.

burgeoning academic disciplines of the nineteenth century. It stirred first in continental philosophy, before passing through history and anthropology. A primary aspect of sacrifice that drew the attention of these various fields—violence—is also the chief aspect that distances their analyses of sacrifice and law from the function that these two concepts perform in the literature of German Realism. Before we can address that, though, we must first come to terms with the more immediate difficulty presented by the multiplicity of definitions and understandings of what sacrifice means in the first place.

In a recent book, Terry Eagleton has outlined several of the foundational theories, beginning with Edward Burnett Tylor's account of sacrifice as the surrender of something valuable in the form of a gift (*Primitive Culture*, 1871), to William Robertson Smith's designation of it as a symbolic feast (*Religion of the Semites*, 1889), or Henri Hubert's and Marcel Mauss's influential explication of it as an attempt to mediate between the sacred and the profane (*Essai sur la nature et la fonction du sacrifice* [*Essay on the Nature and Function of Sacrifice*], 1899). However, as Eagleton observes, the overarching aim of sacrifice, whether in the literal immolation of an object or the figurative (that is, moral) offering up of one's impulses and desires, is always to make possible the establishment and maintenance of civilization.[34] Here one cannot help but think as well of the key points of inquiry in Giorgio Agamben's *Homo Sacer* project, particularly in the inaugural volume's analysis of the ancient Roman concept of "sacred life" as a culturally foundational conjunction of law and sacrifice. According to this precept, Agamben reports, in Roman society the life of a legally designated "sacred man" could be violently extinguished with impunity, yet was forbidden from being extinguished via sacrificial ritual. Consequently, for Agamben it is law rather than religion that serves as the primary context for tracing the possible meanings of *sacer* as both "holy" and "accursed," and thus for understanding

---

34. Terry Eagleton, *Radical Sacrifice* (New Haven, CT: Yale University Press, 2018), 3–19. Another helpful resource in this regard is Julia Meszaros and Johannes Zachhuber, eds., *Sacrifice and Modern Thought* (Oxford: Oxford University Press, 2013).

sacrifice in the first place as a process of "making sacred" (*sacrificare*) a particular object (*sacrificium*) by setting it apart (*sacrare*) for dedication (*sacratio*), either as something hallowed to be offered up or as something unclean to be purged.[35]

Eagleton's and Agamben's studies provide a helpful theoretical backdrop for considering how nineteenth-century culture revised the use of sacrifice as an aesthetic trope, gradually shifting emphasis from the mythic and tragic paradigms of ritual death that had been popular in eighteenth-century classicist drama to an ethical and secular register of self-offering, abstention, and exchange. As Derek Hughes has argued, the specific theme of human (as opposed to animal or vegetal) sacrifice became disentangled from theology in nineteenth-century art and literature. In the preceding century, the symbolism of sacrifice had frequently been utilized in connection with religious and social institutions, but Hughes suggests that this ends with Romanticism, after which "human sacrifice," in particular, "predominantly becomes a means of exploring and articulating the subjective."[36]

In broad terms, then, sacrifice made its entrance into nineteenth-century culture through a gradual process of disassociation from its original mythic, tragic, and spiritual frameworks of meaning, becoming invested with hermeneutic and metaphorical value in place of a traditionally more literal significance. As a consequence, the motif of sacrifice began to dilate and extend, coming to constitute an important aspect of numerous aesthetic and discursive programs, from Friedrich Schlegel's romanticism,[37] to theorizations of the

---

35. Giorgio Agamben, *Homo Sacer: Sovereign Power and Bare Life*, trans. Daniel Heller-Roazen (Stanford, CA: Stanford University Press, 1998), 71–83.

36. Derek Hughes, *Culture and Sacrifice: Ritual Death in Literature and Opera* (Cambridge: Cambridge University Press, 2007), 151.

37. In his *Ideen* (1800), for instance, Schlegel posits the ultimate sacrifice to be that of the artist, the sole figure capable of serving as a "mediator" (*Mittler*) between the human and the divine: "A mediator is whoever perceives the divine in himself, and whoever sacrifices himself to preach, proclaim and present the divine to everyone through morals and actions, words and deeds." Friedrich Schlegel, "Ideas," in *The Early Political Writings of the German Romantics*, ed. Frederick C. Beiser (Cambridge: Cambridge University Press, 1996), 128–129.

tragic,[38] to the actual systems of philosophers such as Hegel, Kierkegaard and Nietzsche.[39]

One could conceptualize this gradual shift in cultural understandings of sacrifice as a pendulum that first began to swing away from themes of ritual violence in the early nineteenth century, then came to rest over the ethics of self-offering during the epoch of German Realism, only to swing back again toward issues of violence and social origins as the century turned. This is certainly borne out by the more influential modern accounts of sacrifice, such as Freud's *Totem and Taboo* (1913), René Girard's *Violence and the Sacred* (1972), Walter Burkert's *Homo Necans* (1972), and the aforementioned works by Agamben and Bataille. What these thinkers all have in common is a basic understanding of sacrifice as a domain of violence, negation, or extirpation that is innate to the origins of human culture. They are salient for modern discourse on sacrifice and its relation to law, and therefore important to keep in mind for any project that deals with it narrowly or broadly (including the present one). However, the texts under investigation in this book call out for readings that frequently lead away from those theoretical edifices. That is because German Realism does not depict bourgeois society as a latent suppression or a lithe manipulation of violent impulses by means of legally and ethically codified institutions. Instead, my chosen narratives tell of ideological, monetary, and moral self-sacrifice carried out by private individuals *amid* established lawfulness. In these stories, sacrifice unfolds upon the small stage of interpersonal and social relationships rather than the grand proscenium of myth or war, and comprises the offering up of one form of order for the sake of another rather than the bloody appeasement of a deity or a political cause.

The nature of this contrast can be helpfully illustrated by tracing an ancient shift that took place within Judeo-Christian thinking

---

38. As Peter Szondi outlines, within the German sphere alone the concept of tragedy and its relation to sacrifice attracted sustained attention from some of the nineteenth century's most iconic figures, including Goethe, Schelling, Hegel, Hölderlin, Schopenhauer, Hebbel, and Nietzsche. Szondi, *Versuch über das Tragische* (Frankfurt am Main: Insel), 1964.

39. See Paulo Diego Bubbio, *Sacrifice in the Post-Kantian Tradition: Perspectivism, Intersubjectivity and Recognition* (Albany: SUNY Press, 2014).

about sacrifice, which Moshe Halbertal describes as a transition from a paradigm of "sacrificing to" to one of "sacrificing for." Halbertal explains that during the Second Temple period, burnt offerings had been a common liturgical practice. After the destruction of the Jerusalem Temple in 70 CE and the concomitant transition to synagogue-based worship and rabbinic theology, however, ritual sacrifice (hitherto the purview of temple priests) was replaced with nonviolent modes of offering and appeasement such as penitence, charity and prayer.[40] In other words, a shift occurs from the semiotic model of immolating an *object* (such as an animal) that *stands for* something else (such as the sacrificer's guilt, a supplicant community's vital resources, and so forth) to one in which the sacrificer *directly* offers a part of the *self* in a non-negational mode, thereby entering the moral and ethical (as opposed to formally ritual) sphere.

While the kinds of sacrifice that appear in the narratives I explore in this book vary—some are conscious, others retroactively acknowledged, some economically rooted, others ideologically so—their mode is that of "sacrificing for" rather than "sacrificing to," in Halbertal's terms. More particularly, the sacrifices that we encounter in the literature of German Realism focalize concrete instants of *decision* in which one possible course of action that accords with order (that is, certain norms, codes and laws) is relinquished for the sake of—or at the expense of—another one. These cases of sacrifice therefore differ significantly from the violently literal rites with which Burkert, Girard, Bataille, or Agamben associate the term.

By addressing the immediate question of how and why the theme of drowning is linked to order (especially various forms of law) and sacrifice in German Realist narrative, it will be possible by the end of the book to address a second, but much larger question: What function does drowning, as an emblem of the interrelation between law and sacrifice, serve in the context of German Realism as a whole? As I will demonstrate in the following chapters, this function is

---

40. Moshe Halbertal, *On Sacrifice* (Princeton, NJ: Princeton University Press, 2012), 48–53, 62. Also see Guy G. Stroumsa, *The End of Sacrifice: Religious Transformations in Late Antiquity*, trans. Susan Emanuel (Chicago: University of Chicago Press, 2009), 63–69; Kathryn McClymond, *Beyond Sacred Violence: A Comparative Study of Sacrifice* (Baltimore: Johns Hopkins University Press, 2008).

comparable to what Schiller's essay on the tragic chorus termed an *Außending*. More specifically, the drowning scene in nineteenth-century German literature comes to function as a narratological mechanism whereby an integral but unobtrusive element of the narrative landscape suddenly transforms into a site in which time gets distended within an instantaneous "blink of an eye" (*Augenblick*), at once "standing outside" the fabric of the story even while remaining intrinsic to it. In order to establish an adequate frame through which to examine this discrete yet consequential feature of German letters, however, it will be helpful for us to pull back once again and consider several dimensions of the drowning motif (and submergence more broadly) that extend beyond the sphere of German Realism while at the same time forming part of the motivic context in which it participates.

III.

One especially crucial such dimension of drowning as a literary motif is its consistent gendering by and within the European (by no means solely German) imaginary. In the art and literature of nineteenth-century Britain, for instance, suicide by drowning came to function as a feminine topos par excellence, though its roots were Elizabethan rather than Victorian:[41] by the 1840s, evocations and depictions of Shakespeare's Ophelia abounded within British as well as French cultural spaces, and it is an interesting detail—one to which I will return in the epilogue—that her popularity as an explicit motif did not attain the same prominence within the German sphere until later in the century. Nevertheless, as I have already in-

---

41. As Barbara Gates suggests, this is evidenced not only by the high number of artistic and literary representations of this motif—including in notable texts by Dickens, Hood, and Wilde, as well as in paintings by Millais, Solomon, and Watts—but also by virtue of the fact that many of these works overtly invoke this motif *as a* motif. In other words, for Victorian artists and authors the trope of the woman who has drowned herself is not simply a noun, but a verb: it is something that is consciously "troped." Gates, *Victorian Suicide: Mad Crimes and Sad Histories* (Princeton, NJ: Princeton University Press, 1988), 135–141.

dicated, the phenomenon of drowning is something that is prevalent within German literature of the nineteenth century as a whole, and remarkably so in the epoch of realism.

Prior even to this, though, the German literary treatment of water and the bodies that drown in it is strikingly diverse with respect to gender as well as age, class, and socioeconomic situation. One of the most distressing discoveries about the nineteenth-century German canon (beginning with Goethe's *Die Wahlverwandtschaften* [*Elective Affinities*]) that this book will relay is the predominance of children who face or succumb to the hazards of water. In texts like Stifter's *Kalkstein* (*Limestone*), Storm's *Aquis Submersus*, or Ebner-Eschenbach's *Unsühnbar* (*Beyond Atonement*), for instance, they do so as supporting characters that in some respect serve to code broad themes like innocence, vulnerability, or passivity vis-à-vis those of guilt, responsibility, and agency on the part of adult protagonists. Contrastively, in texts like Freytag's *Soll und Haben* (*Debit and Credit*), Fontane's *Unwiederbringlich* (*Irretrievable*, which I have written about elsewhere),[42] Keller's *Romeo und Julia auf dem Dorfe* (*A Village Romeo and Juliet*), and numerous late novellas by Storm, the figures who drown range from children to fully grown adults, and are male as well as female.[43] Scholars have demonstrated over the years that German Realism is deeply bound up with issues and discourses of gender and familial relations, which makes it all the more interesting to note that when issues of femininity and masculinity do enter directly into the frame of this literature's drowning scenes, we will see them often doing so subtly rather than overtly, saturating and permeating the narrative fabric rather than leaping in front of it.[44]

---

42. Alexander Sorenson, "The Bride by the Water: Duty, Procession, and Sacrifice in Theodor Fontane's *Unwiederbringlich*," *German Life and Letters* 72, no. 2 (2019): 151–167.

43. If one adds to this consideration subsequent movements such as Naturalism and Impressionism, the list expands (to include, e.g., Gerhart Hauptmann's drama *Einsame Menschen* [1891] and his short story *Fasching* [1887], as well as Eduard von Keyserling's 1911 novel *Wellen*); and were one to open up the generic boundaries to incorporate poetry as well, the list grows longer still. See my epilogue for comments upon a number of entries from that list.

44. On the media-historical precedence for this gendered phenomenon of both diegetic and authorial liminality, see Barbara Hahn, *Unter falschem Namen: Von der*

If, then, the picture of "who drowns" in German Realist literature is more complicated and varied than one might initially anticipate, and if explicit invocations of Ophelia appear in the German-speaking sphere somewhat later than in Britain and elsewhere in Europe, it becomes all the more important to bear in mind the broader (or deeper) theme of submergence as it appears at the *beginning* of the nineteenth century, and not just its middle (realism) or tail end (expressionism and modernism). That theme, which includes but is not reducible to drowning, is but one thread within an elaborate tropological weave that Gaston Bachelard describes in terms of a "metapoetics of water." He distinguishes this from a mere poetics of water—that is, from water's aesthetic function as a *category* of imagery—in order to point instead to its function as a "mainstay" and "founding contributor" of numerous such categories.[45] In this respect, Bachelard argues, the metapoetic role performed by water is that of "an element of materializing imagination"—of imagination *derived* from material elements, which "learns from fundamental substances" as opposed to preceding and encountering them as mere resources for allegory and metaphor.

However universal or collective Bachelard presents these dynamics of the material imagination as being with regard to water, the "metapoetics" that he outlines is heavily gendered and can be found throughout the first several decades of the nineteenth century. Though falling outside of the purview of the present study, it is important to linger for a moment over several crucial instances of this tropology from the first third of the century in order to properly situate this book's more specific subject of drowning within German Realist literature. Bachelard (whose remarks about "the

---

schwierigen Autorschaft der Frauen (Frankfurt am Main: Suhrkamp, 1991); Silvia Bovenschen, *Die imaginierte Weiblichkeit: Exemplarische Untersuchungen zu kulturgeschichtlichen und literarischen Präsentationsformen des Weiblichen* (Frankfurt am Main: Suhrkamp, 1979); Manuela Günter, "'Ermanne dich, oder vielmehr erweibe dich einmal!': Gender Trouble in der Literatur nach der Kunstperiode," *Internationales Archiv für Sozialgeschichte der deutschen Literatur* 30, no. 2 (2005): 38–61.

45. Gaston Bachelard, "Introduction: Imagination and Matter," in *Water and Dreams: An Essay on the Imagination of Matter*, trans. Edith R. Farrell (Dallas: Pegasus Foundation, 1983), 11.

Ophelia complex" I will consider in greater detail in the epilogue) takes a helpful preliminary step in his reading of a paradigmatic example of German Romantic prose—namely, the dream sequence from Novalis's *Heinrich von Ofterdingen* (1802). In Bachelard's account, "after dipping his hands and moistening his lips in a basin that he discovers in a dream," the dreamer "is seized by 'an uncontrollable desire to bathe.' No *vision* invites him. It is the *substance* itself," and it is only after he disrobes and enters the water "that images come. They emerge from the matter...."[46] For Bachelard, part of the "feminine substance" of water in Novalis's text rests in the fact that it produces images (of "charming maidens," notably) only after making *physical contact* with the dreamer's body by "[sticking] to him like a sweet breast" (even more notably). Bachelard's interpretation implies that an imagination that is not simply inspired but derived from matter is, eo ipso, an inherently embodied rather than disembodied feature of human subjectivity. With regard to water, this is particularly true of "Novalis's imagination" insofar as it "is governed by . . . the desire for a hot, soft, warm, enveloping, protective substance, by the need for a matter that surrounds the entire being and penetrates it intimately."[47]

While Bachelard's hermeneutic approach (to say nothing of Novalis's own poetics) betrays numerous presuppositions that reflect the chauvinism of the time and place from which it emerged, it nevertheless (and perhaps unwittingly) lends itself well to gender-conscious analyses of submergence. The text does so, I think, by showing—through the example of its own author—that such imagery is coded not simply in the motivically limited instances of female characters who happen to drown; rather, it lays a path for drawing out the various ways in which the very concept of submergence is often already figured as inherently "feminine" by those authors who, perhaps in cooperation with their own "material imaginations," set it to work in narrative. It is therefore especially interesting to consider texts authored by women from this period

---

46. Gaston Bachelard, "Maternal Water and Feminine Water," in *Water and Dreams*, 126 (emphasis in the original).
47. Bachelard, "Maternal Water," 127.

whose deployment of water imagery is not only innovative but also, to a notable degree, anticipatory of modernist tendencies.

One of the most striking examples in this regard can be found on the first page of Annette von Droste-Hülshoff's 1824 novel fragment *Ledwina*. We find the eponymous protagonist making her way along a riverbank before stopping to gaze at the currents. The setting is presented in a way that establishes a subtle dialectic, demarcating a sphere of oneiric and lyric introversion that will be juxtaposed with the bourgeois sphere of domestic interiors throughout the rest of the text. Yet the water and its environs do not so much stand in opposition to confined indoor spaces and social rituals as intimate a contrast between two kinds of interiority: on the one hand, the constrained order of the home, and on the other, the "open interior" of introspection and reverie that is closely linked to the shoreline that Ledwina wanders along. Several details of this opening scene are recognizably Ophelian: the reflection of her "lovely, pale form" in the current is compared to that of a young linden tree nearby, and her eyes and complexion are likened to various species of flower in an anthropomorphic echo of the other plants growing along the bank. Then things suddenly take a macabre turn as she fixates her "at first bright, then dreaming" gaze upon the river and the objects and reflections carried along by its movement: "But then Ledwina's eyes rested on her own image, as the locks fell away from her head and drifted on, as her clothing was torn apart and her white fingers disintegrated and dissolved. Then she looked dead to herself, decay wearing away her limbs, and each element carrying away what belonged to it."[48] Later, in the fragment's most iconic scene, this thematic framework manifests itself fully: Ledwina, having awoke from sleep and its "dreadful dream-world," looks about her moonlit room. The illuminated window-curtain catches her eye:

> And, as the river was flowing beneath it, the window seemed to undulate like water. Its shadows fell upon her bed and imbued the white duvet with

---

48. Annette von Droste-Hülshoff, *Ledwina*, in *Historisch-kritische Ausgabe*, vol. 5, pt. 1, ed. Winfried Woesler and Walter Huge (Tübingen: Max Niemeyer, 1978), 79.

the same quality, making it appear as though underwater. She regarded this for a while, and the longer she did so, the more horrific it seemed to her; the vision of an undine became that of a corpse submerged in the river, the water slowly and gently eating it away while inconsolable parents vainly dragged their nets through the element's impenetrable dominion. She became so frightened that she decided to get up and pull the curtains closed.[49]

Here, Droste-Hülshoff directly links the liminal—yet domestic—space between waking and dreaming to the uncanny space of imagination, with the window serving as a common portal between them. Insofar as Ledwina's assumed perspective of a drowned corpse from beneath the water constitutes an "impossible" vantage point, her reverie symbolizes the oneiric process of internally confronting a space that otherwise occludes all possible lived experience. In other words, drowning in the first-person perspective casts the act of envisioning one's own de-subjectivization as an inherently *poetic* act.[50] (As we will see in the epilogue, that perspectival facet would subsequently become a hallmark of modernist drowning scenes around the turn of the century, often explicitly invoking Ophelia and, ironically, at the same time marking a break from the more established theatrical mode of an "offstage" incident that gets narratively conveyed in the third person.)

As remarkably innovative as Droste-Hülshoff's text is in its descriptive technique, it is by no means the earliest instance of "oneiric submergence" in nineteenth-century German *écriture féminine*. As a case in point, we can look to Karoline von Günderrode's *Apokalyptisches Fragment* (*Apocalyptical Fragment*, 1801/1804), which explores similar themes of reverie, introspection, embodied perception, and psychic distention in connection with water, albeit in a less eerie mode than *Ledwina*. Günderrode's account unfolds before "a sea, girt in by no shore":

> It was dark within me, as if I had rested in the bosom of the sea, and risen from it like the other forms; to myself I seemed a drop of dew; I moved

---

49. Droste-Hülshoff, *Ledwina*, 97.
50. Brigitte Peucker, "Droste-Hülshoff's Ophelia and the Recovery of Voice," *Journal of English and Germanic Philology* 82, no. 3 (1983): 375–377.

merrily to and fro in the air, and rejoiced, and my life was that the sun mirrored himself in me, and the stars looked upon me.... Once was I aware that all the forms, which had ascended from the sea, returned to it and were again produced in changing forms. This apparition surprised me, for I had known of no end. But now, I thought, my desire is also to return to the source of life.... I seemed no more myself; my limits I could no longer find; my consciousness I had transcended; it was greater, different, and yet I felt myself in it. I was released from the narrow limits of my being, and no single drop more; I was restored to the all, and the all belonged to me. I thought and felt, flowed as waves in the sea, shone in the sun, circled with the stars; I felt myself in all, and enjoyed all in myself.[51]

This striking piece of writing is all the more striking for its prefiguration of twentieth-century women's writing, particularly Luce Irigaray's 1980 text *Amante marine de Friedrich Nietzsche* (*Marine Lover of Friedrich Nietzsche*). Equally presaged by Günderrode's *Apocalyptic Fragment*, but slightly more proximate to it in time and space, is Malwida von Meysenbug's 1876 recollection about how "the riddle of life" had seemed for her to have been "solved" within a single, ecstatic instant (one that five decades later would find more famous echoes in her young friend Romain Rolland's description to Freud of the "oceanic feeling"):

> I was alone on the seashore as all of these thoughts flooded me in liberation and reconciliation. And, as before in those distant days in the Dauphiné Alps, I was once again compelled to kneel down here before the unbounded tides, an emblem of the Endless. I felt that I was praying as I had never prayed before, and now realized what actual prayer is: a return from the isolation of individuation into a consciousness of unification with all that exists . . . earth, sky and sea all rang out as in a great, world-encompassing harmony.[52]

The words of Droste-Hülshoff, Günderrode, and Meysenbug that we have just read all in their own ways communicate a simple yet

---

51. Karoline von Günderrode, "Apocalytpical Fragment," in *Correspondence of Fräulein Günderode [sic] and Bettine von Arnim*, trans. Margaret Fuller (Boston: Burnham, 1860), 12–13.

52. Malwida von Meysenbug, *Memoiren einer Idealisten*, vol. 3 (Stuttgart: Auerbach, 1876), 168.

radical idea: that one can be submerged in and by the world—and even the self—much as one can be by water. Indeed, water does not merely symbolize this, but in fact serves as the material and "matter-real" template for how this happens in the first place. If that is so, then this conceptual and tropological framework of submergence has more to do with literary realism than a simple thematic overlay with drowning imagery; the challenge then becomes to see exactly how and why. As Barbara Nagel nicely puts it, "Realism grapples with the problem of how to make the ordinary appear as such."[53] In this book we will be grappling with a reflection of that problem—namely, with how to understand German Realism's discernment and depiction of the extraordinary within the ordinary.

A brief word on method and structure. Although the readings that follow do not expressly aim to employ an eco-critical approach, they inherently participate in current environmental angles of inquiry by virtue of the core question that motivates them: How is the natural landscape (specifically water) in each text invested with meaning while at the same time directly shaping how this meaning is perceived and given narrative expression in human terms? My attention to the significance of the natural environment charts a modest course between a localized analysis of each text's "aesthetic framing of [its] environmental displays" and a more expansive view toward discovering material in them "from which a planetary ethics can be derived," to cite two different approaches to environmental themes in recent scholarship.[54] This is to say that the ensuing chapters are engaged less in socio-pragmatic, ecological questions than they are in poeto-theoretical, topological ones (though the two are unquestionably linked, as is borne out by work currently being

---

53. Barbara A. Nagel, *Ambiguous Aggression in German Realism and Beyond: Flirtation, Passive Aggression, Domestic Violence* (New York: Bloomsbury, 2021), 75.

54. Sabine Wilke, *German Culture and the Modern Environment: Narrating and Depicting Nature* (Leiden: Brill Rodopi, 2015), 22; Simon Richter, "Goethe's *Faust* and the Ecolinguistics of <Here>," in *German Ecocriticism in the Anthropocene*, ed. Caroline Schaumann and Heather I. Sullivan (New York: Palgrave Macmillan, 2017), 47.

done at the intersection of both).⁵⁵ In setting out to explore water's "place" in German Realism by virtue of its function as a topos in the classically double sense of being both a site and a symbol, my ultimate aim is to demonstrate that water is central to these texts not merely by virtue of being physically situated at the center as well as the margins of the narrative landscapes, but also by virtue of consistently being invested with specific frameworks of meaning that in turn inform the narratives as they unfold within these landscapes. The obvious point of convergence between these domains of the material (landscape, environment) and the semantic (meaning, textuality) is the somatic—that is, the actual bodies of characters who encounter (and often fall victim to) ever-patient and ever-present bodies of water.

Because the chosen narratives all deploy water as an inherent bearer of certain meanings—not just for the reader, but more crucially for the characters themselves—they will not always align organically with every approach within contemporary eco-criticism (particularly those that draw from new materialism and posthumanism in seeking to move past or away from anthropocentric questions of "signification" and "meaning-making").⁵⁶ More applicable, perhaps, to the objects of German Realism under investigation here—as well as to the broader aesthetic objectives of the movement itself as articulated by Schmidt, Fontane, Heyse, and Freytag—would instead be explorations of how the more-than-human and the human *mutually* mean, signify, and suffer. Disciplinarily diverse instances of such an approach include Gernot Böhme's eco-phenomenology, Ursula K.

---

55. Two exemplary recent studies in this regard use the elements of water and air, respectively, as springboards for considering how the concrete encounters between the more-than-human substances of nature and the human "lived body" (in Husserl's sense) open onto numerous areas of political, personal, ecological, and epistemological significance (gender, race, postcolonial consciousness, environmental and social justice, and so on). See Astrida Neimanis, *Bodies of Water: Posthumanist Feminist Phenomenology* (London: Bloomsbury, 2017); Jean-Thomas Tremblay, *Breathing Aesthetics* (Durham, NC: Duke University Press, 2022).

56. See, for example, Jane Bennett, *Vibrant Matter: A Political Ecology of Things* (Durham, NC: Duke University Press, 2010); Donna Haraway, *Staying with the Trouble: Making Kin in the Chthulucene* (Durham, NC: Duke University Press, 2016); Rosi Braidotti, *The Posthuman* (Cambridge: Polity Press, 2013).

Heise's and Thom van Dooren's integration of narrative theory and extinction studies, and other similarly oriented accounts of the porous, co-implicative, and semantically charged relationship between environments and their various inhabitants.[57] Still, even as the narrators and characters of the realist texts under consideration in this book consistently *make sense* of water, to an equal degree the water itself also embodies a primordial antecedence—even preclusion—of sense-making, with drowning frequently serving as an overtly literal image of "return" to this origin and endpoint. One would not need to reach far in order to find points of resonance between these valences of drowning and psychoanalytic accounts of water, from Freud's elaboration upon Rolland's notion of the oceanic feeling in *Das Unbehagen in der Kultur* (*Civilization and Its Discontents*, 1930), to his erstwhile disciple Jung's recurring association of water with the collective unconscious, to Irigaray's articulation of the marine feminine.[58] Appropriately, eco-psychoanalysis has recently emerged as a particularly fecund subfield with regard to the aforementioned project of getting beyond (or perhaps "working through") the stubbornly anthropocentric assumptions of much eco-criticism to date.[59]

---

57. Gernot Böhme, *Für eine ökologische Naturästhethik* (Frankfurt am Main: Suhrkamp, 1989); Böhme, *Leib: Die Natur, die wir selbst sind* (Frankfurt am Main: Suhrkamp, 2019); Thom van Dooren, *Flight Ways: Life and Loss at the Edge of Extinction* (New York: Columbia University Press, 2014); Ursula K. Heise, *Imagining Extinction: The Cultural Meanings of Endangered Species* (Chicago: University of Chicago Press, 2016).

58. Above all in the aforementioned work by Luce Irigaray, which I will take up in the epilogue, *Marine Lover of Friedrich Nietzsche*, trans. Gillian C. Gill (New York: Columbia University Press, 1991). One might also think of Julia Kristeva's necrological (re)vision of the oceanic at various points in *Black Sun: Depression and Melancholia*, trans. Leon S. Roudiez (New York: Columbia University Press, 1989), e.g., 29–30, 73.

59. For instance, Steven Swarbrick has recently examined early modern English poetry in order to articulate a "nonobject-oriented" eco-psychoanalysis based upon the idea "that matter, far from being immediate, knowable, or countable, houses an incognizable lack. This lack underpins the subject of ecocriticism." Drawing a line from Lucretius to Lacan, he proposes that the "constitutive lack" that underlies matter (as well as desire) makes itself felt (like the unconscious) primarily as a lack of *meaningfulness*, as a structural resistance to sense-making. Swarbrick, *The Environmental Unconscious: Ecological Poetics from Spenser to Milton* (Minneapolis: University of Minnesota Press, 2023), 1–3, 10.

With these methodological provisos out of the way, let's now turn at last to an overview of this book's chapters, which together cover roughly the years 1840 to 1890. The bulk of them do so in a successively chronological manner, but chapter 1 takes a slightly different approach in order to examine two key novels from either end of this time frame: Johann Wolfgang Goethe's *Elective Affinities* (1809) and Marie von Ebner-Eschenbach's *Beyond Atonement* (1889). Taking Walter Benjamin's interpretation of the former text (and especially the character Ottilie) as a point of departure, in my own reading I explore how the plots of both works methodically sift a number of paradigmatic discourses at the level of their semantic foundations. These include, in particular, what Benjamin understands as a "mythic" context of fate as well as a modern context of ethical and moral decision. It is within the dynamic play between these two contexts that lawful order, transgression, and sacrifice unfold as guiding themes, and throughout the literature of German Realism bookended by the respective deaths of Goethe (1832) and Ebner-Eschenbach (1916), water—and, more specifically, the ominous theme of death in it—serves as the locus of that dynamic play. The overarching argument of the chapter is that whereas in *Elective Affinities* sacrificiality functions largely in line with the classicist and romantic declensions that I outlined earlier, in *Beyond Atonement* it gradually comes to consist in the offering up *of sacrifice itself* as a possible means of atonement. In both texts, these divergent sacrificial trajectories spring from and in certain respects lead back to scenes of drowning. The chapter therefore intimates the book's full arc by offering a glimpse both of the thematic matrix from which its main subjects emerge near the beginning of the century and of the *telos* toward which they tend in the latter half of the century.

Chapter 2 returns us to the outset of German Realism proper and focuses on Adalbert Stifter's early phase of writing (1842–1853). It first traces the theory of cosmic order that he developed in nonfictional texts on nature as well as aesthetic principles such as his premise of the "gentle law" (*sanftes Gesetz*). I argue that these notions of a universal, underlying order all rest upon a system of invisible cause and visible effect. Crucially, Stifter presents self-sacrifice as the midpoint of this system, bridging the cosmic sphere of natural law and the human sphere of ethics. This motivic framework is then employed in the 1853 novella *Limestone*, which chronicles an ascetic pastor's fervent commitment to protecting the parish children from drowning in the nearby river's regular floods. Stifter's novella thus represents an interesting case of deferred drowning, which by remaining potential rather than actual allows the internal dynamics of this motif, along with the narrative themes of lawfulness and sacrificiality that condition it, to be viewed particularly closely and in a unique light.

Chapter 3 focuses its attention upon Gottfried Keller's novella *A Village Romeo and Juliet* (1856/1876), arguing that it is structured around transgressive acts that consist not so much in overt contradictions of given legal tenets as in the protagonists' imitation of lawful states of being, driven above all by the protagonists' fervent desire for the community to acknowledge them as a properly married couple. However, the lawful status of bourgeois matrimony is occluded precisely by their simulation of this status. At the end, their suicidal drowning on the periphery of the community constitutes a sacrifice of their wish for *public* recognition insofar as it is the culmination of an instant of *private*, reciprocal recognition. I interpret their last act as a sacrifice of the wish for a publicly recognized, married life together in exchange for a momentary, private enactment of it on the banks of the river.

The narratives that occupy chapter 4 develop these themes, gradually moving from the "external laws" of nature and socioethical custom to the "inward laws" of moral obligation (as anticipated in the affinities between Goethe's and Ebner-Eschenbach's respective novels). In this chapter I analyze the later novellas of Theodor Storm (1872–1888), all of which brim with themes of guilt, memory, and regret. Through close readings of two important narratives, along with briefer looks at several others, I propose that in this last period of his writing and life, Storm portrays law as an inheritance of the past, whereas sacrifice emerges as a retrospective means of atonement—a means, that is, of relating to one's future by looking back to the past from out of the present. In each case, these *Augenblicke* of sacrifice culminate in drowning. In the epilogue, I pick up certain threads from the present introduction in order to situate the Poetic Realist drowning motif within a larger arc of German literary history, exploring how it falls between the Romantics' fascination with naiads, nymphs, and other *Wasserfrauen* as metaphors for the individual poetic imagination at the beginning of the century and the modernists' fixation upon Ophelia and other feminine "bodies of water" as avatars of womanhood, societal alienation, and self-estrangement at the fin de siècle. From this vantage point, we will finally be able to gain a more complete appreciation of the enigmatic middle-space within modern German literature that the drowning scene of German Realism occupies—a space situated between Ottilie and Ophelia.

1

WATER AND STONE

The End of Life and of Sacrifice in Goethe's Elective Affinities *and Ebner-Eschenbach's* Beyond Atonement

> Water as the chaotic element of life does not threaten here in desolate waves that bring about humanity's wreckage; rather, it threatens in the enigmatic calm that lets humanity go to its ruin.
> —Walter Benjamin, "Goethe's *Elective Affinities*"

During one of Marie von Ebner-Eschenbach's trips to Rome toward the end of her life, on a spring day in Eastertide, she made her way to the Campo Cestio, the eternal city's "non-Catholic cemetery" (*Cimitero Accatolico*). As an entry from her posthumously published diary recounts, she paid her respects at the grave of Theophanie Schücking (daughter of the writers Levin and Louise von Gall) before visiting the nearby resting place of Malwida von Meysenbug, for whom life's "riddle" had been solved in that ecstatic instant on the seashore, "before the unbounded tides, an emblem of the Endless," and who now shares the same vicinity as John Keats, the like-minded poet of negative capability "whose name was writ in water." They and numerous others lie beneath the impressive shadow of the Cestius Pyramid looming overhead, but it is to a smaller, more melancholy site close by that Ebner-Eschenbach guides us next, directing our attention downward in order to show us the memorial of Princess Maria Obolensky. The diary offers an ekphrasis of the tomb, which is flanked by ivy.

> [Through the ivy] the light, slightly muffled, falls onto a small marble sculpture—a crypt. One of its ironclad doors is ajar. Two tall steps lead down to the entrance, and on the uppermost one rests a young, female figure.... She has turned her head away from the grim depths and gazes ahead, inconsolable, as if asking: "Must this be? I am so young and yet not young enough in order to die easily, the way children die because they do not sense how beautiful life *could* be, how delectably beautiful!" These thoughts hover on her brow, and her face pronounces them. It is the face of a patient sufferer; the entire sculpture exhales a sorrow that is breathed through each and every detail—through every fold of her garment, every strand of her soft, thick hair, every finger of her clasped hands. These lie folded on her right knee; the left one is stretched out and her foot is already poised on the next step down to the ominous entryway.... You poor child! The more I submerge [*versenke*] myself in the sight of you, the more you seem to stir with life.[1]

This captivating depiction of a young woman made from stone, dead before her time yet seeming to sigh with a still-living grief, is not an unfamiliar one in Ebner-Eschenbach's prior written work—particularly her 1889 novel *Unsühnbar* (*Beyond Atonement*), which will be the primary focus of this chapter. Yet in observing how the narrative's heroine, Maria, slowly takes on these ethereal traits over the course of the plot, we will in fact be witnessing a Poetic Realist

---

Epigraph: Walter Benjamin, "Goethe's *Elective Affinities*," in *Selected Writings*, vol. 1, *1913–1926*, trans. Stanley Corngold (Cambridge, MA: Harvard University Press, 1996), 303 (translation modified). / Benjamin, "Goethes *Wahlverwandtschaften*," in *Gesammelte Schriften*, vol. 1.1, ed. Rolf Tiedemann and Hermann Schweppenhäuser, 125–201 (Frankfurt am Main: Suhrkamp, 1974), 133: "Das Wasser als das chaotische Element des Lebens droht hier nicht in wüstem Wogen, das dem Menschen den Untergang bringt, sondern in der rätselhaften Stille, die ihn zu Grunde gehn läßt."

1. Marie von Ebner-Eschenbach, *Aus einem zeitlosen Tagebuch* (Berlin: Paetel, 1916), 81–82 (emphasis added).

echo of (and perhaps even a reply to) one of the most iconic figures of early nineteenth-century German fiction—namely, Ottilie from Goethe's 1809 novel *Die Wahlverwandtschaften* (*Elective Affinities*). Both characters die young, but slowly, first slipping into liminal, almost statue-like conditions that make them into objects of observation, even aesthetic viewership; toward the end of *Beyond Atonement*, Maria's father will catch sight of her sitting in an autumnal garden, not far from a sculpture of the Virgin Mary, "transparently pale, thin in her close-fitting black dress," and soon after perceives her as "someone who has half departed this world."[2] Near her own end, Ottilie ceases to eat, drink, or even speak, and becomes enveloped in "stone-coldness" and "silence," "pale, ethereal," and even after her lifeless body is at last laid in a casket, onlookers are drawn to marvel at "the continuing beauty of Ottilie's state, more like sleep than death."[3] Both women begin to hover somewhere between life and death after having been submerged in mournful regret over the same tragedy: drowning. Both undergo a sorrow reminiscent of the one that the stone effigy of Maria Obolensky "breathes out" and that "breathes through" the whole of her form in turn. That form comes thereby to resemble a "genuine sculptural figure" in Hegel's understanding by being able to be "immersed [*versenkt*] in the substantial nature of its spiritual content" at the same time that this "inner and spiritual life is effused [*ergossen*] over the entirety of the sculptural form and is grasped as a whole only by the spirit, the spectator, contemplating it"—namely, by Ebner-Eschenbach as she "submerges" [*versenke*] herself in the sight of it.[4]

---

2. Quotations from Ebner-Eschenbach's novel are taken from the following translation: Marie von Ebner-Eschenbach, *Beyond Atonement*, trans. Vanessa Van Ornam (Columbia, SC: Camden House, 1997), 116–117 (hereafter cited parenthetically in the text). Any references to the original German will likewise be included in parenthetical citation, with respective page numbers preceded by the abbreviation *U*, referring to the following edition: Ebner-Eschenbach, *Unsühnbar*, ed. Burkhard Bittrich, in *Kritische Texte und Deutunge*, vol. 1, ed. Karl Konrad Polheim (Bonn: Bouvier, 1978).
3. Johann Wolfgang Goethe, *Elective Affinities: A Novel*, trans. David Constantine (Oxford: Oxford University Press, 2008), 230, 234, 238 (hereafter cited as *EA*).
4. G. W. F Hegel, *Aesthetics: Lectures on Fine Art*, vol. 2, trans. T. M. Knox (Oxford: Oxford University Press, 1975), 732. / Hegel, *Vorlesungen über die Ästhetik*,

The exhaled sorrow becomes a medium of exchange between statue and viewer, as something aerious that is "breathed" and simultaneously as something aqueous in and by which effusion, immersion and submergence also occur.

The terrible irony of these parallels rests in the lethal juxtaposition of water and breath that is also at the crux of both novels' plots: Ottilie, racked with guilt over the accidental drowning of the child in her care, submits to an unrelenting program of penitent ascesis, ultimately enacting a "renunciation" (*Entsagung*) not just of "flesh" in the Pauline sense, but of life itself, and thereby entwining self-sacrifice with atonement in her gradual "being toward death." By comparison, following the tragic drowning of her husband and firstborn son, for Maria the very act of *staying alive* ultimately becomes the sole remaining means of potential expiation that focalizes the life of her second son as he will continue to live it in the future. Rather than sacrificing herself in a literal way, Maria instead immolates the very framework of negational sacrifice (whether of the self or of other objects) in order to assume a *kenotic* framework of self-sacrifice; having renounced renunciation, Maria instead consumes herself with *self-withdrawal* in orientation around the good and life of another person. However, ultimately it is not sacrifice but law—and specifically, the formal mechanism of legal "renunciation" (*Verzichtleistung*)—that presents itself as a socially sanctioned redress of transgression. Throughout this late novel of German Realism, sin and guilt only lie "beyond atonement" as long as sacrifice remains "before the law."

I.

Before turning to my reading of *Elective Affinities* and *Beyond Atonement*, some preliminary remarks are due on how their plots bear

---

in *Werk*, vol. 14, ed. Eva Moldenhauer and Karl Markus Michel (Frankfurt am Main: Suhrkamp, 1986), 390. For an illuminating account of this and contemporaneous theorizations of sculpture vis-à-vis its appearance as a literary motif, see Catriona MacLeod, *Fugitive Objects: Sculpture and Literature in the German Nineteenth Century* (Evanston, IL: Northwestern University Press, 2014), esp. 43, 17–47.

upon the paradigmatic depictions of "female death" in novels of love, seduction, and adultery that enjoyed widespread popularity across the eighteenth and nineteenth centuries. Christine Lehmann offers a taxonomic account of these depictions that looks back to Samuel Richardson's 1748 novel *Clarissa* as a motivic progenitor. In that text, Lehmann finds a case study in the combination of emerging bourgeois sexual morality and pietistic introspection (amplified by *Clarissa*'s epistolary form) that would recur in the subsequent "novel of seduction" (*Verführungsroman*) and the similarly structured "novel of love" (*Liebesroman*), with a female protagonist who demonstrates the "deadly consequences" of extramarital passion being a mainstay of each. However, Lehmann suggests, in the nineteenth-century incarnations of such novels the protagonists never directly question or challenge the assumed necessity of marriage, with the consequence that their dramatic arcs tend to be set in motion by a manifestation of suppressed or unacknowledged tensions—or even simple boredom—that emerges from within their accepted habitus.[5]

This broaches the important context of the gendered mores and double standards of the patriarchal society (and even more specific aristocratic milieu) in which Ebner-Eschenbach lived and wrote, and of which she made a frequent subject throughout her writerly career.[6] B. J. Kenworthy suggests that the "novel of adultery," in placing the institution of marriage under the microscope, became a means for depicting, and also for interrogating, the standard position of women in nineteenth-century society.[7] This is particularly true of *Beyond Atonement*, which enjoys a special status as one of the few such novels not authored by a man. Though this work is less well known to general readers, its scholarly reception has accorded it a place along-

---

5. Christine Lehmann, *Das Modell Clarissa: Liebe, Verführung, Sexualität und Tod der Romanheldinnen des 18. und 19. Jahrhunderts* (Stuttgart: Metzler, 1991), 9–10, 61.

6. Patricia Herminghouse, "Women and the Literary Enterprise in Nineteenth-Century Germany," in *German Women in the Eighteenth and Nineteenth Centuries: A Social and Literary History*, ed. Ruth-Ellen B. Joeres and Mary Jo Maynes (Bloomington: Indiana University Press, 1986), 78–93; Ulrike Tanzer, *Frauenbilder im Werk Marie von Ebner-Eschenbachs* (Stuttgart: Akademischer, 1997), 122–123.

7. B. J. Kenworthy, "Ethical Realism: Marie von Ebner-Eschenbach's *Unsühnbar*," *German Life and Letters* 41, no. 4 (1988): 479.

side *Madame Bovary*, *Anna Karenina*, and *Effi Briest*, with the latter being an especially frequent point of comparison.[8] However, as I hope to demonstrate in this chapter, we can discover quite a bit more about the dimensions of Poetic Realism that are the core concern of this book if we approach Ebner-Eschenbach's 1889 novel by way of one from the beginning of the century—namely, Goethe's *Elective Affinities*—as opposed to simply comparing it with another one from the end of the century (such as *Effi Briest*).

Before moving forward, though, I first would like to add the disclaimer that my intention in turning to Goethe's text is not to advance new (or to intervene in previous) readings of it, but instead, firstly, to trace its themes of decision, fate, law, and sacrifice, in order to, secondly, establish the groundwork for my investigation of those very themes in the subsequent literature of German Realism (as represented in this particular chapter by *Beyond Atonement*). In light of this, my discussion of *Elective Affinities* will hew closely to the itinerary of Walter Benjamin's influential (and contentious) interpretation of it. Here too, my objective is not to defend or critique Benjamin's claims, but instead simply to allow my analysis of the above-mentioned themes in Ebner-Eschenbach's novel to benefit from the level of detail with which Benjamin delineates remarkably similar ones in Goethe's. By looking at both works side by side, we will be able to achieve an intriguing picture of the three guiding subjects of this study—order, sacrifice, and submergence—in their early and late nineteenth-century manifestations, and thereby to set a course for the chapters that follow.

Ottilie's *Augenblick*

Toward the beginning of his wide-ranging essay on Goethe's novel, Benjamin claims that, despite all outward appearances, the main subject of the story is not marriage: "Nowhere in this work are its

---

8. See, for instance, Kenworthy, "Ethical Realism," 481; Agatha C. Bramkamp, *Marie von Ebner-Eschenbach: The Author, Her Time, and Her Critics* (Bonn: Bouvier, 1990), 113, 115; Peter C. Pfeiffer, "Genre, Gender, and Aesthetic Evaluation of Novels of Adultery: Theodor Fontane's *Effi Briest* and Marie von Ebner-Eschenbach's *Unsühnbar*," *Colloquia Germanica* 52, no. 1–2 (2021): 142.

[marriage's] ethical powers to be found. From the outset, they are in the process of disappearing, like the beach under water at floodtide."[9] Instead, he regards the true issue of the narrative to be how this very dimension of the ethical gets overwhelmed by that of the mythic. As Benjamin puts it, Goethe "did not want . . . to establish a foundation for marriage but wished, rather, to show the forces that arise from its decay. Yet these are surely the mythic powers of the law."[10] This "mythic law" becomes interlaced in the novel with the broad concept of "nature" and is first manifested in the eponymous principle of elective affinities, which the book's own characters interpret simply as a metaphor, but which they thereby fail to recognize as an actual operative force in their lives and reality. With the "dissolution" of marriage as an "ethical problem" as well as a "social problem" in the plot, Benjamin writes, "everything human turns into appearance, and the mythic alone remains as essence."

Scholars such as Kir Kuiken have pointed out that much of Benjamin's somewhat curious claim rests upon the distinction he makes early in the essay between "material content" (*Sachgehalt*)—that is, the explicit or "phenomenal" events, topics, and images—and the "truth content" (*Wahrheitsgehalt*), that which is "unsaid" in the novel, the "secret" that the critic is able to discover as being what the novel is actually about.[11] Thus, while the "material content" of *Elective Affinities* is marriage, its truth content is something else: "the powers that emerge from the disintegration of the marriage must necessarily win out. For they are precisely those of fate".[12] As Kuiken emphasizes, the hinge upon which the novel's material as well as truth content turns for Benjamin is the theme of decision (and, even more, the question of what true decision consists in, as opposed to mere choice).[13]

---

9. Benjamin, "Goethe's *Elective Affinities*," 302.
10. Benjamin, "Goethe's *Elective Affinities*," 301.
11. Benjamin, "Goethe's *Elective Affinities*," 313.
12. Benjamin, "Goethe's *Elective Affinities*," 308.
13. Kir Kuiken, "On the Delineation of Choice and Decision in Benjamin's 'Goethe's *Elective Affinities*'," *Canadian Review of Comparative Literature* 31, no. 3 (2004): 289–290.

Decision, Benjamin argues, is the primary domain within which the ethical becomes actualized and is rooted first and foremost in language and speech.[14] Centering the bulk of his analysis on the figure of Ottilie, Benjamin reads the crux of the novel's drama—a drowning—as corresponding to her inability to enunciate her own interior; she is silent, "reserved," and enveloped in "plant-like muteness," which for him is key both to her lack of character and to her resulting incapacity for ethical decision. Ottilie is not alone in this latter respect, though; Benjamin regards the other characters as also sharing in the illusion that their actions are products of deliberate, freely willed decision, when in actuality they derive from arbitrary choices bound up with the natural force of election (*Wahl*), a fellow traveler of myth and fate.[15] And, as the essay's epigraph from Klopstock's *Odes* (1750) declares, to be subject to such forces is to operate in darkness and to court sacrifice: "whoever chooses blindly is struck in the eyes / by the smoke of sacrifice."[16]

In order to more clearly distinguish the relationships between decision, choice, and sacrificiality that Benjamin presents in his analysis, it will be helpful to look at another valence of nature with which he associates the mythic law that silently yet decisively drives the novel and its characters. Along with the titular law of blind choice intrinsic to elective affinity, Benjamin pairs his focus upon Ottilie with attention to the key material element that anticipates the works of German Realism that will be explored in this book, for he emphasizes the significance of *water* as a topos in each character's trajectory. Water, he writes, appears, not as a violent agent of justice or the divine, but instead as a stage for the unfurling of fate as "the nexus of guilt among the living."[17] Like fate, guilt is registered within the passive but ever-present inevitability of consequence following from apparent deci-

---

14. Benjamin, "Goethe's *Elective Affinities*," 336.
15. "Only the decision, not the choice, is inscribed in the book of life. For choice is natural and can even belong to the elements; decision is transcendent." Benjamin, "Goethe's *Elective Affinities*," 346. Compare Kuiken, "Delineation of Choice and Decision," 296–297.
16. "Wer blind wählet, dem schlägt Opferdampf / in die Augen." Klopstock, "Die Grazien," lines 6–7 (Benjamin, "Goethe's *Elective Affinities*," 297).
17. Benjamin, "Goethe's *Elective Affinities*," 307.

sions that have been unmasked as mere choices: "Water as the chaotic element of life does not threaten here in desolate waves that bring about humanity's wreckage; rather, it threatens in the enigmatic calm that lets humanity go to its ruin."[18] Marcus Bullock singles out water and speech as two major motifs of the novel, suggesting that the latter reflects a desire for "fixity of judgment" whereas "water figures throughout this work as a contrary presence, the boundary of judgment.... In the novel, the dark and treacherous realm of the lake is constantly woven into a background of peril looming before the ornately enlightened weave of language that unites the [main characters] in their plans for the estate."[19] Alluding to the same landscaping project that occupies the background of the novel in its first part, David Constantine echoes both Benjamin and Bullock:

> Ironically, by merging the ponds they were returning them to their former and in that sense more natural state; for they were once, as the Captain has found out, a mountain lake. Nature, especially water, "the unsteady element," constitutes a threat throughout the novel; or, we might say, it is present as an alternative to the rigidity of the estate. That alternative, the way of greater naturalness, appears as a threat, and in the end as a deadly threat, to people afraid to embrace it. So life itself, the fate which is hounding them, must appear monstrous; indeed, must appear at last in the form of death. (*EA* xvi)

This atmosphere of unobtrusive, patient catastrophe is conveyed by the "damp scents around the lake" and the fading light of dusk in which Ottilie, hurrying back from her tryst with Eduard, thinks to glimpse the white folds of Charlotte's dress on the balcony. Her nerves unsettled, Ottilie opts to forego the footpath leading around the lake in favor of the shorter, more direct route across the "stretch of water" (*Wasserraum*) by boat (*EA* 208).[20] This momentary choice

---

18. Benjamin, "Goethe's *Elective Affinities*," 303 (translation modified). / Benjamin, "Goethes *Wahlverwandtschaften*," 133.
19. Marcus Bullock, "Goethe versus Benjamin: *Elective Affinities* and Marriage Equality," *Monatshefte* 112, no. 1 (2020): 92–93.
20. Goethe, *Die Wahlverwandtschaften*, in *Werke: Hamburger Ausgabe in 14 Bänden*, vol. 6, *Romane und Novellen I*, ed. Benno von Wiese (Munich: C. H. Beck, 1996), 456 (hereafter cited as *W*).

proves to hold a dual significance for the remainder of the novel: first, within the symbolic framework of the plot, her abandonment of the path signals the abandonment of law, as Ottilie herself will later indicate in her penitent declaration, "I went off course, I broke my laws [*Gesetze*]" (*EA* 214 [translation modified]/*W* 462). Second, it is this instant of abandonment that leads to the drowning of the child, a scene in which the narrative voice suddenly switches to the historical present tense in a distention of the terrible moment being recounted.

With her senses reeling, Ottilie clambers unsteadily into the boat, "the child on her left arm, the book in her left hand, the oar in her right.... She lost the oar on one side and, as she sought to steady herself, the child and the book on the other, all overboard" (*EA* 208). She at last manages to retrieve the baby, but his breathing has already stopped. "At that moment [*Augenblick*] her good sense returned to her, but her anguish, correspondingly, was all the greater.... Cut off from everything, she drifted on the faithless, impenetrable [*unzugänglichen*] element as its prisoner" (*EA* 208–209 [translation modified]/*W* 457). Adrift in every possible sense, Ottilie cradles the lifeless infant against her breast and tries to nurse in a desperate attempt to revive him, but to no avail. The scene concludes with a multilayered vignette of stasis: the distention of narrative time (conveyed by the historical present tense of the narration up to this point in the sequence), the halted rhythm of young life, and the consciousness of irretrievable choice all come to rest in a single image of a suspended *Augenblick*: "The child lay motionless in her arms, and the boat motionless on the surface of the water." This water is the locus of an interpenetration of law and human subjects, one that has culminated in a drowning possessing hallmarks of what Benjamin will term "mythic sacrifice"; yet he will turn out to reserve this description primarily for *Ottilie's* trajectory in the final phase of the story rather than the child's death that precipitates it.

Since Ottilie's decision to starve herself—one in which her "deepest being speaks as nowhere else"—is secret, silent, and "shroud[ed] in darkness," Benjamin regards it as an outgrowth of the fateful mythic law that has overpowered all other human forms of law in the novel and supplanted them with its own demands. "Furthermore, what that darkness conceals does emerge clearly from everything else: the possibility, indeed the necessity, of the sacrifice according to the deepest intentions of the novel." On this reading, Ottilie's slow, self-imposed death is sacrificial, not in the mode of an agentive decision to immolate one good (her life) for the sake of another, higher good (personal atonement), but instead in the mode of a mythic—and, for Benjamin, natural rather than tragic necessity.[21] This necessity antecedes and predetermines her "will to die" and ultimately reveals that "what underlies it is not a decision but a drive."[22] "Thus," he claims: "not only is it as a 'victim of destiny' that Ottilie falls—much less that she actually 'sacrifices herself'— but rather more implacably, more precisely, it is the sacrifice for the expiation [*Entsühnung*] of the guilty ones. For atonement [*Sühne*], in the sense of the mythic world that the author conjures, has always meant the death of the innocent. That is why, despite her suicide, Ottilie dies as a martyr."[23]

It is worth noting that in both biblical and juridical contexts, atonement (*Sühne*) traditionally designates the means for attaining the desired end result, expiation (*Entsühnung*). Expiation, however, lies beyond the final control of the atoning subject, whose authority extends only to her own actions (the domain of penitence). Given Benjamin's angle of interpretation, it therefore makes sense for him to highlight Ottilie's *death* as a sacrificial expiation (since this implies a certain closure inherent to its status as a fait accompli) more than her *dying* (as a processual activity). Additionally, Benjamin's association of atonement with the "mythic world" in the quote above is part of a larger pattern of his thought that falls in line with the religious (both Judaic and classical) context of violent atonement.[24] For instance, in one of his other, more famous essays written

---

21. Compare Bullock, "Goethe versus Benjamin," 81.
22. Benjamin, "Goethe's *Elective Affinities*," 336.
23. Benjamin, "Goethe's *Elective Affinities*," 309. / Benjamin, "Goethes *Wahlverwandtschaften*," 140.
24. See, for example, Hartmut Gese, *Zur biblischen Theologie: Alttestamentliche Vorträge* (Munich: Kaiser, 1977), 85–106; Alfred Marx, *Les systèmes sacrificiels de l'Ancien Testament: Formes et fonctions du culte sacrificiel à Yhwh* (Leiden: Brill, 2005), 15–51.

around this same time, "Critique of Violence" (1921), he makes a similar move: "If mythic violence is lawmaking, divine violence is law-destroying; . . . if mythic violence brings at once guilt and retribution [*verschuldend und sühnend zugleich*], divine power only expiates [*entsühnend*]."[25]

In grammatical terms, one might say that Benjamin's account of Ottilie's death has to do with something like the middle voice: the actions that bring about the end of her life (and the story) comprise a process, not so much of her sacrificing *herself*, but of *being a sacrifice* in such a way that she functions as an object, subject, and medium of expiatory activity all at once. Benjamin's emphasis upon her passivity—as well as, throughout the essay, the connected themes of her "chastity" and beauty—introduces a clearly gendered dynamic to the reading, though it is fair to say that in doing so it simply accentuates what Goethe's own text has already coded as such.[26] Nonetheless, Benjamin's notable fusion of passivity, fragility, and sacrificiality in his analysis of Ottilie certainly qualifies it as part of the broader "genealogy of gender" that Eva Geulen has traced across his writings.[27] Benjamin himself succinctly brings all of these threads together in remarking that "Ottilie's passing away emerge[s] unmistakably as a sacrificial action," albeit one in which, "in her seeming and her becoming, *subjected* until her death to a fateful power, she vegetates *without decision*."[28]

However, agreeing with Benjamin's insistence that this "sacrificial action" occurs in a mythic register (that of passive victimhood) as opposed to an ethical one (that of conscious decision and agentive action) would seem to require recognizing that the prior event of the child's death possesses as many, if not more, characteristics of "mythic

---

25. Walter Benjamin, "Critique of Violence," in *Selected Writings*, vol. 1, *1913–1926*, ed. Marcus Bullock and Michael W. Jennings, trans. Edmund Jephcott (Cambridge, MA: Harvard University Press, 1996), 249. / Benjamin, "Zur Kritik der Gewalt," in *Gesammelte Schriften*, vol. 2.1, ed. Rolf Tiedemann and Hermann Schweppenhäuser (Frankfurt am Main: Suhrkamp, 1977), 199.
26. Benjamin, "Goethe's *Elective Affinities*," e.g., 335, 338–339, 342, 344, 348–350, 353.
27. Eva Geulen, "Toward a Genealogy of Gender in Walter Benjamin's Writing," *German Quarterly* 69, no. 2 (1996): 166, 168.
28. Benjamin, "Goethe's *Elective Affinities*," 309, 337 (emphasis added).

sacrifice" as Ottilie's own death.[29] In fact, she will use the active language of atonement rather than sacrifice to describe her plans for this final phase of her life, exclaiming to Charlotte, "God has opened my eyes to the crime in which I am caught up. I will atone [*büßen*] for it." In her stated intention to atone, decision on her part is not merely implicit but something that she invokes explicitly: "I have set out my new course for myself. I have decided [*Ich bin entschlossen*] . . . . [A]nd do not anybody seek to dissuade me from my intention [*Vorsatz*]" (*EA* 214/W 463). By comparison, Benjamin's understanding of Ottilie's suicide as a "death of the innocent" arguably applies more organically to the wholly unchosen drowning of the wholly innocent child, as a truly passive "victim of destiny," than it does to her penitential ascesis afterward "for the expiation of the guilty ones."[30] Earlier in the same scene, the Captain himself (having attained the rank of Major during his absence) is shown to regard the drowning as a sacrifice, though he conceptualizes it as a cost of future contentment rather than as a casualty of past passions. "The Major left. Though he felt the deepest sympathy for Charlotte he could not grieve over the poor departed child. Such a sacrifice [*Opfer*] seemed to him necessary for the happiness of them all" (*EA* 213/W 461). Shortly thereafter, we learn that "with all secrecy Charlotte had removed the child to the chapel. It rested there as the first victim [*Opfer*] of the fate still lowering over them" (*EA* 215/W 464).

Here, several paradigms of sacrifice come into contact with each other in a way that will similarly mark Ebner-Eschenbach's *Beyond*

---

29. Compare Bullock, "Goethe versus Benjamin": "At the crucial point of *sacrifice that carries the baby to its death*, Goethe brings the interaction of water and language into the foreground. It is Ottilie's attachment to her book that precipitates her moment of ineptitude and causes her to let the child slip from her confused grasp" (81, emphasis added). Also see Norbert Bolz, "Ästhetisches Opfer: Die Formen der Wünsche in Goethes *Wahlverwandtschaften*," in *Goethes "Wahlverwandtschaften": Kritische Modellen und Diskursanalysen zum Mythos Literatur*, ed. Norbert Bolz (Hildesheim: Gerstenberg, 1981), 69; Elisabeth Herrmann, *Die Todesproblematik in Goethes Roman "Die Wahlverwandtschaften"* (Berlin: Erich Schmidt, 1998), 246–251; Volkhard Wels, "Opfer und Erlösung: Eine Auslegung von Goethes *Wahlverwandtschaften* nach ihrer theologischen Begrifflichkeit," *Euphorion* 4, no. 88 (1994): 409–414.

30. Benjamin, "Goethe's *Elective Affinities*," 309.

Atonement, and indeed many other works of late nineteenth-century German Realism. On the one hand, there is the "mythic" paradigm that Benjamin associates primarily with Ottilie, according to which the child could be read as an innocent sacrificial victim that "monstrous" fate seeks out for itself.[31] On the other hand, there is a second mode of sacrifice that Ottilie's subsequent self-renunciation at the end of the novel more clearly embodies: namely, *pace* Benjamin, that of a conscious decision to offer something up (here, health and ultimately life) for the sake of something else (repentance, if not atonement, for the child's death). Both of these paradigms briefly intertwine in the moment (*Augenblick*) encompassing the drowning and the final, darkly poignant image of Ottilie adrift in the boat with the motionless child at her breast—a *Pathosformel* that conjugates powerlessness and presence, much like the Christian iconographical motifs of the Nativity and the *Pietà* which cooperatively inform it. However, there is arguably a third, synthetic register of sacrifice that can be discerned in this laden final section of the novel as well, for while the child's death can be understood as sacrificial, I propose that one should do so not merely in the sense in which the Major does, but also in the sense that Ottilie and the narrator both imply: insofar as the drowning is a consequence (however unintended) of Ottilie's choice to abandon her "laws"—symbolically marked by her abandonment of the path *around* the water in favor of a new path "on" it[32] —it constitutes an exchange of innocent life for that act of choice, one for which she later feels she must atone by means of a self-sacrificial exercise of her own. Yet in addition to having no possible inkling of the sacrifice that her alternative path will end up leading to, Ottilie also does not realize that this single, undeliberated *Wahl* is already woven into a larger tapestry of *decision* whose full scope is revealed only at the end of the story. However cruel fate may be, the

---

31. As Constantine notes (*EA* xiv), when the adjective "monstrous" (*ungeheuer*) appears in the novel, it is frequently in reference to the idea of fate or otherwise ineluctable circumstances (see, for instance, 78, 89, 174, 211, 216, 218).

32. Idris Parry, "Footpath on the Water," in *Speak Silence: Essays* (Manchester, UK: Carcanet, 1988), 23–24.

cold explicability of cause and consequence is much crueler in its own way. (*Introit* realism.)

Each of these registers of sacrifice centers, crucially, upon the question of lawfulness or of order more generally, whether regarding the thing that is sacrificed or the thing for sake of which a sacrifice must be made. Incidentally, an encounter between these two paradigms is also at the center of Ebner-Eschenbach's novel, against which echoes of Goethe's seem to reverberate from the other side of the century. In hers too, as we will now see, water serves as both the site and the symbol of that encounter and as the carrier of those echoes.

II.

Burst Banks—Order and Transgression

The categories of duty and lawful order with which Ebner-Eschenbach sets the stage of her story are standard fare for late nineteenth-century novels that feature an adultery plot. In a recalled scene from her youth, for instance, the protagonist Maria Dornach (née Wolfsberg) is described as having "fulfilled all the filial duties her father expected of her" while preparing tea for him (3). From this early point, the text establishes a framework of lawfulness in terms of the dutiful obligation that children bear to their parents. What's more, here as elsewhere in the narrative, the gender dynamics are often such that the Austrian nobility's patriarchal structures appear in literal, personified form vis-à-vis its female members. Several lines earlier, for instance, we read that Maria's mother had not felt a vocation to marriage but eventually gave in to her brother's and future husband's pleas that she accept his proposal and take up residence as his wife. That decision is described by Wolfsberg's sister as "a great sacrifice," thus adumbrating a connection between the discourses of duty and sacrifice from the outset of the text (2).

The gendering of these discourses will continue to be underscored in the novel, especially through the recurring juxtapositions between Maria and her mother, in terms of both their personalities as well as their personal trajectories.[33] This is also accomplished by the more subtle contrast that the narrative draws with the "filial duties" that are performed by male characters; Hermann Dornach's uprightness and "obedience to his mother's wishes" suggests them to be forms of parental obligation reserved for males insofar as they are agentively assumed and thereby assigned a certain virtue, whereas the "feminine" versions of this order are not taken up as a matter of choice but instead inculcated with the implicit expectation that they will be fulfilled (10).[34]

With so many structures of social and moral lawfulness on display in the novel's preliminary chapters (not to mention its very title), the reader is alerted to the central importance of transgression in the story. Equally central, though, both as a motif and as a thematic framework unto itself, is water, and it will become increasingly clear that developments in the text's core drama can be effectively traced by way of water scenes. In other words, the gradual intensification of watery imagery throughout the novel corresponds to that of its key themes—namely, transgression, guilt, sacrifice and atonement. We see this as early as Hermann's proposal to Maria: "Two words, the extent of her youthful wisdom, fell almost inaudibly from her lips . . . the words of her father, which he had impressed upon his willing pupil: 'Stay calm!' Long ago, when she had

---

33. Tanzer points out that much as their respective marital fates are reverse images of each other (for instance, Maria "betrays" her marriage vows, whereas her mother was agentively betrayed by Wolfsberg), so too are their temperaments: Maria radiates "resolve, fortitude, clarity," whereas her mother exudes "idiosyncratic melancholy and helpless diffidence." Tanzer, *Frauenbilder*, 120.

34. Drawing upon Ingrid Aichinger's discussion of "Entsagungsmut" with a view to Ebner-Eschenbach's corpus as a whole, Edith Toegel says that "for the women protagonists renunciation becomes a way to self-fulfillment and in turn promotes individuality and independence." She suggests that even though Ebner-Eschenbach's male characters also practice renunciation, they do so in ways that are self-serving and "entrenched" in social conventions and mores of the time. For the female characters, by contrast, it is a decision that gets forced upon them with a degree of consistency that allows renunciation to "becom[e] the author's political statement about gender and ideology at a time of drastic social and political changes." Toegel, "'Entsagungsmut' in Marie von Ebner-Eschenbach's Works: A Female-Male Perspective," *Forum for Modern Language Studies* 28 (1992): 141.

thrown herself in despair over the body of her dead mother ... And, much, later, while hunting, when her horse had shied and raced toward the millstream" (14–15).

It is impossible to overlook this passage's stark symbolization of nature, instinct, and emotion in the speechless movements of water and bodies (both human and animal), on the one hand, and of control and self-possession in the organizing structures of thought and language, on the other—not to mention the overt binary opposition that is set up between them. However, lest we make the mistake of reading this vignette merely as a parochial depiction of a young woman being "carried away" by "nature" (as figured by the paired physicality of her runaway horse and her distraught embrace of her mother's remains), we should duly note how the passage complicates them by introducing a more subtle dialectic of control and immobilization. The novel's early pages already hint at this dialectic on the level of ambiguously threatened boundaries of physical affection, as when Hermann holds Maria's hand tightly when she tries to pull it away, much like her father pulls her into an embrace so tight that she cannot breathe (14, 19). Both instances can be read as gestures of male control that foreshadow the adultery scene itself, in which the language of bodily force is combined with metaphors of natural forces, causing the lines between mutual passion and one-sided coercion to become distressingly blurred. We later learn that Tessin is only able to surprise Maria on her own in the summerhouse through the machinations of her embittered and vengeful half-brother, and once there he makes the darkly ironic assertion that if Maria were to call for help from her attendants, he would have to "yield to force." But the inverse situation plays out: "He grasped her resisting hand" and "assailed her more and more fervently," and after Maria admits her own feelings for him and, "struggling in this most difficult battle," allows him to kiss her hand in a gesture of farewell, he pulls her into a passionate embrace. Maria "wanted to pull herself away from him—she wanted to save herself— but she lay on his breast, irresistibly drawn to him as though by the force of nature" (55). Unlike in the scene of narrowly averted disaster on horseback, Maria is unable to redirect one natural force away from another, with the result that she and Tessin, as "two ecstatic people," both lose "all consciousness of honor, duty, and fidelity."[35]

This scene of submergence in, and by, a particular "force of nature" presages that of another, more tragic (and externally literal) kind still awaiting her at the novel's climax. Prior to that, another sequence near water introduces the framework of moral (and nonviolent) sacrifice that will play such a central role in the latter part of the story. Not long after the affair Maria discovers that she is pregnant and, suffused with guilt, finds herself by a gentle stream that "flowed peacefully through the meadows, navigated there by rowboats, became a torrent in this narrow ravine. Seething and roaring, the spraying current circled and formed deep whirlpools, turned round and round, rose in pillars of foam, then madly threw itself back into its rocky bed, luring the onlooker to participation in its gushing, inexhaustible high spirits [*Lebenslust*]" (61/U 70). The language of "participation" in the water's "Lebenslust" recalls Bachelard's notion of material imagination, according to which a given natural element *conditions* specific modes of feeling, forms of thought, and modes of psychic life, rather than serving, in a secondary capacity, as a mere symbol for them. Nature, that is, becomes a vessel for human attunement as opposed to an object for metaphorization. For example, Bachelard suggests that it isn't the case that the virtue of "purity" as understood within the ethical and moral domain is something for which clear water simply serves as one of many possible images; rather, placid water stands as the very source— the *Quelle*, so to speak—for how the notion of purity is conceived and articulated in the first place, reflecting "the kind of *natural morality* learned through meditation on a fundamental substance."[36]

---

35. Pfeiffer argues that the adultery plot of Ebner-Eschenbach's novel centers, not upon an act of marital deception born out of lust (as in most examples of this genre authored by men), but instead upon the (Trillingian) theme of Maria's sincerity and authenticity to her sense of self in the face of constraints imposed by her patriarchal society—including, most overtly, the adultery itself. Pfeiffer, "Genre, Gender," 141.

36. Gaston Bachelard, *Water and Dreams: An Essay on the Imagination of Matter*, trans. Edith R. Farrell (Dallas: Pegasus Foundation, 1983), 14 (emphasis in the original).

What kind of "material imagination" might correspond to the water that Maria gazes at from the top of the ravine? Having changed from a tranquil, peaceful stream into a churning, hazardous torrent, it seems at first glance simply to mirror Maria's own moral trajectory from clarity and "purity" to chaos; however, this water graduates from the level of basic symbolism to that of material imagination insofar as it appears to inform (rather than merely reflect) Maria's psyche in the instants that follow. After all, it is here, at the point of her internal convergence with the water's material quality of tempestuous confluence, that she feels a sudden *compulsion* to *become one* with it: "Maria pictured it all to herself, saw herself step onto the bridge and move forward and then slowly and deliberately slip at just the right spot . . . totter, fall, be shattered on the rocks that, always shining, always wetly glistening, projected from the water" (61/U 70). Yet the fact that this water surges precisely with *Lebenslust* aligns seamlessly with what she chooses to do in the next instant: arrested by the thought of the growing child in her womb, she decides against suicide. "Perhaps, without her knowledge, the life force [*Lebenstrieb*], now doubled, struggled against annihilation" (62/U 71).

At a loss, she yearns for atonement through some other means but swiftly eliminates the possibility that it might consist in simply confessing to Hermann, since she suspects that his goodness would keep him from punishing her, or even allowing word of her misdeed to spread and her name to be stained. Moreover, she thinks to herself, "Then you will have taken on a new burden of gratitude and destroyed in vain the best of all that fills his heart and elevates his soul. You have nothing to lose, while he will lose everything." She therefore resolves at last to *sacrifice* this desire for absolution, dispelling the option of penal atonement (suicide or retribution) and thereby entering instead into a long-term exercise of ascetic atonement: "The atonement she longed for lay certainly in the realization that she was unable to atone. Fate's decree for her was this: 'You love truth; now live a lie.'" As we will see by the end of the novel, *this* is the form that her Bachelardian "participation" in the water ultimately takes—not self-destruction, but a penitent dedication to remaining alive in reconciliation with the fact that, like the swirling currents in the chasm, neither her body nor her conscience will come to lasting rest of their own accord.

However, hers is a course with many twists, turns, and eddy-like regressions. Following the birth of her second son, Erich (whose true provenance she keeps secret), she feels yet another pull toward water—this one, though, unambiguously operates under the aegis of the death drive rather than the "Lebenstrieb." We find her, as in her previously recollected memory of youth, once again alone on horseback:

> A green and grassy hollow bordered on the field and formed the bank of the clear, full stream. It was the same one that, up in the mountains, at the foot of the castle ruins, raged with such magnificent bravado through the rocks. Even from afar Maria could see its smooth surface glisten. There, taking its placid course in the shallow river bed, it had lost its rage. . . . A scream rose from Maria's breast and resounded weirdly through the silence. But listen—there was an answer: a dull, monotonous sound that came from a distance. At the entrance to the forest glen was a mill, and its gigantic wheel turned ceaselessly, driven by the falling stream. . . . Onward, toward it! Hadassa [her horse] does not swerve. A bitter smile twisted Maria's mouth. Life is poor, even in invention. Everything repeats itself. This is just what had happened years ago when she, hardly more than a child, was carried toward the death she now races to meet. . . . "Maria!" a voice suddenly rose above the rushing of the stream, "Maria!" and she, called back suddenly into the awareness of reality, started and pulled up on the reins. (74–75)

By this point, the steadily accumulating intimations of death in water have sounded a clear note of foreboding, which is certainly heightened by the above passage's rather Nietzschean accents of the millwheel that turns "ceaselessly" and the declaration that "everything repeats itself," yet which becomes even more discernible in conjunction with a key intertextual echo of *Elective Affinities*: namely, the fact that the features of Maria's second son are described as containing "a trace of the anguish of mind [*Seelenpein*] that had accompanied his development" (70/U 80). While in Goethe's story the features of the infant mysteriously constituted a trace of the psychological and spiritual event of *imagined* union (of Eduard with Ottilie, and of Charlotte with the Captain) which coincided with his actual conception by Eduard and Charlotte, Ebner-Eschenbach keeps her text firmly within the boundaries of realism insofar as the adulterously conceived child resembles both of his biological parents ("'He has a stranger's eyes and his mother's face,' decided the nurse"). This distinction will turn out to make *Elective Affinities* an even more powerful as a point of comparison, though, because the knowledge of what befalls the child in that novel stokes the reader's anticipation that the imminent catastrophe in *Beyond Atonement* will likewise center upon the innocent child who physiognomically manifests the transgressive circumstances of his origin. However, the tragedy that Ebner-Eschenbach has in store is in a way even more wrenching than this, for the innocent characters who end up drowning—Hermann and his son—in every objective sense bear no "mark" of transgression in the way that Erich or the baby in *Elective Affinities* do. This dynamic assumes preliminary shape in Hermann's declaration to Maria shortly before the drowning that *he* carries a "debt" (*Schuld*) to her—namely, that he had pursued her when she did not want to marry him—which "fate" (*Schicksal*) has reciprocated with "gifts of grace," leaving him to wonder when he will at last be "punished" for this "crime against you—one beyond atonement" (71/U 81).

I do not think it would be overstating matters to suggest that Hermann's closely packed allusions to fate, grace, punishment, and atonement do not simply evoke but actually invoke the mythic paradigm of sacrifice that Benjamin detected within every nook and cranny of Goethe's novel, but with this additional dose of cruel irony: deeming it unsafe, Hermann had on several occasions removed a "rickety footbridge" spanning the river that ends up serving as the (literal) launching point for the terrible accident lurking on the horizon, but woodcutters kept putting the footbridge back so that they could avoid a longer route from the mountain (98). In an almost Sophoclean twist, the conditions for the event that will claim both Hermann and his son as victims had been unknowingly removed by him and then unknowingly reestablished by strangers under wholly unrelated circumstances. Ebner-Eschenbach's narrative is suddenly injected with the recognizably realist modalities of coincidence, cause, and consequence, which enter into a contrapuntal dance with the discourse of tragic (perhaps even "mythic") fate that has been threaded through the novel up to this point.

On the ill-fated day, during a group outing to the surrounding countryside, one of Maria's and Hermann's friends, standing with them on a hill on the opposite side of the river from their son, suddenly chooses to make a "fateful joke" and calls down to the boy, daring him to join them. Maria and Hermann both scream at the boy to stay away from the bank, but "the child seemed to have made a quick decision and was running toward the footbridge" (99). Like the conditions that have led to the unsafe crossing's continued presence, these two impulsive choices, made in quick succession, add a further inflection of coincidence to the tragic events that are about to take place. As the adults hurry down the hillside toward the bank, their son's "little white tunic shimmered through the branches of the willows, and then he appeared on the footbridge." Goethe's Ottilie haunts this heart-wrenching sequence, for she too "stood confused and agitated" and "looked across to the house on the hill and thought she saw Charlotte's white dress on the balcony," and she too made a chance—but no less fateful—choice: "In her thoughts she was already over, as she was with her eyes. The risk of going on the water with the child vanished in her urgency" (*EA* 207–208).

The points of comparison between the two novels continue to mount: Maria and Hermann's son loses his balance and falls into the coursing water, and his father's attempt to save him appears at first to recapitulate the Captain's rescue of the drowning boy in *Elective Affinities*: "Overtaking all the others, Hermann had reached the bank. Keeping his eyes fixed on the child, who, without sinking, was being swept away by the current, he threw off his coat and leapt into the turbulent water" (99). Likewise, Goethe's Captain "made up his mind, he threw off his outer garments, all eyes were upon him, and his solid and powerful form filled everyone with confidence" (*EA* 95). Hereafter, though, the two scenes abruptly diverge: the Captain, "being a strong swimmer, [had] reached the boy and brought him, but dead as it seemed, to the dam. . . . [E]veryone was safe." By contrast, in *Beyond Atonement* nature takes on the mythic characteristics of a vengeful adversary: "Hermann, with superhuman strength, was holding out against the force of the current"; the others try desperately to reach him, but to no avail: "The enormous spiral of the whirlpool had already encircled father and son and pulled them down and with savage fury thrown them up again, gasping, covered with foam. A last, horrible struggle. Exhausted, overcome, flung mercilessly against the rocks, Hermann still attempted to cover his child's body with his own" (100).

Unlike the boy in *Elective Affinities*, the father and son in Ebner-Eschenbach's scene do not merely *seem* lifeless when they are at last retrieved from the water. In this, there is an even more rending contrast with Goethe's text, and specifically with the embedded novella, "Strange Neighbors." The climax of that intradiegetic narration describes how a young lover succeeds in rescuing and resuscitating his nearly drowned beloved: "Water is a friendly element for whoever knows it well and is able to manage it. It bore him up, and being a good swimmer he mastered it. He had soon reached the girl carried away ahead of him; he seized her, raised, and bore her.... Now the intense desire to save overrode every other consideration. Nothing was left undone that might bring the beautiful, stiffening, naked body back to life. It worked. She opened her eyes'" (*EA* 191). For Maria, the opposite scenario unfolds with brutal starkness as she "pressed her mouth to that of the dead man and breathed into it until her breath failed her. She did not arouse the slightest response from him. And now she understood that she had lost him.... Close to madness, she prayed, she begged for a miracle" (101).

Years before, in a flush of happiness over the birth of her first son and her overall situation in life, Maria had regarded it as her "duty to count herself among" those whom "fortune" (*Schicksal*) had "chosen" (39/U 46). But chosen in what sense, and for what? The implicit answers to both questions had seemed decidedly positive in tone at that early juncture of the narrative, but now get retroactively transposed into a darker key. As it turns out, her husband and firstborn have in a certain respect been "chosen" too: namely, as *Opfer* in both available senses of the term. They appear as innocent *victims* of catastrophic (but wholly chance) misfortune, yet Hermann, in his desperate final moments, also introduces a kenotic register of *sacrifice* in giving his own life in the attempt to save his son's. After their remains are brought back to Castle Dornach, their intertwined fates are physically literalized when the rescuers are unable to "disengage the hand of the child from that of his father, and so the two of them lay next to each other on one bed and would lie in one coffin as well" (101).

With notable subtlety, Ebner-Eschenbach's drowning scene evokes the mythic paradigm of fateful victimhood while simultaneously lending itself to entirely causal, realist explanation. Both of these narrative registers are then thrown into relief against a moral register of self-sacrifice, which will ultimately occupy the foreground of the novel's last chapters. The conjunction of all three of these frameworks—fate, coincidence, and decision—is movingly externalized in the rigor mortis of the clasped hands of father and son, and will also soon be internalized in Maria's actions near the end of her own life.

III.

Before turning our attention to the novel's final arc, it will be useful to note how up to this point, when the motif of water has appeared, it has been in the mode of a Bachelardian "material image" for the complex dynamics of sacrificial decision (Maria's as well as Hermann's). An additional and related theme it has conveyed is, appropriately, that of relationality itself. That is, the key scenes involving water thus far have centered upon characters deciding whether or not to offer up something for the sake of something else—of one's sense of justice for the sake of an other's happiness, and vice versa; or most pivotally, of one's life for the sake of an other's. Consequently, these scenes have also concerned numerous different relations—of the human to the nonhuman, of the individual to the other, of men to women, of children to parents, and so forth. A strikingly synthetic image of this occurs prior to the drowning, when Castle Dornach hosts a lavish hunting party. Surveying the guests at the evening ball, Maria perceives the sight of them as a seething "storm-tossed sea" of vanity and diversion, convulsed by "a roaring and tumbling":

The waves towered to the sky, plunged to unfathomable depths, climbed up only to sink again: an eternal rising and falling. And a howl of pain burst forth from this ghastly churning of waves—hunted, hunting, devouring, devoured—for they consisted of the bodies of animals and humans, they were the tortured family of the living, and the ocean that drove this tide was an ocean of suffering. Occasionally a twinkling star appeared high on the horizon, and millions of human hearts rose up, yearning eyes drank in its trembling light. But it was not long till they knew that the glow that smoldered and promised was only the reflection of the longing for comfort, of the hope—in their own hearts. (81)

In spite of its brevity, this passage is deft in its demonstration of how capacious water imagery can be, particularly in Ebner-Eschenbach's hands. It could, for instance, be read as an index of the pronounced social criticism that critics have identified across her writing as a whole.[37] Or more specifically, it could be seen as an index of the "ambivalence" ascribed to many of her female characters as one of several "more subtle forms of resistance" to the patriarchal structure of her biographical time and place.[38] The image yields still more hermeneutic possibilities than the sociopolitical alone, however, as when Burkhard Bittrich, in his accompanying commentary on the novel, rightly recognizes in these lines a clear echo of the metaphysical pessimism that Arthur Schopenhauer had famously distilled within an almost identical image of his own (*U* 341–342):

---

37. Aichinger identifies a discrepancy between Ebner-Eschenbach's seemingly simple narratives, often regarded as escapist, and her personal "remarks about corrupt jurisprudence and a lacking sense of justice overall; the dominant state apparatus's determinations at the expense of the individual; and, lastly, incensed commentary in connection with growing anti-semitism and nationalism." Referring to another work, but in terms very pertinent to *Unsühnbar*, Aichinger describes "the narrator's overarching consciousness" as one in which "skepticism . . . bears its witness in a critical distance from out of which the question of guilt is problematized and relativized through the pragmatic unfolding of the conflict between the 'I' and its social environment." Aichinger, "Harmonisierung oder Skepsis? Zum Prosawerk der Marie von Ebner-Eschenbach," *Österreich in Geschichte und Literatur* 16 (1971): 484.

38. Tanzer takes previous feminist criticism to task for overlooking these characters as a result of their subtle modes of resistance, as opposed to more explicit or even radical ones (*Frauenbilder*, 5).

> Just as a captain sits in a boat, trusting the weak little vessel as the raging, boundless sea raises up and casts down howling cliffs of waves; so the human individual sits calmly in a world full of sorrow, supported by and trusting in the *principium individuationis*, which is how the individual cognizes things as appearance. The boundless world, everywhere full of suffering, with its infinite past and infinite future, is alien to him—in fact, it is a fairy tale: his vanishing little person, his unextended present, his momentary comfort, these alone have reality for him.[39]

Water, then, certainly appears in a variety of forms and with a variety of implications in *Beyond Atonement*, but in doing so also evokes a rich array of themes that were also of interest to a contemporary of Ebner-Eschenbach (and a sharp reader of Schopenhauer)—Friedrich Nietzsche, whose philosophical writings on precisely those themes provide a helpful frame for our analysis of the novel's final act.

The Ladder of Offering

Nietzsche's 1886 text *Jenseits von Gut und Böse* (*Beyond Good and Evil*) at one point develops a speculative ethnography of sacrifice and religiosity. In §55, Nietzsche describes a "ladder of religious cruelty" that stretches through human history. The first rung is said to comprise the practices in which "people used to make human sacrifices to their god, perhaps even sacrificing the one they loved the best." The two rungs that succeed this first one, however, are the most applicable to Maria's inner drama: "Then, during the moral epoch of humanity, people sacrificed the strongest instincts they had, their 'nature,' to their god. . . . . Finally: what was left to be sacrificed? In the end, didn't people have to sacrifice all comfort and hope, everything holy or healing, any faith in a hidden harmony or a future filled with justice and bliss? Didn't people have to sacrifice God himself and worship rocks, stupidity, gravity, fate, or nothingness out of sheer cruelty to themselves?"[40] In broad terms, these rungs of Nietzsche's ladder depict a gradual evolution in the sacri-

---

39. Arthur Schopenhauer, *The World as Will and Representation*, vol. 1, trans. Judith Norman et al. (Cambridge: Cambridge University Press, 2010), 379 (§63).
40. Friedrich Nietzsche, *Beyond Good and Evil*, trans. Judith Norman (Cambridge: Cambridge University Press, 2002), 50.

ficial psychology of qualification—a transition from offering beloved *objects*, to offering up specific desires and apparatuses of comfort, to at last relinquishing the possibility of immanence or purpose within existence as such (including, perhaps, the very logic underpinning sacrifice itself).

For the sake of argument, let us briefly compare the "middle rung" with Maria's trajectory following the affair: Following human sacrifice in primeval religions, Nietzsche claims that a new sacrificial model of self-abnegation arose. In other words, the individual self and its "nature" take the place of external objects and living beings as offerings. In Maria's case, pregnant with Tessin's illicit child, a comparable transition begins with her deferral of the moral gratification that invests the possibility of expiating her marital guilt (whether by drowning herself or by confessing to Hermann), which she construes as a secondary form of atonement in itself ("you love truth, now live a lie"). In so doing, she consciously avoids accruing additional guilt that would result from either method of expiation: firstly, "she realized that she could not die without committing a double murder. To be sure, a thought flamed up in her: bury the fruit of transgression with you! But to *kill* in order to atone? She was still pious and devout" (62, emphasis in the original). Secondly, as she silently exclaims to herself atop the ravine, to reveal the infidelity to Hermann in the hopes of receiving punishment would in turn destroy his happiness, and yet she intuits that "he will demand respect for you from others. Then you will have taken on a new burden of gratitude.... You will have made him miserable to no purpose" (62). The irony, of course, is that even though Maria decides against either of these courses of action, her firstborn *and* Hermann both die anyway. Faced with this much worse tragedy of which she is personally innocent, it is almost as though her original guilt accrues an "interest" that can only be "canceled" by other means. Let's look more closely at how Maria arrives at those means (and, with them, at the third rung of Nietzsche's ladder).

As Maria's cousin Wilhelm reads aloud the deceased Hermann's will and testament in the presence of Maria, her father, and Hermann's mother, Countess Agathe, the official document's stirring references to its author's love for Maria in praise of her goodness become too much for her conscience to bear, and she abruptly confesses by way of declaring that Erich is not eligible to inherit Hermann's title or estate (106). A hole in the fabric of positive law suddenly becomes a channel for communicating the hitherto concealed breach in moral law that has formed the central arc of the novel's plot.[41] There are various interpretive as well as philosophical implications to be drawn from this. For example, it is possible to see Maria's admission as highlighting a distinction (*qua* relation) between "natural law" (*physis*) and the human laws of custom (*nomos*) à la Aristotle.[42] Alternatively, the fact that these two categories of law fall together as part of the larger event of truth's revelation recalls one of Plato's definitions of law as that which "tends to be discovery of reality."[43]

The sudden discovery of Maria's secret elicits shocked and outraged reactions from those present, and it is swiftly established that Wilhelm is next in line to inherit the estate, but he insists that the law protects Erich's claim to it since he was technically born within the marriage (just not fathered by Hermann). Maria's father promises that in spite of his legal claim, Erich will not inherit and will be raised "as befits him, and once he is of age he will sign his renunciation [*Verzichtleistung*] of the title with the awareness that the act of signing is a mere formality," to which Maria agrees (107/U 121). An attempt is thus made for the breach in moral law to be atoned for by a legal means of renunciation (*Verzichtleistung*), which forms an ironic counterpoint to Ottilie's penitential act of physical and lin-

---

41. Compare Kenworthy, "Ethical Realism," 485.

42. The distinction between *physis* and *nomos* is important for Aristotle in many places (for example, *Nichomachean Ethics* 1135a), but his *Rhetoric* offers one of the more succinct explications of it. At one point in book I.13 (1373b), he remarks that there are "two sorts of laws.... I mean that law is on the one hand special and on the other hand common, the latter being unwritten, the former written, and special being what each [community] has defined relative to itself, and common in accord with nature." Aristotle, *Rhetoric*, trans. C. D. C Reeve (Indianapolis: Hackett, 2018), 45 (brackets in the original).

43. Plato, *Minos*, in *Plato in Twelve Volumes*, vol. 12, trans. W. R. M. Lamb (Cambridge, MA: Harvard University Press, 1955), 395 (315A). An alternative translation of "Ὁ νόμος ἄρα βούλεται τοῦ ὄντος εἶναι ἐξεύρεσις" might read something like "law wills to be the discovery of that which really is."

guistic renunciation (*Entsagung*) at the end of *Elective Affinities*. That is, both Ottilie's *Entsagung* and Erich's future *Verzichtleistung* center upon the refusal or negation of something in order to fill in a gap that has appeared within the moral order; for both, that is, renunciation involves the redress of one lack by means of another lack. As we will see, Maria ultimately seeks to redress her own lack—that is, to atone—not via negation, as Ottilie and the *Verzichtleistung* do, but instead via the continuation of her life. This begins, though, with her "withdrawal" of a different sort: not from life per se, as in Ottilie's case, but from life in society.

Maria returns to live alone with Erich at her father's estate; after winter passes, she is described by her aunt as having become "rather unwell" (114). Soon after, her father learns from the family doctor that her condition is precarious, and that "all excitement, no matter how trivial, may have the worst consequences for her" (115). He at last goes to see her, finding the grounds overgrown and the house in disarray, and Maria herself "transparently pale"; when she later demands of her father that he not involve himself in Erich's future in any way, even after her death, "her unshakeable composure moved him to the depths of his soul. It seemed to him to be the composure of someone who has half departed this world, who no longer hopes or desires" (116–117). When he suggests that she relocate with her son to cheerier and healthier surroundings, she declines sharply: "Let me bury myself here, let me be dead for everyone; it's the only way I can bear to be alive" (118). The precise status of this new life of hers, shorn of her former status and persona and relocated from the *polis* to the *oikos*, becomes clearer when Tessin unexpectedly visits her one last time. He perceives her as a "faded woman," and tells her that she looks to be "ailing." "'And dreadfully changed,' he added mentally" (120). When Maria spurns his amorous declarations by expressing regret over her betrayal of Hermann, his manner abruptly changes and he asks, cruelly, if she wishes to commit suicide. She replies: "No, I want to live in order to raise my child. . . . I want to teach him to be upright and true and strong, and enemy of all that glitters and pretends and lies" (121).

With this declaration, Maria evokes the two Aristotelian registers of "life," which Giorgio Agamben has elucidated as the organic or animal life common to all living beings (*zoè*), and the "mode" or "form" of life proper to the political and ethical-moral existence of human beings (*bios*).[44] Within the contours of Maria's penitential project, however, these two registers could be said to interweave, *zoè* blending with *bios*, insofar as the act of staying alive becomes intrinsic to her effort to inculcate a specific form of life in Erich as a counterbalance to her transgression. This blurring of Aristotle's distinction between *bios* and *zoè* considerably predates nineteenth-century realism, however. Indeed, Agamben argues, that is exactly what one finds in the third-century philosopher Plotinus's description of the "happy life" in terms of a *bios* whose form is nothing less than *zoè* itself (*Ennead* I.4.3). In this Neoplatonist articulation, "life is never separable from its form and, quite to the contrary, is always its mode of being, without for that reason ceasing to be one.... The happy life here appears as a life that does not possess its form as a part or a quality but *is* this form, has completely passed into it." Maria's penitence thus resembles, at least analogically, one of the core features of the happy life according to Plotinus, for in resolving to keep living for the sake of instilling a new mode of living in Erich, her own *zoè* becomes a *bios* unto itself, such that the latter days of her existence demonstrate "that there can be a *bios*, a mode of life, that is defined solely by means of its special and inseparable union with *zoè* and has no other content than the latter (and, reciprocally, that there is a *zoè* that is nothing other than its form, its *bios*)."[45]

The possibility of precisely this seems to be almost within reach when Maria eventually extracts a promise from Tessin that he will not lay claim to Erich and will sever all ties with them. However, like Eduard's affirmative reply to Ottilie's final words to him— "Promise me you will live!" (*EA* 235)—Maria's resolution proves to be doomed. As soon as Tessin leaves the room, Maria falls into a faint, which the doctor will attribute to "a rupture of the heart,"

---

44. Giorgio Agamben, *Homo Sacer: Sovereign Power and Bare Life*, trans. Daniel Heller-Roazen (Stanford, CA: Stanford University Press, 1998), 1–2.

45. Giorgio Agamben, *The Use of Bodies*, trans. Adam Kotsko (Stanford, CA: Stanford University Press, 2015), 218–219 (emphasis in the original).

and she is soon on the threshold of death (125). In this sense, the locus of her potential atonement has shifted from *her* life or death—and from the potential for either to constitute an act of sacrifice—and is now situated instead in Erich's life as he will go on to live it; the success or failure of her atonement is now out of her hands.

After recovering consciousness, she asks Lisette, her loyal former nanny, whether she thinks it will be permitted for Maria to be buried beside Hermann in the family crypt. "There, where he is now . . . we will lie hand in hand behind the stones. Not a single sound will reach us, not a single voice—not even the voice of conscience" (123). In her final hour, surrounded by members of her household, it becomes clear that this vision of the hereafter is very much limited to the "here," and that it houses the "after" in a strictly temporal (rather than transcendent) sense:

> Helmi had knelt down before her. "Maria, dearest, beloved Maria," she implored in a low voice, "do not depart this life unreconciled with God; fulfil your duty as a Christian . . . prepare yourself to lay your head on the heart of the All-bountiful."
> "The—All-bountiful?"
> "In whom you believe—"
> "In whom I believe?" Longingly she repeated Helmi's words in a whisper. "All is lost, Helmi—the belief in providence . . . even the belief in my free will . . . and yet I still have only one wish. . . ." Her last strength exhausted itself in the words, "Oh, if only I had never done wrong!" (126)

In claiming to have lost her faith on multiple counts, Maria recapitulates a pivotal stage from her mother's own life. She discovers this early in the novel after finding a letter that her mother had written to her father following the discovery of his illegitimate son (Maria's half-brother, Wolfi), which contains a stronger, Manichean refutation: "Have I not faithfully fulfilled all my duties? Was I not devout and pious? If God were good and just, He would have answered my prayers. But there is no God at all in heaven, only a devil, and he is punishing me" (33). In another place, her mother's writing shifts focus from the transcendent to the earthly realm, declaring, "I would not have sacrificed for you what she [Wolfi's mother] did: her parents, her home, honor and duty" (33). The categories of duty and lawfulness (both domestic and doctrinal) are therefore introduced at this early juncture as part of a sacrificial economy in which Maria's own past is implicated.

Not long after her clandestine reading of the letters, we learn that Maria has begun to regard her mother as, not the "victim [*Opfer*] of a crime, but the martyr to an unavoidable fate, a saint transfigured by suffering" (39/U 46). Maria's own case is somewhat more complicated, however, at least in the eyes of scholarship on the novel, some of which has argued that she does indeed function as an *Opfer*, though there is little consensus upon the sense in which this is so. Ulrike Tanzer suggests that she should be seen as a victim not of mythic fate (as in Benjamin's account of Ottilie), but of a "patriarchal power struggle" by Tessin and Wolfi to exact revenge against her father.[46] Ingrid Aichinger, meanwhile, says that an analysis of guilt should not reduce it simply to social factors, because these appear in the text as part of a more general "inclination to see human existence at the same time as determined by ahistorical forces like heredity and fate." In light of this, she writes, "Maria is to be regarded as a victim not only of societal dictates but also of her own weakness—though a weakness that is, at least in part, biologically motivated."[47] Charlotte Woodford offers a third alternative reading, in which Maria's sacrificial status is construed, not as passive victimhood (whether of biological determinism, mythic fate, or patriarchal social forces), but instead as freely willed self-sabotage: "Maria's virtue . . . is the basis for Hermann's happiness and his honour, and so she conceals Erich's illegitimacy, the ultimate crime against the patriarchal order. . . . She sacrifices her moral integrity and the opportunity of seeking forgiveness."[48]

---

46. Tanzer, *Frauenbilder*, 126.
47. Aichinger, "Harmonisierung oder Skepsis?," 488.
48. Charlotte Woodford, "Realism and Sentimentalism in Marie von Ebner-Eschenbach's *Unsühnbar*," *Modern Language Review* 101 (2006): 156. As we have seen, though, that initial sacrifice must be understood in context with the more dramatic sacrifice that Maria ultimately performs at the end in revealing Erich's illegitimacy. The dynamics of this subsequent sacrifice come to the fore in a remark that Ebner-Eschenbach herself makes in a letter to Julius Rodenberg (March 12, 1889), in which she refers to the real incident in Austrian society that inspired *Unsühnbar* and how she had been occupied by the "thought . . . of motivating the he-

In whatever sense one wishes to interpret Maria's *Opfertum*, its intrinsic connection to the mission of atonement is plain. The precise nature of the desired atonement does invite further consideration, however. Whereas Ottilie's drawn-out death resembled (or was made to resemble) a penitential act in itself, Maria has already indicated that it is precisely by *staying alive* that she hopes to atone—survival becomes its own form of sacrifice. As in the two earlier scenes where Maria, alone near water, is drawn to the possibility of suicide, here again any despair-driven desire for "annihilation" is offered up instead to "the life force" that struggles against it (62). From this vantage point, her imminent death represents a deferral rather than a fulfillment of atonement: "You see that I will not be permitted to live for the child . . . nor will I be permitted to expiate any part of my sin," she tells Wilhelm and Helmi in her last hours. She continues, saying that she has "repented, but not atoned" for her guilt. "I could never have done that. . . . The awareness of that makes life difficult . . . and death, too." (125). These pivotal words—some of her last in the book—recall the ones she had used in her final conversation with Tessin to describe "a sin that can no more be washed away by tears of remorse than a cliff by the waves that break at its base" (121). All of this suggests, finally, that there remains a "surplus value" of guilt that cannot be discharged with the cessation of her life, only defaulted upon. In what sense might this be so?

One answer is that sacrifice has disappeared as a viable mode of pursuing atonement. If one were to read Ebner-Eschenbach's drowning scene through the mythic lens that Benjamin applies to *Elective Affinities* and construe it as a "choosing" of innocent victims by fate, one immediately comes up against the fact that, far from somehow "settling" or balancing out the *Schuld* (guilt/debt) that Maria feels for the affair, this tragic event actually intensifies and extends it. To an equal degree, the moral declension of sacrifice that we noted in Maria's prior decision to undergo "inner" atonement by giving up (or *renouncing*) the possibility of "external" atonement for the affair—by either drowning herself or seeking

---

roic resolve of a noble and broadly admired woman to destroy her immaculate reputation in order to honor the truth." (Quoted in Tanzer, *Frauenbilder*, 111.)

punishment by Hermann—likewise failed to discharge either the marital guilt or its subsequently compounded form. And finally, insofar as she understands the act of continuing to live in orientation around Erich's moral formation as a last form of atonement, her own death soon forecloses the possibility of any fully realized expiation; in lieu of her own survival, her guilt survives her like an uncanceled debt. As a consequence, the future of this debt can remain open only through means other than her own—namely, via two kinds of order: the legal means of Erich's renunciation of his inheritance, and the moral means of the way of life that Maria hopes he will go on to actualize. Because *her* life has already supplanted sacrifice as a path to atonement, at the moment of her death *Erich's* life, with its two incorporate orders, becomes the new locus of atonement's potentiality—not just the life of his body (*zoè*) and of his being in the *polis* (*bios*) under the aegis of law (*Verzichtleistung*), but perhaps also the life of his "flesh" in Eric Santner's sense, within which the other two *vitae* converge in an enveloping "jointure of the somatic and the normative dimensions of human life."[49]

The question of sacrifice's supplantation broaches a second key point of comparison between Maria and her mother; namely, the issue of lost faith. Maria, for her part, does not articulate this loss by reference to God (as her mother had in her letters), but instead by the notion of divine providence (*Vorsehung*) and even to her "free will" (*U* 142). Both losses were arguably presaged on that tragic day by the river, when Maria tried to resuscitate Hermann by "pressing her mouth to that of the dead man [*dem Entseelten*]" (101/*U* 114). Ebner-Eschenbach's language reverses the biblical account of creation in Genesis 2:7, in which God breathes the "breath of life" (Lat. *spiraculum vitae*; Grk. *pnoēn zoēs*) into the human form made from clay, which thereby becomes "a living soul" (*animam viventem/ psychēn zōsan*). Neither by will nor by providence can Maria's own breath catch hold of the departed soul that has left behind the body she cradles against her own (as in Ottilie's *Augenblick*, adrift

---

49. Eric L. Santner, *The Weight of All Flesh: On the Subject-Matter of Political Economy* (Oxford: Oxford University Press, 2015), 238.

on the water with the lifeless child at her breast); in this de-creation scene, God is nowhere to be found, and, "close to madness, she prayed, she begged for a miracle." None comes.

By the time she declares her loss of faith just before passing from life into death, Maria seems to have reached, albeit gradually and via several circuitous routes, a variation of the third rung of Nietzsche's ladder: her belief, she says, is gone, though not because it has been sacrificed—indeed, even the potential for sacrifice has faded for her as well. All that remain are her unfulfillable wish and the undiminished need for atonement with which it corresponds, a need for which neither sacrifice nor God any longer serve as possible recourses. The stones of the crypt mark these conceptual remains and absences as much as the literal ones lying beneath them, echoing Maria's aforementioned depiction of her moral predicament as "a sin that can no more be washed away by tears of remorse than a cliff by the waves that break at its base" (121). In the measure that this is a story about order, transgression, sacrifice, and atonement, it is also a story about water and stone.

What we see in this late novel of Poetic Realism is, finally, a portrayal of sacrifice's "end" in the classical double sense—a portrayal not only of its aim but also of its dissolution. Concomitantly, we also witness the twofold "end" of Maria's life as conditioned by sacrifice.[50] The possibility of a sacrificial negotiation of transgressed law has faded; now only a literalization of law itself (that is, Erich's enforced "renunciation" via the legal procedure of *Verzichtleistung*, in contrast to Ottilie's sacrificial *Entsagung*) can attend to it. Nor can Maria reenact her decision in the first half of the book, following the affair with Tessin, to "sacrifice" the potential for punishment as a form of atonement in its own right: *life* has replaced death as the only fitting form of penance for her, such that its

---

50. Here one could detect yet another resonance with Goethe's novel and its depiction of "the historical-cultural process" of disintegration and "collapse of the symbolic" which, as a "not merely aesthetic but general cultural phenomenon," is "thus always related to an order that has the character of law." David E. Wellbery, "Die Wahlverwandtschaften (1809)," in *Goethes Erzählwerk: Interpretationen*, ed. Paul Michael Lützeler and James W. McLeod (Stuttgart: Reclam, 1985), 291–292.

eventual usurpation by death at the end of the novel dispels the possibility of further atonement (*Sühne*), let alone expiation (*Entsühnung*). Both of these categories (which we also saw invoked by Benjamin) are now, like the drowned Hermann and his son, *entseelt* (unsouled) and incapable of being revived by human attempts alone; and unlike the "cliff" of Maria's accrued guilt, sacrifice can be and has been eroded and submerged beneath the "waves" of tears and regret. In her last moments, Maria, like the statue of the cognominal Russian princess that Ebner-Eschenbach would behold over a decade later in Rome's Campo Cestio, "exhales a sorrow that is breathed through each and every detail" of her character, almost in response to—or continuation of—the instant in which she had thrown herself down onto the riverbank next to Hermann, and, desperate, "pressed her mouth to that of the dead man and breathed into it until her breath failed her." And yet the atmosphere surrounding her own deathbed is not purely mournful but also tinged with a certain tone of quietude, even peace, for as the final lines of the text recount, Maria's lifeless gaze had settled on a moonlit patch of the distant horizon: "There, where it was bright, where the transfiguring glow radiated outward—lay Dornach" (127). In this concurrence of moonlight, resignation, and rest, we can make out a Virgilian signature that Erwin Panofsky eloquently describes as a "vespertinal mixture of sadness and tranquility" in which one seems to "feel evening silently settle over the world."[51] With just such an evening Ebner-Eschenbach's narrative draws to a close.

Much remains to be said about how *Elective Affinities* and *Beyond Atonement* present drowning—interestingly, of nonfemale characters in both cases—in connection with the gendered sacrificial dynamics at work within the (patriarchal) honor paradigms that determine the ideals of marriage and virtue, which in turn form the backdrop of both novels' plots (along with those of much German Realist fiction). Previous scholarship on Ebner-Eschenbach's novel has rightly dis-

---

51. Erwin Panofsky, "*Et in Arcadia Ego*: Poussin and the Elegiac Tradition," in *Meaning in the Visual Arts* (Chicago: University of Chicago Press, 1982), 300–301.

cerned that its central themes of transgression, guilt, sacrifice, and penitence (if not atonement) must be understood within this modern sociohistorical context, which itself appears in the story as a theme in its own right.[52] At the same time, we have observed how the context of fateful chance stubbornly haunts Ebner-Eschenbach's story, much as Benjamin argued fate per se to have done Goethe's. Both contexts become interwoven within the motif of drowning, through which these two novels from either end of the nineteenth century interweave in turn. Appropriately, we have also seen that both texts feature a dialogical interplay between two different paradigms of sacrifice and atonement, respectively: a recognizably "modern" genre of personal decision to relinquish something for the sake of something else, accompanied by atonement in the mode of interior purgation; and a "mythic" genre of a victim (or here, victims) being "taken" by fate in seemingly reciprocal response to a transgression committed by someone other than the victims themselves.

A further attribute of German Realism that has made itself known in both *Elective Affinities* and *Beyond Atonement*—again via the symbolism inherent to water—is the narratological tension between the presentable and the unpresentable, between the "surface" and "depths." The imagery of submergence that suffuses German Realism nearly always instances this formal liminality—or, better,

---

52. The issue of how exactly to understand Maria's guilt has been a source of divergent interpretations, however. For instance, Bramkamp argues that the novel should be read as a critique, not of Maria's "immoral" behavior, but instead of the sociosexual and moral double standards of her milieu (both the Viennese aristocracy specifically, as well as modern culture in general): "It is not only Maria's personal sin that by her own adherence to a flawless image of herself is unredeemable. Beyond atonement is the guilt of generations that have subjugated women.... The title *Unsühnbar* then is not only to be interpreted as a moral judgment concerning the main character, but is at the same time an indictment of a whole society." Aichinger, meanwhile, analyzes Maria's guilt on its own terms and argues that it is rooted in her "half measure" (*Halbheit*), because despite her professed passion for the truth, she "is able neither to admit her love ... nor later to address the consequences of her adultery." It is only when Maria is near death that she attains authenticity via skepticism: "Insofar as Maria acknowledges her doubt in the face of her life's contradictions, she is more true than her environment with its weddedness to mere appearance." Bramkamp, *Marie von Ebner-Eschenbach*, 122; Aichinger, "Harmonisierung oder Skepsis?," 487.

littorality—insofar as it constitutes a narratological *vanishing point* par excellence. In Goethe's and Ebner-Eschenbach's respective texts, as in the ones by Stifter, Keller, and Storm that I will examine in later chapters, we are rarely, if ever, provided access to what takes place below the surface. There as elsewhere in nineteenth-century German literature, scenes of drowning do not so much draw our gaze down and out of the everyday lifeworld (*Lebenswelt*) of perception and experience, as Husserl would later term it; rather, they somewhat ironically refocus our gaze upon precisely this latter sphere. True to its name, realism, unlike subsequent modernist instantiations of the drowning motif, anchors us within the realm of the familiar and observable even as it announces this realm's imbrication with that of the uncanny and unseen.

Having been placed at the interstice of surfaces and depths, we will come to discover in the drowning scenes of German Realism a poetics of the ever-present threshold. It is therefore perhaps not surprising that the literature of this epoch fixates as much on the dynamics of watery surfaces as on those of its depths.[53] Somewhat like Schiller's notion of the theatrical *Außending* discussed in the introduction, then, a core function of water in German Realist literature will prove to be the disclosure of truth as a space of jointure *between* perception and intuition. In that measure, drowning—as a phenomenon precisely of fluid passage between the spheres of what can be seen and what can only be imagined—stands in a rela-

---

53. Vera Bachmann suggests that "postmodernity" is generally interested in the paradigm of surfaces over and against "the long-preferred depths," and that this "prehistory of the postmodern celebration of surfaces" begins in the nineteenth century. Bachmann argues that whereas the depths were favored as a key metaphor (and the surface proportionally disregarded) since antiquity, in the eighteenth century the images of surface and depths begin to "mutually stabilize" one another as aesthetic and epistemological topoi in discourses such as geology, physiognomy, and aesthetics (starting with Winckelmann, in particular). Interestingly, Bachmann maintains that "the heroes of bourgeois [German] Realism" tend to avoid—indeed, even "shy away from"—the question of depths in favor of the surface as a matter of post-Romantic principle: "To still be earnestly celebrating the depths as a dimension of truth and meaning seems entirely ridiculous in the late nineteenth century." Vera Bachmann, *Stille Wasser—tiefe Texte? Zur Ästhetik der Oberfläche in der Literatur des 19. Jahrhunderts* (Bielefeld: Transcript, 2013), 9, 12, 279.

tion to truth that is similar to what Benjamin designates as the relation between beauty and truth. Beauty is not "truth become visible," he writes in the final pages of his Goethe essay. "For the beautiful is neither the veil nor the veiled object but rather the object in its veil.... Never yet has a true work of art been grasped other than where it ineluctably represented itself as a secret."[54]

---

54. Benjamin, "Goethe's *Elective Affinities*," 350–351.

2

The Wide Sea of Light

Hidden Law and Works of Love in Stifter's Early Writing

> Beneath me—alas, vanished from the light—
> The lovelier of my hours are already dreaming.
> Out of the blue depths yesterday calls:
> Are there many sisters of mine left in the light?
> —Conrad Ferdinand Meyer, "Eingelegte Ruder"

Two months before his death, Adalbert Stifter penned the autobiographical account *Aus dem bairischen Walde* (*From the Bavarian Forest*), which documents the unprecedented snowstorm that swept down upon the Dreisesselberg region in November 1866. The effect that this event had upon Stifter—he refers to it at one point as "the white behemoth"—was due in part to its utter transformation of the woods near Lackenhäuser in which he had sought and found a source of tranquility in the preceding months. This text was one of the last works Stifter completed in his lifetime, yet in certain passages devoted to the healing properties of the natural environment one can still recognize the principles of cosmic law that he had first formulated more than thirty years before. One such passage describes the experience of walking into the forest:

> We believe that the world is full of serenity and splendor; and when we pass from one form of this tranquility into another one—say, into that of a great forest—it seems to us at once to be truly the same and truly of a different sort. Things begin to close in upon one's gaze, and although only the nearest ones press themselves into view there is still an unfathomable multitude of objects.... Out there, beyond the woods, the wide sea of light had held sway, but in here it has shattered into countless shimmering droplets that hang from all of the branches, flecking the tree-trunks, burning like fire on mossy stones and causing the brooks and streams to blaze like silver. And often, when one comes to a gap in the trees, the darkness of the forest gets cut through by a glowing line.... And in everything one hears the sound of ceaseless, rushing water.... Here, it is within the smallest things that the magnitude of omnipotence reveals itself.[1]

With these reflections upon how light and water serenely coalesce before the human eye, Stifter intimates a system of laws in which magnitude and simplicity become one and the same. As we shall see, it is a system that had remained notably consistent in its form and content throughout his life's work.

In the present chapter I look to these two natural elements of light and water—and particularly their more disconcerting manifestations, such as solar eclipses and floods—as guiding motifs for examining Stifter's writings between 1842 and 1853. These two topoi enframe the central point of focus for my reading—namely, the relation between law, as perceived in the natural world as well as in the human community, and self-sacrifice. In the first section of this chapter, I consider *Die Sonnenfinsterniß am 8. Juli 1842 (The Solar*

Epigraph: Conrad Ferdinand Meyer, "Eingelegte Ruder" (1869), lines 5–8. ("Unter mir—ach, aus dem Licht verschwunden— / traümen schon die schönern meiner Stunden. // Aus der blauen Tiefe ruft das Gestern: / sind im Licht noch manche meiner Schwestern?")

1. Adalbert Stifter, *Aus dem bairischen Walde*, in *Sämtliche Werke*, vol. 15, *Vermischte Schriften II*, ed. Gustav Wilhelm (Reichenberg: Sudetendeutscher, 1935), 327–328.

Eclipse of July 8, 1842), which makes a helpful entry point for our exploration of Stifter's work because it immediately presents its reader with a dynamic relationship between the spheres of nature, human experience, and a hidden order of law that becomes "visible" only by seeming to be suspended altogether. Moreover, this text establishes the motif of sacrifice (via the image of Christ's crucifixion) as a crucial element in Stifter's depictions of cosmic law and of how the human observer perceives this law to be in or out of effect.

I then consider two important principles of cosmic law that Stifter developed during this same period: the "chain of flowers" (*Blumenkette*), formulated in the introductory passages of his 1843 novella *Abdias*; and the "gentle law" (*sanftes Gesetz*), laid out, similarly, in the preface to his 1853 novella cycle *Bunte Steine* (*Motley Stones*). Both principles integrate notions of exception into their very understanding of lawfulness itself, and the gentle law in particular occludes a codified space for the miraculous insofar as it allows lawfulness in general to seem simultaneously in and out of effect, yet without being "suspended" by a supernatural force. In this phase of Stifter's thinking, universal law begins to manifest itself in nature as well as in human action, but by this very token it becomes possible for law to appear out of joint with itself from the vantage point of human perception and experience. Unlike cosmic phenomena, however, human behavior is shown to have a special capacity not only to form a bridge between nature and ethics but even to set universal law back into joint with itself. For Stifter, the domain of human action in which this becomes possible is love. In order to explore this, I draw upon Søren Kierkegaard's conceptualization of self-sacrifice and devotion to the other as the visible "fruit" by which an invisible "royal Law" of love can be both identified and fulfilled. However, while *The Solar Eclipse* first introduces sacrificiality within the context of light and shadow, the text that I will focus on in the second part of this chapter does so in terms of water—and more specifically, the possibility of drowning.

That second part of this chapter is a reading of Stifter's 1853 novella *Kalkstein* (*Limestone*), which tells the story of a country pastor's tireless and abstemious efforts to protect the parish children from the nearby river's regular floods. And this is where sacrifice becomes key for tracing Stifter's evolving conception of law: whereas *The Solar Eclipse* uses the crucifixion to signal law's apparent suspension, in *Limestone* self-sacrifice evinces law's uninterrupted cohesion. This cohesion comes about in Stifter's early writings when the potential for irregularity is incorporated into the very form of law. In the fictional world of *Limestone*, sacrifice weaves irregularity into order, ultimately making it possible for exceptions to law to become manifestations of lawfulness.

I.

Whatever their differences in hermeneutic opinion and approach, readers of Stifter often have the impression that in spite of his aesthetic program's predication upon an affinity for the natural world, many of his writings nevertheless convey a sense of uncanniness and disjunction with it. W. G. Sebald, for instance, would speak for many with his observation that "Stifter, moved by the chaotic goings-on in his innermost self as well as by his scientific insights into nature's terrible vulnerability, spent his entire life working away at a kind of literary auto-therapy of portraying a brighter world."[2] There is a certain amount of irony in the thought that Stifter's lifelong project was to portray a "brighter" world, given that one of his earlier texts presents a detailed and affect-laden description of the sun's temporary disappearance. *The Solar Eclipse* establishes a correspondence between the natural phenomenon of sunlight and an assumed order of cosmic law. Crucially, at the instant of complete eclipse the text alludes to Christ's crucifixion, invoking the Christian paradigm of kenotic sacrifice shortly before going on to reflect upon whether the divine becomes most theophanically "visible" precisely within the apparent disappearance of nature's laws (that is, within miracles).

---

2. W. G. Sebald, "Helle Bilder und dunkle: Zur Dialektik der Eschatologie bei Stifter und Handke," in *Die Beschreibung des Unglücks: Zur österreichischen Literatur von Stifter bis Handke* (Frankfurt am Main: Fischer Taschenbuch, 1994), 174.

"Never Shone Such an Unearthly Light, and So Awfully"

An overarching duality that structures this text—and arguably the bulk of Stifter's work—is the opposition between the rational, a posteriori understanding of a given natural phenomenon and the nonrational, even existential, fear it instills.[3] As Martin and Erika Swales point out, Stifter was a skeptic regarding exactly how much science could truly reveal about nature, and he expressed a faith that the "darkness" left by lacunae in scientific knowledge could be approached as indices of a divinely meaningful order.[4] Nevertheless, Stifter had studied several natural sciences, including astronomy, and as a consequence he was well acquainted with the causes and characteristics of a solar eclipse.[5] And yet he exclaims at the beginning of his account of the eclipse he witnessed in Vienna on July 8, 1842, "Never, ever in my entire life was I so shaken, from terror and sublimity so shaken, as in these two minutes—it was nothing other than if God had all at once spoken a clear word and I had understood it."[6]

The notion of divine revelation being conveyed through the fluctuations of sunlight has its own rich literary legacy, and Stifter's pronounced use of biblical and apocalyptic tropes in his descriptions of the spiritual anxiety that the eclipse instigated in him suggests a link between *The Solar Eclipse* and this poeto-theological tradition.[7] However, one obvious facet of Stifter's text that distinguishes

---

3. Friedrich Wilhelm Korff claims that this eclipse proved to be Stifter's definitive "Experience because at that time the poet was in a state of desolation and a kind of creative distance [*Entfernung*] from himself—the overcoming of which became the inner theme of his production from then on." Korff, *Diastole und Systole: Zum Thema Jean Paul und Adalbert Stifter* (Bern: Francke, 1969), 28.

4. Martin Swales and Erika Swales, *Adalbert Stifter: A Critical Study* (Cambridge: Cambridge University Press, 1984), 29, 32–33.

5. Barbara Potthast, "'Ein lastend unheimliches Entfremden unserer Natur': Adalbert Stifters 'Die Sonnenfinsterniß am 8. Juli 1842' als Dokument einer anderen Moderne," *Scientia Poetica* 12 (2008): 122–123.

6. Stifter, "The Solar Eclipse on July 8th, 1842," trans. Jocelyn Holland, *Configurations* 23, no. 2 (2015): 253.

7. One thinks of the lamentation from Milton's *Samson Agonistes* (1671): "O dark, dark, dark, amid the blaze of noon, / Irrecoverably dark, total Eclipse / Without all hope of day! / O first created Beam, and thou great Word, / Let there be

it from strictly religious accounts of phenomena such as eclipses is its implicit suggestion that nature cannot be grasped solely with the instruments of reason or of religious faith; instead, such a grasp requires the cathartic merging of both frames of mind that leaves room for the one alternately to triumph over the other.

A fine illustration of this parallax is offered by Stifter's assertion that he had closely studied the empirical qualities of eclipses, "and really so well that I thought to be able to describe a total solar eclipse beforehand as faithfully as if I had already seen it" (253). However, his subsequent depiction of the preliminary seconds of the eclipse is devoid of the naturalistic *sangfroid* that this initial statement might lead one to expect: "Finally, at the foretold minute—as if from an invisible angel it received the gentle kiss of death—a fine stripe of its light faded back from the breath of this kiss, the other side swelled onward tender and golden in the glass of the telescope" (254). Here, the scientific precision of Stifter's act of observation through his telescope "at the foretold minute" joins forces with metaphor in order to make sense of an unprecedented experience. One is reminded of Michel de Certeau's allusion to metaphor as something that can travel across distances between (and even within) distinct swaths of knowledge and language, like a vehicle that moves along a "spatial trajectory."[8] In this brief passage, Stifter's chosen metaphor enables his language to traverse the gap between naturalistic knowledge drawn from observation and the inexplicable experience of theophany, just as his eye moves between two different images of the darkening sun: one in the expanse of the heavens and one in the small enclosure of the telescope lens. In this respect, the "invisible angel" that is closely observed as it steadily envelops the sun with its "kiss of death" is emblematic of much of Stifter's writing for its attempt to reconcile the predictable rhythms of nature

---

light, and light was over all; / Why am I thus bereav'd thy prime decree? / The Sun to me is dark / And silent as the Moon" (lines 80–87). Another frequent point of comparison with Stifter's text is Jean Paul's *Die Rede des toten Christus vom Weltgebäude herab* (1796); for a discussion of the latter intertextual relationship, see Korff, *Diastole und Systole*, 11–37.

8. Michel de Certeau, *The Practice of Everyday Life*, trans. Steven Rendall (Berkeley: University of California Press, 1988), 115.

with the mystery of a hidden law that seems to be immanently at work in things.

This fusion between different modalities of subjective perception is foregrounded in the climactic sequence of the text, which describes the actual moment of eclipse: the darkness continues to eat away at the sun, and although Stifter knows this shadow to be "our moon—the beautiful and gentle moon," it nevertheless appears to him "like an evil animal... this uncanny, clumplike, deep black thing" (255). The dread exuded by Stifter's language echoes that of numerous other images and texts throughout European history similarly consumed by the troubling fact that a part of nature (which is to say, creation, in his vocabulary) can be known to be "beautiful and gentle" and thus reflective of the Good as such, even as another part of it can simultaneously appear as an "evil" and beastlike "thing" that hungrily de-creates creation. In this regard, Stifter's description of the solar eclipse of 1842—in a less literal way than, say, Jeremias Gotthelf's theodicean account of a catastrophic deluge in Switzerland several years prior (*Die Wassernot im Emmental am 13. August 1837*)—recalls the biblical Flood narrative, which unfolds its natural theology in illustration of a chiastic, almost riddle-like idea: the created, creative, and "good" cosmos can, without paradox, be destroyed and become destructive as a consequence of uncreated "evil" (which Neoplatonist and Christian writers like Augustine would later gloss simply as a "privation of good" [*privatio boni*]). The key question, then, is in what sense the good and an absence of the good can co-inhere. And for answering this question, images drawn from nature seem to hold particular explicatory power, as instanced by Stifter's treatments of light and water that are the focus of this chapter.

An eerie twilight spreads over the rooftops of Vienna, and Stifter notes how it is now possible to behold the sun with "the naked eye," a detail that confirms the interruption of astronomical normalcy to correspond with an interruption of physiological normalcy as well; suddenly, in this climactic instant of cosmic exception, Stifter and all of his fellow citizens become able to gaze directly at the sun without having to look away. However, this equivalence is swiftly upended in the instant of the sun's transition from a state of full obscuration to its reemergence from behind the black orb of the moon, and the narrative accordingly shifts from the passive framework of human observation to the active framework of revelation: "It was actually this moment that had the effect of being truly heart-shattering . . . it was the moment where God spoke and men hearkened" (255). Stifter describes how the gradual extinguishing of the light had transported him and his fellow spectators into "a kind of death," and how the withdrawal of this "holy" light, which is taken for granted throughout human life, leaves an unfathomable lack and induces a "deathly still majesty" (256). In a moment of utmost importance for our analysis, Stifter directly aligns this privation of light with synoptic Gospel accounts of the eclipse during Christ's death on the cross, when, as he quotes, "the sun darkened, the earth shook, the dead arose from their graves and the curtain of the Temple tore from above to below" (256).[9] What this biblical allusion implicitly declares is that the liminal space of transition between darkness and light—as well as between a quotidian and a miraculous register of experience—is occupied and mediated by sacrifice, and specifically kenosis.

The Christian theological notion of kenosis (κένωσις), which translates as "emptying," has two traditional resonances. The first of these denotes a metaphysical process of self-emptying, which pertains, first, to the withdrawal of God's absolute divinity in order to "make room" for Being as such (and therewith for creation *ex nihilo*) as well as for becoming human through the Incarnation; and, second, to Christ's withdrawal of his own divine nature in order to suffer a mortal, self-sacrificial death. A second sense of kenosis concerns the religious-ethical practice of *imitatio Christi* whereby one "empties" one's own comforts and desires for the sake of a fellow human being. As Paolo Diego Bubbio has argued, the concept and symbolism of kenotic sacrifice assumed an increasingly influential role in post-Kantian thought, and the majority of nineteenth-century

---

9. Stifter's quotation actually combines several verses from three of the synoptic Gospels—Luke 23:45, Matthew 27:52, and Matthew 27:51, respectively.

German philosophers, theologians, and aestheticians regarded the figure of Christ—and particularly his crucifixion—as the *locus classicus* of both the supernatural and moral registers of kenosis.[10]

Stifter's decision to invoke the eclipse that supposedly accompanied Christ's death at the climax of his own description of the 1842 eclipse as a "gradual dying" of "holy" light thus accords sacrificiality an important position within the text's motivic economy (255). Equally important to this economy, as the concluding paragraphs of the text suggest, is the coincidence of self-sacrifice with a "suspension of normality" that marks the simultaneous suspension of natural law and revelation of the God that created this law.[11] "Why, since all laws of nature are, of course, miracles and God's creation, do we notice his presence in them less than when all at once a sudden change, a disturbance of them as it were occurs, where we then suddenly see him standing there, and with terror? Are these laws his shining robe that covers him, and must he raise it so that we see him for ourselves?" (257). This evocative passage raises the question of whether disturbances and interruptions of the normal order of things, "since all laws of nature are . . . miracles and God's creation," paradoxically allow us to see what would otherwise remain

---

10. Paulo Diego Bubbio, *Sacrifice in the Post-Kantian Tradition: Perspectivism, Intersubjectivity and Recognition* (Albany: SUNY Press, 2014), 61–85; compare Peter Szondi, *Versuch über das Tragische* (Frankfurt am Main: Insel, 1964), 20–28. This lineage arguably reaches into twentieth-century continental philosophy as well; for instance, in a key work of modern ethical thought, Emmanuel Levinas describes "the Infinite" as being a condition for relationality—and thus for ethics per se—in terms highly redolent of kenosis: "Infinity is produced by withstanding the invasion of a totality, in a *contraction* that leaves a place for the separated being. . . . An infinity that does not close in upon itself in a circle but *withdraws* from the ontological extension *so as to leave a place* for a separated being exists divinely." The consequence of this, echoing the incarnational cosmology of theologians like Maximus the Confessor and Duns Scotus, is the intrinsic "paradox of an Infinity admitting a being outside of itself which it does not encompass, and accomplishing its very infinitude by virtue of this proximity of a separated being—in a word, the paradox of creation." Emmanuel Levinas, *Totality and Infinity: An Essay on Exteriority*, trans. Alphonso Lingis (The Hague: Martinus Nijhoff, 1979), 103–104 (emphases mine). See Karl Shankar Sengupta, *Otherwise, then Being: Kenosis in the Thought of Emmanuel Levinas*, Ph.D. diss., University of Texas–Dallas (2021), 65–88.

11. Jutta Müller-Tamm, "Farben, Sonne, Finsternis: Von Goethe zu Adalbert Stifter," *Goethe-Jahrbuch* 125 (2008): 171.

invisible to both our external and our internal "vision." In this respect the text's conclusion echoes its own beginning, for in the opening passages Stifter had also used the distinction between vision and feeling—and specifically between the eyes and the heart—to illustrate the paradox of a rationally conceivable occurrence in nature nevertheless becoming incomprehensible to us. The specific word he uses to designate this natural phenomenon that at the same time seems to be supernatural is crucial: at the moment of the eclipse, he writes, "we ... direct our eyes and eye-pieces toward the sun ... and the understanding already triumphs," and yet in this same moment, "such a moral force is imbued in this process that it surges in our hearts to an incomprehensible *miracle*" (253, emphasis added).

Solstitium, Iustitium, Eclipsis

Stifter's essay thus circles around a central tension: even though the eclipse is understood rationally to be consonant with natural order, on a phenomenological level it nevertheless has the effect of a suspension of natural law—or, in Stifter's words, of a miracle. But does the miracle for him constitute a divine suspension of natural order, or the very revelation of "true order" in what only *appears* to be a suspension? If, as Stifter suggests above, God becomes most present and intelligible to humanity while seeming to dissolve rather than uphold his own cosmic laws (which Stifter has already described as "miracles" in their own right [257]), then any "true" experience of nature in turn becomes predicated upon the miraculous—that is, upon an exception to law that is nonetheless a part of law as well.

Stifter was certainly not the first, and by no means the last, to link the modality of exception to that of the miracle. Less than a century after *The Solar Eclipse* was published, Carl Schmitt would seize upon the religious category of the miracle in order to lay out the salient characteristics of his theory of the state of exception (*Ausnahmezustand*). While doing so, Schmitt famously claims that "all significant concepts of the modern theory of the state are secularized theological concepts," and notes in particular the example in which "the omnipotent God became the omnipotent lawgiver."

Within the context of this shift in semantic register from divine power to legal authority, the relation between the miracle and the state of exception becomes clear: "The exception in jurisprudence is analogous to the miracle in theology."[12]

The roots of this paradigm reach even further than the Judeo-Christian theological tradition, however. Giorgio Agamben has investigated the Roman law precursor to Schmitt's state of exception, *iustitium*, which pertained to a "suspension not simply of the administration of justice but of the law as such."[13] Interestingly, Agamben notes that ancient jurists explicated the term *iustitium*—a compound derived from "law" (*ius*) and the verb "to stand still" (*sistere*)—through analogy with the etymologically related "solstice" (*solstitium*), during which the sun comes to a "standstill."[14] It is worth underscoring how in this particular instance of Western legal thought, the suspension or "standing still" of law is expressed by way of not only metaphor, but metaphor tied to a natural—and specifically solar—phenomenon.

If we regard *The Solar Eclipse* within this context, Stifter's use of the eclipse as a topos suddenly takes on significant implications. As Agamben and Schmitt respectively suggest, the Roman concept of *iustitium* and the theological concept of the miracle both form the backdrop to modern notions of law as something that can occasionally "stand still," as if enacting its own solstice, or even give way to a state of exception established by "direct intervention," just like a miracle brought about via divine "transgression of the laws of nature."[15] When viewed in this light, *The Solar Eclipse* falls in

---

12. Carl Schmitt, *Political Theology: Four Chapters on the Concept of Sovereignty*, trans. George Schwab (Chicago: University of Chicago Press, 1985), 36.

13. Giorgio Agamben, *State of Exception*, trans. Kevin Attell (Chicago: University of Chicago Press, 2005), 41.

14. Agamben, *State of Exception*, 41. This particular reference can be traced to the *Commenta Bernensia*, an anonymous tenth-century commentary on Lucan's *Pharsalia* (61/65 AD). In book 2 of the *Commenta*, we read the following: "*iustitium* is when law stands still, just like they say of the solstice, and no cases are pleaded" [*iustitium quando ius stat nec causa agitur, sicut solstitium dicitur*]. In Hermann Usener, ed., *Scholia in Lucani bellum civile: Commenta Bernensia* (Hildesheim: Georg Olms, 1967), 49. Translation mine.

15. Schmitt, *Political Theology*, 36. Interestingly, the Greeks also used the sun as a trope when discussing the relationship between *nomos* and *physis*. As Hans Kelsen notes, Heraclitus's ninety-fourth fragment describes a scenario of the sun

with a long tradition of portraying law's dual capacity to vanish and to be present, like the sun during an eclipse.[16]

II.

Stifter's text thus begins and ends with the same key question: How should we understand a phenomenon that simultaneously appears to correspond with the laws of nature and with a divine suspension of law itself? This question is given voice in much of Stifter's work from this time frame, including in his metaphysical and aesthetic conceptions of cosmic law that are of concern to us in this chapter. The first of these is the principle of the "chain of flowers," which is presented at the beginning of the 1843 novella *Abdias*.

"The Gaps Which Now Exist"

In the opening passages, the narrator of *Abdias* describes humankind's impression of nature's simultaneous visibility and obfuscation, as though an "invisible arm" were hidden behind the phenomena unfolding "before our eyes."[17] This seamless cooperation between the unseen, seemingly disinterested machinery of nature and its visible effects in the environment is illustrated with an unsettling allegory: "Here for example the beautiful silver mirror of a river swells, a boy falls in, the water ripples sweetly around his locks, he sinks—and after a short while the silver mirror swells as before" (21).

The reader is first presented with the image of a tranquil river, whose quiet surface suddenly and for the briefest instant surges and parts to receive a young boy in a "loving" embrace redolent of the "kiss of death" with which the sun was enveloped in *The Solar*

"transgressing" against the precepts of nature (*physis*) and then being corrected by law (*nomos*). Kelsen paraphrases Heraclitus as follows: "If the sun doesn't keep to its prescribed path, then the Erinyes, the attendants of justice, will put it in its place [*zurechtweisen*]." Kelsen, *Reine Rechtslehre* (Vienna: Deuticke, 1960), 88.

16. "Eclipse" derives, via the Latin *eclipsis*, from the Greek εκλειψις, which means "disappearance" or "abandonment."

17. Adalbert Stifter, *Abdias*, trans. Helen Watanabe-O'Kelly (London: Angel Books, 1990), 21.

Eclipse, before returning just as quickly to its previous stillness. In a fashion markedly similar to the eclipse of 1842, this tripartite movement of nature—though here water rather than light—comprises an oscillation between a visible topography, the sudden appearance and disappearance of an object, and a final reinstatement of the initial image. The text associates these linked movements with the equanimity of nature, whose regularity and normality can momentarily become host to an "incomprehensible" or "terrible" event that unexpectedly takes place.

The narrator goes on to say that throughout history, humans have sought to explicate or at least reconcile nature's unpredictability with concepts such as blind fate (*fatum*), destiny (*Schicksal*), or divine will. While Stifter certainly seemed partial to the latter paradigm in his description of the 1842 eclipse, here his narrator opts for a system of disinterested cause and consequence, articulated with a striking metaphor:

> A serene chain of flowers hangs through the infinity of the universe and transmits its shimmer into men's hearts—the chain of cause and effect—and into man's brain was cast the most beautiful of these flowers, reason, the eye of the soul, in order to attach the chain to it and by means of it to count his way down flower by flower, link by link, until he comes finally to that hand in which the end rests. (22)

Several phrases immediately leap out at the reader, particularly the central idea that the "most beautiful of these flowers" is contained within human reason—"the eye of the soul." The narrator claims that if one is successful in surveying the links of the flower chain with this psychic eye of reason, a full view of the true order of things can eventually be attained: "then chance will no longer exist for us, but consequence, not misfortune but only guilt" (22). Here, as in the opening passage, the reign of normality and the regularity of truth are linked with a Platonic paradigm of visibility, and more specifically with both a metaphysical and metaphorical symbolism of visual access to nature. However, here too the "visible" realm of reason, understanding, and cosmic lawfulness is interwoven with an invisible patchwork of unknowability, for in surveying the flower chain of consequences and culpability that hangs in place of destiny and ill fortune, humanity's inner eye will inevitably stumble across empty spaces that obtain between the blossoms of causal uniformity, and "the gaps which now exist are the cause of the unexpected."

The image seems straightforward enough: if causes and effects of events in the world are the blossoms forming a chain that hangs through time and space, and if the most beautiful blossom is the "eye of the soul," or reason, then the gaps in this chain might also be understood as "blind spots" of the psychic eye that regards it. Much like "the invisible" that suddenly reaches out from a solitary cloud or the impassive currents of a river, the unexpected and the incomprehensible are those unseeable spaces in the chain that constitute the other side of the seeable, predictable, and comprehensible workings of nature and its familiar laws. The narrator provides a simple reason as to why these inexplicable and seemingly random blind spots can be accommodated within what is allegedly a cohesive chain of causes and consequences—namely, that only a small proportion of the countless blossoms that constitute this great chain of flowers have yet been found and understood through the course of human history: "The supply [of blossoms] is immeasurably big so that each coming generation can find something for itself—the little that has been discovered is already a great and splendid treasure, and the more people in the future who live and reveal it, the bigger and more splendid this treasure will become—and we can divine scarcely a thousandth of a thousandth of what lies behind the great wave of the future" (22). That which remains invisible, the text suggests, should be thought of, not as a consequence of "blindness" or absent knowledge, but instead as a prelude to eventual "sight" and future discovery.

The idea with which the passage concludes is therefore that the terrifying and exceptional phenomena that appear to bespeak a disappearance of nature's governing principles are not actually aberrations, but instead merely seem so to human observers due to our finite and fixed vantage point in time and space. This subtly contrasts with the musing in *The Solar Eclipse* as to whether God might be most "visible" to human experience precisely by way of the apparent disappearance of his laws, for what the narrator of *Abdias* suggests is that the interstitial gaps in the cosmic chain of causes and effects are temporarily veiled sites of an immanent (but not necessarily miraculous) cosmic pattern.

These two texts thus underwrite an important distinction. Something in the experience of the eclipse cannot be reconciled with reason, for even though Stifter declares that he understands the cause of the eclipse, he still continues to feel the split between the scientific and the phenomenological perspectives. In the chain of flowers, by contrast, we are dealing, not with the experience of a parallax between natural order and divine suspension, but instead with a continuum of comprehension. At first glance, then, it would seem that the miraculous has fallen out of view and been replaced with nothing less than law itself; what the spectator of the eclipse experiences as an "incomprehensible miracle" is simply one of the flower chain's many "gaps." Or has "miracle" instead come to mean something else for Stifter? Perhaps it is now closer to Idris Parry's definition of the miracle as "something unusual but not unnatural," something that "does not uncover anything new; it reveals the marvelous which is always present but veiled and nameless."[18]

As with the concept of *iustitium*, here too a rich epistemology hovers in the background. Spinoza, for instance, adamantly claimed that miracles were not divine suspensions of natural law, but instead wholly "lawful" natural phenomena that humans simply could not yet explain.[19] In chapter 6 of his *Tractatus Theologico-Politicus*, Spinoza remarks that the majority of people believe God to be revealed via apparent violations of nature's laws. This belief, Spinoza continues, rests on the implicit assumption that divine law and natural law are not conjoined. He takes the opposing view, arguing that nature's laws operate solely by virtue of divine will, and that because according to divine law everything willed by God is eternal and true, it follows that if any natural event were ever to "violate" natural

---

18. Idris Parry, "Stream and Rock," in *Speak Silence: Essays* (Manchester, UK: Carcanet, 1988), 282.
19. Benedict de Spinoza, *A Theologico-Political Treatise and Political Treatise*, trans. R. H. M Elwes (New York: Dover, 2004), 81–84.

law, it would also necessarily violate divine law (a logical impossibility, he notes). Nature is instead always at work in accordance with a set order of laws—whether or not we can perceive or comprehend it—and as such, "miracles are only intelligible as in relation to human opinions, and merely mean events of which the natural cause cannot be explained."[20] Consequently, Spinoza suggests, God's essence should be sought, not in miracles, but instead in "the fixed and immutable order of nature."

These opposed paradigms of the miracle, as modeled by Schmitt's state of exception and Spinoza's *Tractatus*, will prove to be helpful lenses through which to trace Stifter's own changing conceptualizations of cosmic law and theophany. Moreover, within this same change we can also observe a parallel shift in emphasis from supernatural exception to natural cohesion. To a significant degree this has happened as part of a reconceptualization of law itself, not as something that might seem to be suspended by a divine force, but instead as something that can integrate exception—or what appears to us as exception—*into itself*. One is led to wonder whether for Stifter this paradoxical capacity of law also extends to the human dimension—the ethical realm—in addition to the natural realm. Stifter's theory of the gentle law, formulated in the preface to his novella cycle *Motley Stones*, addresses precisely this question while shifting focus from the sphere of cosmic law to that of ethical law.

"To Glimpse the Gentle Law"

Stifter's definition of the gentle law begins in one of the more frequently quoted passages in his oeuvre, but as it contains the most concise summary of this principle, it is worth doing so once again here:

> The wafting of air the trickling of the water the growing of the grain the surging of the sea the budding of the earth the shining of the sky the glimmering of the stars is what I deem great; the thunderstorm that looms in splendor, the lightning that cleaves houses, the storm that

---

20. Spinoza, *A Theologico-Political Treatise*, 84.

drives the breakers, the fire-spewing mountain, the earthquake that buries whole lands, these I do not deem greater than those first phenomena, indeed I deem them smaller, for they are the mere effects of much higher laws. They occur in isolation, and are the results of one-sided causes.[21]

The semantic inversion of "small" and "great" that is the focal point of these lines is rooted in two fundamental premises: (1) that a higher degree of significance resides in totality than in singularity, and (2) that there is a higher degree of significance in a cause than in its effect. For Stifter, the small and serene phenomena of nature are in some way "greater" than violent or traditionally sublime ones. This is because the unobtrusive regularity of, say, a murmuring stream evinces what he regards as an underlying principle of reality itself. The sudden force of a flood, by contrast, evinces not regularity but singularity, and stands apart as an extreme *effect* of reality's "much higher laws" rather than as an *embodiment* of those laws in their regular and regulating operativity.

Before going any further, we must ask ourselves just how to understand these qualifications of "greater" and "higher," for if a gentle phenomenon is as much an effect of nature's "much higher laws" as a violent phenomenon is, then by what metric does the one become "greater" than the other? As it happens, this puzzling relation between the pairs small/great and high/higher also caught the attention of Walter Benjamin in a brief 1917 essay on Stifter's poetics. Benjamin's critique begins from the view that Stifter's writings unfold along a "path of false foundational convictions."[22] For Benjamin, this false path is especially evident in the preface to *Motley Stones*, though he finds it to course through most of Stifter's work, suggesting that Stifter's ceaseless—in more modern terms one might say pathological, as Thomas Mann would later do[23]—attention to minutiae of the

---

21. Adalbert Stifter, "Preface," in *Motley Stones*, trans. Isabel Fargo Cole (New York: NYRB Classics, 2021), 3–4.
22. Walter Benjamin, "Stifter," in *Gesammelte Schriften*, vol. 2.2, ed. Rolf Tiedemann and Hermann Schweppenhäuser (Frankfurt am Main: Suhrkamp, 1977), 608.
23. Thomas Mann, "Neigung zum Exzessiven, Elementarischen, Katastrophalen, Pathologischen," in *Die Entstehung des Doktor Faustus: Roman eines Romans (1949)* (Frankfurt am Main: Suhrkamp, 1984), 95.

ordinary signals a hidden desperation to divert focus away from something else he does not wish to see.[24] However, Benjamin detects a certain exhaustion that drags at this effort from within, and cites the aforementioned preface as a case in point. Stifter's reconceptualization of smallness, greatness, and height in particular strikes Benjamin not just as speculative, but as "deceptive, inessential . . . relative." This faulty alignment becomes most troubling to him when, as he sees it, Stifter subsequently attempts to transpose the blithe simplicity of nature into "the grand relations of fate."[25] In his inability to discern or comprehend the boundary between these two spheres, Benjamin says, Stifter becomes servant to a "convulsive impulse" to bind destiny (*Schicksal*) and "the ethical world" to the natural world, a move that at first glance might appear harmless and quaint but in fact is "demonic and spectral."[26]

This is not the proper place to address the complex epistemology that informs Benjamin's objections to the "false path" of Stifter's metaphysics.[27] But we can take as a cue his remark that Stifter sees the spheres of nature and ethics to be closely linked. The schematic ranking of cause and effect in terms of the qualities small/great/high may have been nebulous from the vantage point of nature, but within an ethical context, as we shall see shortly, it comes into focus. This new vantage point will in turn provide a clearer view of how, between 1842 and 1853, law takes on a new form for Stifter, no longer as an order that simply stands in opposition to disorder or exception, but instead as an order that can incorporate exception into itself. By developing a concept of law that applies both to the natural environment and to human interaction, Stifter

---

24. As Eric Downing suggests, the fact that Stifter privileges the internal "eye of science" over the empirical eye reflects his projection of God as the guarantor of unity and transcendent meaning, which the Realist *Menschenforscher* can investigate within the sphere of objective reality. Downing, *Double Exposures: Repetition and Realism in Nineteenth-Century German Fiction* (Stanford, CA: Stanford University Press, 2000), 32.

25. Benjamin, "Stifter," 608. Compare W. G. Sebald, "Bis an den Rand der Natur: Versuch über Stifter," in *Die Beschreibung des Unglücks*, 18.

26. Benjamin, "Stifter," 609.

27. See Peter Demetz, "Walter Benjamin als Leser Adalbert Stifters," *Neue Rundschau* 91, no. 1 (1980): 151.

accords law a new potential to be in effect (in one domain) while simultaneously being out of effect (in the other).

Let's look more closely at how the preface to *Motley Stones* executes this shift in focus. As was the case in the natural sphere, in the societal sphere, too, that which is visible and tangible evinces a hidden order of laws standing behind it:

> As is outward Nature, so too is inward nature, the nature of the human race. A whole life filled with righteousness simplicity self-mastery rationality efficacy within one's sphere admiration of beauty joined with a cheerful serene death is what I deem great: powerful stirrings of passion's wrath rumbling emergence the thirst for vengeance the inflamed spirit striving for action, tearing down, altering, destroying, and in this excitation often casting away its own life, these things I deem smaller, not greater, for they are but the product of isolated and one-sided forces, like storms fire-spewing mountains earthquakes. We seek to glimpse the gentle law that guides the human race. (5)

In a key sense, then, Stifter's concepts of the "moral law" (*Sittengesetz*) and "natural law" (*Naturgesetz*) are essentially modulations of one another, mutually reflecting the invisible but ever-present gentle law.

Stifter's description of the natural world's coextension with human affect once again brings Spinoza to mind. In the preface to part III of the *Ethics*, for instance, Spinoza writes that "nature's laws and ordinances, whereby all things come to pass and change from one form to another, are everywhere and always the same."[28] As a consequence, he says, these "universal laws" and principles of nature should also form the basis and "method of understanding the nature of all things whatsoever," including the spectrum of human passions. For Stifter, it is specifically the simple, everyday textures of feeling that add up to a totality in correspondence with both the form and content of the cosmic whole. By contrast, the violent and vitriolic expressions of human nature that Stifter lists are merely "the product of isolated and one-sided forces," extreme effects and singular perversions of the regulating and mild force of the gentle

---

28. Benedict de Spinoza, *On the Improvement of the Understanding/The Ethics/Correspondence*, trans. R. H. M Elwes (New York: Dover, 1955), 128.

law—"this law alone" being for him "the only universal the only sustaining and never-ending one" (6).

Whether or not the cosmic gravitas with which Stifter invests his descriptions of the gentle law is merely rhetorical, its Christian bent becomes increasingly tangible as the preface goes on.[29] This is especially the case in the passages on moral law, which "decree[s] that each should stand respected honored unmolested beside the others, ... that he be cherished as a gem, as each person is a gem for all other people. This law is found wherever people live alongside others, and is shown whenever people act upon others. It lies in the love of husband and wife the love of parents for their children of children for their parents in the mutual love of siblings of friends" (6). This juncture of the text introduces an important difference between the natural law and the moral law, and more specifically between the consequences of either one being disrupted. In contrast to the violent phenomena of nature, which distort but do not necessarily violate the gentle law, Stifter assigns graver implications to interpersonal behaviors that prevent the "law of justice and morals" from being "seen" in "certain movements within the human race": "When the law of right and morals is not apparent in these movements, when they struggle toward one-sided and selfish goals, the student of humankind turns away in disgust, however tremendous and terrible they be, and regards them as a small thing unworthy of humanity" (6). Thus, whereas the "smaller" events in the natural world should simply be recognized as such, those in the ethical domain are to be *looked away from* altogether, as if to mirror the way they have caused the moral law itself to become "unapparent" (*nicht ersichtlich*). The concept of one-sidedness is reiterated for a third time here as an index of these smaller forces. It initially appeared in the denunciation first of violent natural occurrences as "results of one-sided causes" (4), and then of incontinent or intemperate human action as products of "isolated and one-sided

---

29. On the question of whether Stifter's religiosity was genuine, see Downing, *Double Exposures*, 31; Walter Silz, "Stifter, *Abdias*," in *Realism and Reality: Studies in the German Novelle of Poetic Realism* (Chapel Hill: University of North Carolina Press, 1954), 60.

forces" (5). Here it is "one-sided and selfish goals" that veil the moral law from view.

Notably, Stifter regards the case of lawfulness being "unseen" in the realm of ethics as more hazardous than sublimely terrifying and deleterious occurrences in the natural world. Although the text goes on to affirm optimistically that the "law of right and morals" will always triumph in the end, one might nevertheless ask why Stifter feels that unethical behavior poses such a threat to it. Why should the "student of humankind... turn away in disgust" from this very specific variety of smallness within the sphere of human relationships, but not necessarily from "small" events that occur in the landscape?

One explanation for why one-sided and self-interested activity might be considered more dangerous than natural catastrophes can be sought in the duality of cause and effect that underpins the entire preface. Whereas violent or destructive events in nature were defined as simply extreme products or effects (*Wirkungen/Ergebnisse*) of primary forces, human actions or motivations that are antithetical to the gentle law are not merely effects of it. Instead, by virtue of free will, these behaviors can become singular and independent causes unto themselves, for a person can choose to act unilaterally out of his or her own self-interest in contradiction to the moral law.[30] By contrast, a bolt of lightning is not spoken of as "transgressing" against the natural law by "deciding" to strike a house. As was shown in the description of the chain of flowers in the foreword to *Abdias*, the terror of the "invisible arm" is that even as it extends into the world in order to upend, destroy, and bereave, nature's "indifferent innocence" remains intact. The terror of human will is precisely the opposite, however. When people go astray of the moral law, *they* are the cause of their straying, not the true and essentially gentle law which they freely violate; one could invert the *Abdias* narrator's words and say that it is a person's *visible* arm and *non*-indifferent *guilt* that together render "the law of right and morals" *invisible*. Just as the gaps in the chain of flowers that baffle or frighten us nevertheless cohere with the causality of its overall form, the ungentle and unlovely incidents in

---

30. Compare Martin Beckmann, "Stifters 'sanftes Gesetz': Selbstwiederholung in der Wirklichkeit," *Neophilologus* 80, no. 3 (1996): 435–459.

nature are ramifications of a single cosmic order. As a consequence, the ethical domain of human impulses and decisions seems to possess a uniquely autonomous potency for Stifter—namely, the capacity either to accord with the law alongside its other effects or to diverge from it as a self-governing cause. If regularity and predictability epitomize the gentle law, then it is understandable that the caprice and unpredictability of the human heart provide the most apt conditions for it to be infringed upon (hence the "rigorism" that attends gentleness in so many of his texts).[31]

It has been remarked that the contemporary political dimensions of Stifter's time and place, and revolutionary discourse in particular, offer the most important context for understanding his conception of both lawful order and its disruption. For Hans Höller, it is the socio-aesthetic ramifications of the Industrial Revolution in Central Europe, beginning in the 1830s, that can be felt behind Stifter's devotion to seemingly small and simple phenomena. On this reading, his pastoral settings and meticulous attention to the description of objects in the world bespeak not a naive idyllicism but instead an active defense of the essence and meaning of nonhuman things of the world vis-à-vis industrialized capital. According to Höller, a key step in this defense involves exiting the urban sphere in order to purposively engage with the natural world in an attempt to shake off the clammy tenacity of capitalistic reification, which in turn allows the natural world to retain (or regain) an inherently "aesthetic" quality in lieu of merely materialist applicabilities and functions.[32] Martin Tielke, on the other hand, is less ready to presume that Stifter's writings reflect a purposive critique, let alone elusion, of the subliminal ideological influences of political economy. Rather, for Tielke it is mainly against the "passions" and disorderliness of overtly political revolutionism that Stifter reacts with his doctrine of

---

31. Hans Dietrich Irmscher argues that this rigorism "can only be understood from the perspective of Stifter's elementary fear of a dissolution of the bonds that make human co-existence possible in the first place." Irmscher, *Adalbert Stifter: Wirklichkeitserfahrung und gegenständliche Darstellung* (Munich: Winkler, 1971), 50.

32. Hans Höller, "Die Sozialgeschichtliche Bedeutung der ästhetischen Wahrnehmung bei Adalbert Stifter," *Wirkendes Wort* 4 (1982): 259.

the gentle law. Just as Stifter posits the laws of morals and of nature as two sides of a single coin—the gentle law—his literary portrayals of orderliness and disruption within both of those spheres correspond with a consistent metaphorical framework that is inherently sociohistorical rather than metaphysical in its concerns.[33]

In any case, for our present purposes we must leave aside the question of whether the impetus and underlying valences of Stifter's formulation of cosmic principles, from the flower chain to the gentle law, are more political, economic, or phenomenological in their orientation, and return to the issue of law becoming invisible. This invites us to recall Stifter's description of the 1842 solar eclipse, which was framed as a wholly natural phenomenon, yet one so moving that it nevertheless created the sense of natural law having been suspended by a divine hand. His subsequent reference to the crucifixion introduced the category of sacrifice as a kind of bridge extending through the now darkened horizon of natural law to affirm a link between human existence and a hitherto veiled order of divine law. In the preface to *Motley Stones*, by comparison, Stifter specifically refers to law becoming nonvisible within the ethical realm, whose guiding moral law is linked to neighborly love. Perhaps he designates one-sidedness and self-interest as the prime culprits in ethical law becoming "unapparent" because both of them militate against the conditions for such love—a concern that has clear echoes within the overarching didactic project of Biedermeier literature more generally.[34] Might self-sacrifice therefore also play a role here, not only in bridging the realms of nature and ethics, but also in somehow allowing a "shadowed" law to become illumined and visible once more?

---

33. Martin Tielke, *Sanftes Gesetz und historische Notwendigkeit: Adalbert Stifter zwischen Restauration und Revolution* (Bern: Peter Lang, 1979), 111.

34. "The Biedermeier poet equates the biblical Fall (*Sündenfall*) with the self-consciousness that leads to a dissociation of the people, to loneliness, and to dissatisfaction." Friedrich Sengle, *Biedermeierzeit: Deutsche Literatur im Spannungsfeld zwischen Restauration und Revolution, 1815–1848*, vol. 1 (Stuttgart: J. B. Metzler, 1971), 127.

III.

In *Limestone*, beneficent acts that appear as works and gestures of selfless love emerge not only as the mode in which the human subject might reconcile herself with apparent "suspensions" of law in the cosmos, but also as the proper register of ethical action in which to redress interruptions of both the natural law and the moral law. Most importantly, this dynamic relation between sacrifice and law ultimately inverts the categories that Stifter had established as a foundation of the gentle law at the beginning of the preface: through acts of self-sacrifice, effects will become "higher" than their causes. Ultimately, pursuing this line will allow us to see how Stifter looks to the narrative arc of an individual life—and particularly the assembly of actions that form its stage—as a space within which the much larger apparatus of natural order can be glimpsed in miniature. Hannah Arendt beautifully encapsulates a sentiment we will soon observe to be quite akin to Stifter's own in her thesis that "just as, from the standpoint of nature, the rectilinear movement of man's life-span between birth and death looks like a peculiar deviation from the common natural rule of cyclical movement, thus action, seen from the viewpoint of the automatic processes which seem to determine the course of the world, looks like a miracle."[35]

The Surveyor and the Priest

We can approach *Limestone* as a narrative composed of two primary elements: the now familiar dialectic of hidden or "unseen" causes and their perceivable effects, and the two protagonists' variant attempts to resolve this dialectic. Both of these elements are introduced in the opening passages of the story, which begins with a recollection of several friends debating how to account for the distribution of capacities in each individual. Some point out that human abilities

---

35. Hannah Arendt, *The Human Condition* (Chicago: University of Chicago Press, 1998), 246.

typically exist either in relatively equal proportion with one another, or in decidedly disproportionate constellations. Others suggest that the presence or absence of reason, as the foremost human trait, necessarily determines the operation of all the others. The frame narrator is inspired to begin his story, however, only after a member of the company hypothesizes that "God had created human beings as he had created them, we could never know how he had distributed his gifts, nor could we debate the question, it being uncertain what might yet come to light in the future."[36] This division of an unseen, interior quality and its exterior, visible manifestations within action will prove decisive not only for the role of the narrative's two main figures—a parish priest and a land surveyor (who is the narrator)—but also for the function of sacrifice that determines their respective experiences of the core events in the plot. This becomes particularly evident if one reads the pastor's acts of sacrifice and self-abnegation alongside Kierkegaard's 1847 treatise *Works of Love*, which posits that love, like the biblical proverb that a tree can only be known by its fruits, is a hidden force that can only be recognized by way of its external effects—that is, within human works and deeds.[37]

Kierkegaard underscores a key distinction between traditional forms of reciprocal sacrifice and works of "true" (kenotic) sacrifice, the latter of which he traces to Christ's commandment in Matthew 22 to "love thy neighbor as thyself." Much like in Stifter's preface, Kierkegaard's concept of a work of love is closely linked to his conception of law; indeed, he defines the biblical imperative to love as the "royal Law."[38] Kierkegaard interprets this injunction as suggesting that to fulfill the law by loving one's neighbor as oneself is, concomitantly, to love oneself in the proper way—"as a neighbor."[39] In

---

36. Stifter, "Limestone," in *Motley Stones*, 41–42.
37. Kierkegaard begins his book with this quote from Luke 6:44, declaring that "every tree is known by its *own* fruit ... we are also saying that in a certain sense love itself is hidden and therefore is known only by its revealing fruits." Søren Kierkegaard, *Works of Love*, ed. and trans. Howard V. Hong and Edna H. Hong (Princeton, NJ: Princeton University Press, 1998), 7–8 (emphasis in the original).
38. Kierkegaard, *Works of Love*, 61.
39. Kierkegaard, *Works of Love*, 20–23.

turn, what this "royal Law" inveighs against above all else is selfishness, just as Stifter identifies self-interest and one-sidedness as the primary banes of the moral law.[40] (In this respect, they both bear traces of Augustine; namely, his characterization of sin as a "person curved in upon themselves" [*homo incurvatus in se*].)

The works that Stifter's pastor—as the eponymous "Poor Benefactor" (*Der arme Wohltäter*) of the original serialized version of the story from 1848—performs are outwardly determined by a sacrificial denial of his own health and comforts for the sake of others. These acts are related by the tale's narrator, who can be (and has been) understood as an exemplum of the programmatic "student of humankind" alluded to in the preface, for in addition to his formal occupation as a land surveyor, he also performs an aesthetic and ethical function as a surveyor of humanity. The kind of writer Stifter describes in the preface is a recognizably Aristotelian one, whose observation of the patterns of reality is intrinsically linked to theorization; that is, to contemplative "looking" (*theoria*) within the "theater" of both human and natural action.[41] In *Limestone*, the narrator-protagonist's most crucial observation relates to the central leitmotif in the entire narrative, the fine white linen that emerges as the sole luxury the priest allows himself to own. The very first time the narrator sees him, he makes careful note of the latter's composure and black attire, save for "two tiny white lappets—the only white thing on his person" (43). The narrator then notices that "as he sat there, some sort of ruffle would sometimes emerge ever so slightly from his sleeves, and he was always covertly tucking them back." Years later, after the two men have established a friendship, the narrator recalls having noticed at their first meeting how the pastor "kept furtively tucking his ruffled shirt cuffs back into his jacket sleeves, as though he were ashamed of them. Now he kept doing the same thing" (48). Subsequently, while taking shelter from a thunderstorm in the

---

40. Kierkegaard, *Works of Love*, 52–53.
41. For a recent account of this concept's possible meanings in Aristotle (and of precedent scholarly perspectives on them), see David Roochnik, "What is *Theoria*? *Nichomachean Ethics* Book 10.7–8," *Classical Philology* 104, no. 1 (2009): 69–82. For a brief remark on affinities between *theoria* and the aesthetic program of Poetic Realism, see my introduction.

pastor's home, the narrator is given a glimpse of the status that this concealed fabric holds for his host, who bustles about preparing a makeshift bed: "Then he opened one of the yellow chests, took out a sheet of extraordinary beauty delicacy and whiteness, unfolded it and spread it over my bed. When I saw the superb quality of the linen in the candle's faint light, and involuntarily glanced at him, he blushed" (54).

As will gradually become apparent, this external, visible realm of effects and actions is consistently juxtaposed with a nonvisible, subterranean realm of motivation and unspoken intention. This contrast is equally operative in the domain of nature, as indicated in an early remark by the pastor that the austere landscape of "the Corrie" (*Kar*) "is as God created it" (45). This nearly verbatim iteration of the introductory frame's description of the division between the hidden facets of a person and their observable manifestations implies that the narrator's occupation as a surveyor applies to both the geographical and the human landscape, and in so doing bespeaks a broader cultural ethics of panoramic visibility that came to prominence in the nineteenth century.[42] It is in the former, external sphere that this division is first portrayed.

On the morning following the torrential thunderstorm, the narrator gazes through the window of the parsonage, where he had stayed the night at the priest's insistence. The day is clear and pristine, and the unobstructed field of visibility instills in the narrator a sense of nature's immensity as he surveys the vista before him. He looks into the sky, watching as "the sun rose resplendent in measureless blue," and reflects upon the thunderstorm's origins within the "the sky's fine invisible vapors" that had quietly compounded "in measureless space" during the previous day until, at last, "the

---

42. Swales and Swales, *Adalbert Stifter*, 207. Vance Byrd has examined how the panorama represents a broader cultural and medial history of attempts to bring a "tamed" version of wild nature into the social and domestic interior. Stifter's texts play with this fault line in their emphasis of immersive and occasionally baleful landscapes that are countered with frameworks and structures of order (often articulated in a visual register, as is the case in *Kalkstein*). Byrd, *A Pedagogy of Observation: Nineteenth-Century Panoramas, German Literature, and Reading Culture* (Lewisburg, PA: Bucknell University Press, 2017), 71–96.

night's measureless rain" dispersed them and cleansed the sweltering air (57). The triple repetition of "measureless" (*unermeßlich*) signals that the narrator—a practitioner of surveyorship (*Meßkunst*) by both trade and diegetic function—here confronts an aspect of nature that cannot be uniformly (let alone mimetically) depicted.[43] This measurelessness will also inform the hidden, interior topography of human motivation that is the other half of the narrative's core theme. However, before we can adequately analyze both halves together, we must first consider more thoroughly the natural elements that form the stage for the story.

As in *The Solar Eclipse*, light plays an important symbolic role. On the day of the thunderstorm, for example, an oppressive heat is accompanied by "an unsubstantial light" that drenches the bare land, yet the sun cannot be located at a distinct point in the sky (48). Rather, this "strangest lead-colored light" (49) seeps over every surface of the Corrie, just as the storm's "flashes of lightning, bright though they were, were not yet snaking lines, but merely diffuse flares" (51). Like the uncanny twilight that both illuminates and enshrouds Vienna during the eclipse of 1842, this "essenceless" (*wesenloses*) light pervades everything and washes objects of their contours and distinctions. It is then juxtaposed with the smaller, beneficent forms of light that appear in the pastor's domestic rituals. For instance, as the storm gathers and the two men have installed themselves in his sitting room, the pastor explains "that it was his custom, when storms came at night, to set a candle on the table and sit quietly by the light as long as the storm should last" (50–51). This contrast between the habitual candlelight and the intermittent flashes of lightning from the storm outside recalls the contrast between the constancy demanded by moral precepts and the exceptions to the gentle law occasionally entailed by natural phenomena.[44] Most importantly, as in *The Solar Eclipse* this strange light

---

43. Martin Selge, *Adalbert Stifter: Poesie aus dem Geist der Naturwissenschaft* (Stuttgart: W. Kohlhammer, 1976), 61–64.

44. Claudia Nitschke, "Chaos und Form, Raum und Ethos in Stifters *Bunte Steine*," *German Life and Letters* 68, no. 4 (2015): 561; John Reddick, "Tiger und Tugend in Stifters 'Kalkstein': Eine Polemik," *Zeitschrift für deutsche Philologie* 95 (1976): 253; Swales and Swales, *Adalbert Stifter*, 216.

prefigures sacrifice; however, here the natural element that will occasion the most revelatory view into the relation between the cosmic and the human is not light, but water.

"Pits and Hollows"

As a case in point, *Limestone* places the river in the foreground of its thematic framework of sacrifice and abstention. A symbolic affinity between water and self-imposed order is subtly choreographed to come into focus gradually. Stifter initially portrays the river as an agent of restraint by having it function as the topographical border of the tale itself. The water physically demarcates the terrain of the Corrie, a bare and low-lying region that strikes the narrator on his first visit as "abominable" (45). He notes that he is partial to "wilds gorges chasms cliffs and plunging waters," and therefore the uniform and slack lines of the landscape cause him a certain degree of unease. The river and its banks "were all that relieved and refreshed the eye" in this otherwise undifferentiated environment of pale limestone slopes and silent space devoid of middle distance or natural objects to occupy the surveyor's attention (44). The violent storm and flood, as archetypically ungentle manifestations of Stifter's natural law, thus stand at the opposite extreme from the Corrie's pervasively monochrome and unchanging forms while at the same time underscoring the aesthetic as well as psychological value of the river in its ability to conjugate movement and stillness.[45]

In addition to offering visual refreshment and relief, the river's current also becomes an element of *interrupted* predictability, repetition, and habit by bursting its banks and threatening the local inhabitants. The water is also described as merging with light at decisive moments

---

45. As Isolde Schiffermüller has shown, these very same facets of water are known to have been of interest to Stifter in his other artistic endeavors of this same time, particularly in the series of *Bewegung* (movement) paintings that he produced beginning around 1854. Schiffermüller, "'Jenes Ding . . . das Licht': Zum Glanz in der Prosa von Adalbert Stifter," in *Fleck, Glanz, Finsternis: Zur Poetik der Oberfläche bei Adalbert Stifter*, ed. Thomas Gann and Marianne Schuller (Paderborn: Fink, 2014), 15–19.

of the story, such as in the flooding of the meadow that results from the ferocious thunderstorm. The sight has a marked aesthetic impact upon the narrator due to the combined capacity of water and light to uniformly envelop and redetermine a formerly innocuous space with a new beauty: "[The river] had overflowed its banks and flooded part of the meadow. . . . The high bridge, as it descended, led straight into the water. Yet disregarding the damage the flood must have caused by washing sand onto the meadow, even this was a beautiful phenomenon. The great expanse of water gleamed in the rays of the sun, adding to the green of the meadow and the gray of the rocks a third chiming, shimmering note, and the bridge stood out bizarrely like a dark line over the silvery mirror" (58). This passage anticipates Stifter's 1867 portrayal of the optimal tranquility that he would find in the Lackenhäuser woods, where the "wide sea" of sunlight is transposed into "countless shimmering droplets" by the forest's objects and shadows, such that "the darkness of the forest gets cut through by a glowing line." However, a more specific figural characteristic of water is at the fore of *Limestone*—namely, its bifurcation of the perceived world into the visible space above the surface and the nonvisible domain beneath the surface. Fittingly, it is precisely this dichotomy that determines self-sacrifice throughout the narrative.

The key scene takes place in this flooded meadow and is an emblematic instance of the pastor's self-giving nature that we have observed up to this point. After all, his offer to shelter the narrator from the storm the night before had fulfilled a central tenet of the moral law, as signaled by the pastor's response to the narrator's gratitude with the words "I gave what I had. . . . People live side by side, and can do one another many good turns" (58). However, we learn early in the text that he does not have very much to begin with; at several points the narrator makes note of the pastor's abstention from physical comforts. For instance, he has neither a bed nor a pillow, but has instead accustomed himself to sleeping every night on the hard bench of his table, with a Bible propped under his head. He is also abstemious with food and drink, eating sparingly from his habitual meal of bread, strawberries, and milk.

After the narrator has taken his leave of his host and is making his way homeward, he notices that children have begun to assemble on the opposite shore of the swollen river. They seem to be preparing to ford the currents, removing their shoes and stockings and beginning to wade into the water from the nearly submerged footbridge; and then, suddenly,

> To my surprise I now saw a tall black figure in the middle of the water, none other than the poor priest of the Corrie. He stood in it nearly up to his hips. I had not seen him wade in, for my eyes had been fixed on the bridge the whole time, and only as the children moved in my direction had I shifted my gaze to the foreground. The children all waded toward the pastor, and after pausing beside him and talking to him a while, they set out toward the bank where I stood. As they picked their way with more or less care, they scattered across the water as they came, standing out like black dots on the gleaming surface, and reached me one by one. (60, translation modified)

Only when the narrator encounters the pastor soon afterward does he discover the reason for the remarkable spectacle he has just witnessed. The pastor explains that "pits and hollows" (*Gruben und Vertiefungen*) had been left in the meadow after the local farmer extracted stones from the soil, and that because the ground is now inundated with rushing water, the children might have unwittingly waded into the indentations and slipped beneath the surface. "And so he thought to stand next to the pit to avert any danger. But as its sides were steep, he had slipped in himself, and once standing in it he had remained there. One of the smaller children could even have drowned in the pit, deep as it was dug. The meadow would have to be leveled again, for the water was murky when it flooded, and concealed the depth and the irregularity of the ground underfoot" (62).

The narrator's act of observation thus involves seeing as well as not seeing in multiple senses. Due to the literal lack of visibility caused by the floodwater's obscuration of the treacherous ground, he is also unable to decipher the reason for the pastor's presence there. The formal characteristics of this vignette recall Hans Blumenberg's analysis of the division between land and sea, and more specifically of the ancient topos of a shipwreck seen from the shore. For Blumenberg, the metaphorical salience of this image is rooted in the elemental boundary between land as the symbolic domain of lived experience, subjective perception, and contemplation, and the water as the symbolic domain of that which forms the horizon to one's perception and thought—of that which can be "seen" but not wholly known. In short, the metaphor of beholding another's peril in the water from a removed and secure vantage point relates to a foundational ontological division in subjective experience between the "exterior that is unreachable from within" and "the interior that is unreachable from without."[46]

What the narrator witnesses from land could thus be described as the pastor's literal mediation of the symbolic dichotomy inherent to water, for he physically bridges the division between the unseen realm beneath the surface that is proper to death and the unknown, and the visible realm above it that is proper to life and recognition. His literal (and littoral) suspension between water and light foregrounds him as a figure in whom Blumenberg's categories of "within" and "without" will continue to collide throughout the rest of the story.[47] A critical point for our analysis of *Limestone* is that the sacrificial resonances of the pastor's behavior are in a way rooted within the liminal semiological space between the unseen and the seen. The image of his "tall black figure" half-submerged in the river becomes retroactively salvatory in the eyes (or hindsight) of the narrator and the reader alike as soon as the pastor contextualizes this image with his explanation about the uneven ground beneath. In this way the selflessness actualized by the pastor's actions in the water suggests that a primary function of sacrificiality is the negotiation of the dialectic introduced

---

46. Hans Blumenberg, *Schiffbruch mit Zuschauer: Paradigma einer Daseinsmetapher* (Frankfurt am Main: Suhrkamp, 1979), 17.

47. This motif also plays a decisive role in another novella from the *Motley Stones* cycle. In *Katzensilber* (*Cat-Silver*), a similar scene of flood and rescue (in this case by the mysterious "braunes Mädchen") centers upon a transformed body of water and its eradication of visual boundaries (Stifter, *Motley Stones*, 192.) Like the pastor in *Kalkstein*, the girl enters the swirling currents in order to locate and indicate a safe route for the children, who otherwise might choose the wrong footing. Both of these characters mediate the gap between obscured peril and visible objects by turning their own bodies into "visible proof" that transposes an invisible order of unknown hazards beneath the water into a visible order of knowledge and safety above the surface.

in the opening pages—namely, that of a nonvisible order and its observable effects (or, to speak with Kierkegaard's language, its "fruits"). The priest's physical presence in the water, with his lower half beneath the surface and his torso extending above it, mediates these two spheres as he seeks out and guards against the hazardous underwater "pits and hollows."[48] This figural division between the known and the unknown is intrinsic to the function of sacrifice in *Limestone*, for we soon learn that the pastor's numerous monetary and material sacrifices, though beneficent in their effects, do not derive from pure selflessness. Paradoxically, however, it will turn out to be the *morally* problematic motivations behind the pastor's self-giving behavior that end up making it possible for the *ethically* sound objective of this behavior to be fulfilled. As such, a deviation from certain dimensions of the moral law will ultimately allow the overarching order of the gentle law to remain whole.

Old *Habitus*

The key to grasping this complicated but elemental function of sacrifice is revealed several years after the day of the flood, when the pastor falls ill and is visited by the narrator. What follows is a frame narration by the pastor of several episodes from his past that, in light of the recounted content, resembles a confession and at last provides context for his stringent self-abnegation in things both fleshly and financial. As we soon learn, this context pertains directly to his obsession with white linen and the furtive shame he has demonstrated in connection with it.

As a young man working for his family's business, the pastor had taken to looking into the adjoining garden, where the neighbor (a widow with a young daughter) would hang fresh laundry and linen to dry. "I so loved to look at her," he recounts. "Sometimes I stood at the window and looked over at the garden where washing always hung on the lines, except when night fell, or bad weather came, and I was very fond of those white things" (78). He continued to observe her, taking special note of the fact that "on her body, at her

---

48. Compare Reddick, "Tiger und Tugend," 242.

neck or at her sleeves, I had always seen the finest white linen" (79–80). He eventually built up the courage to attract her attention by leaving peaches for her to find, and the young romance at last blossomed. All the while, the young man also began to spend his humble earnings on fine white linens, in which, as the narrator would notice during their first meeting many years later, he clothed himself from then on, adorning his own body in the same manner as the girl's that he had studied so closely.

The events that follow are decisive for his trajectory: paradise is lost when the girl's mother discovers the two of them together in the garden one day ("We were ashamed of ourselves indeed, and ran away from each other"), and soon thereafter she is sent away. The young man, alone and penurious following the deaths of his father and elder brother, joins the priesthood and is assigned to the parish of the Corrie, where he has lived ever since. He tells the narrator that during this time, he has been rigorously pursuing a particular goal, donating his furniture and saving every penny he earns toward it. Though he does not yet specify what this high aim is, he does make a critical confession: "Over this long span of time my way of life has become a habit, and I love it. But there is one sin against this frugality that weighs upon my conscience: I still have the fine white linens. . . . It is a grave error, but I have sought to atone for it by skimping still more on my physical needs and other things. I am too weak to do without them" (83). Only at the end of the novella, following the pastor's death, does the narrator at last discover that the object of these many years of self-sacrifice and austerity has been to fund the construction of a new schoolhouse that will allow the children to avoid crossing the river, thus eliminating the risk of their drowning during times of flood.

Between this later revelation and the pastor's previous admission to the secret impetus of his ascetic lifestyle, it becomes possible to discern a temporal underpinning of sacrifice in *Limestone*: On the one hand, the narrator eventually learns, at the end, that the pastor's devotion to protecting the children from the water had concrete aims that would extend well beyond his lifetime. And yet, on the other hand, the narrator has also already been told that this devotion is not purely preventive, but also expiatory; in other words, it is both rooted in and addressed to the past as well as to the present and the future. Thus, we can begin to see that water is significant in *Limestone* not only because it is at the center of the narrative setting, but also because it figuralizes the ceaseless movement and coalescence that is so innate to lived time as the pastor describes it, and in turn so interpenetrative with the ethical and moral substance of his sacrifices.

This relates to the earlier discussion of how water symbolizes sacrificiality as a mediation of the seen and the unseen. While the pastor's physical presence in the river could be interpreted as a literal mediation of the underwater "hollows" and the visible realm above the surface, his self-sacrificing poverty and abstinence turn out to qualify more as acts of atonement rather than an unconditioned, kenotic neglect of his own well-being for the good of the other *without* an expiatory logic of exchange. His offerings, in other words, do not constitute unincited works of love in Kierkegaard's sense, for the constancy of his giving and self-denial that he describes as hard-won "habit" (*Gewohnheit*) functions in part as compensation for his continued failure to "do without" (*abgewöhnen*) the white linen.[49] By contrast, his obsession—whether with the materiality of the linen itself or with the memory of its referent—constitutes a transgression from the vantage point of his spiritual vocation.

It warrants considering the deeper implications of *Gewohnheit*, which, as the pastor himself conveys, consists in a rigorism that allows isolated and potentially variable actions and impulses eventually to be restructured as habit: "[People] grow accustomed ... and believe it must be so. But it can also be otherwise. People grow accustomed to everything, and habit becomes very easy then, very easy" (56). In considering the opposition between the pastor's moral habituation and his retainment of the linen in which he secretly clothes himself—a literalization of the ancient relationship between

---

49. Kierkegaard's definition of sacrificial love leaves little room for negotiation with respect to underlying motivation: "The self-denial, the self-control, and the self-sacrifice that are still only transactions within temporality, within the horizon of the human, are not truly Christian.... The movement of [temporal] sacrifice accordingly becomes specious; it makes a show of forsaking the world but still remains within the world" (*Works of Love*, 131).

outer appearance and inner will that is intrinsic to *habitus*[50]—it might also be helpful to borrow from modern philosophical distinctions between lawful regularity and transgressive repetition. For instance, Gilles Deleuze takes law to consist in "similar form and ... equivalent content"; that is, in a normative consistency distinct from repetition, which by contrast consists in "a singularity opposed to the general ... a distinctive opposed to the ordinary, an instantaneity opposed to variation and an eternity opposed to permanence."[51] An echo of the pastor's assiduous adherence to domestic habit and ritual can be heard in Deleuze's description of moral law as being rooted within a normative generality of habituation; that is, within Hegel's notion of "second nature."[52] In this context, then, the *repetition* associated with the linen—and not merely as a recurring motif, but more crucially as a "ritualistic" object of compulsive behavior and memory—contrasts decisively with the *repetitiousness* of habit.[53] Yet, in good Deleuzian (and, as we will see presently, Kierkegaardian) fashion, both are ironically oriented more to the unpredictable, ever-morphing horizon of the future than they

---

50. As John Cassian's fifth-century *Institutes* insist, a monk's garb (or "habit") is merely an external expression of his life's inward regulation by faith and duty— that is to say, by pious habits: "After having exposed their outward appearance to view we shall then be able to discuss, in logical sequence, their inner worship." Cassian, *The Institutes*, trans. Boniface Ramsey (New York: Newman Press, 2000), 21.

51. Gilles Deleuze, *Difference and Repetition*, trans. Paul Patton (New York: Columbia University Press, 1994), 2–3.

52. "Habit is rightly called a second nature—*nature*, since it is an immediate being of the soul; and a *second one*, since it is an immediacy *set* by the soul." According to Hegel, the subject graduates from its natural state by codifying certain actions and experiences into habits, allowing the self to emerge into consciousness and make way for the eventual emergence of Spirit. Thus, like the role of sacrifice in Stifter's dialectic of hidden cause and perceivable effect, *Gewohnheit* in Hegel's system operates as a middle bridge between two poles: nature and Spirit. G. W. F. Hegel, *Enzyklopädie der philosophischen Wissenschaft im Grundriss III*, in *Werke*, vol. 10, ed. Eva Moldenhauer and Karl Markus Michel (Frankfurt am Main: Suhrkamp, 1979), 183 (§410, emphases in the original).

53. Sabina Becker and Katharina Grätz, "Einleitung," in *Ordnung—Raum—Ritual: Adalbert Stifters artifizieller Realismus*, ed. Sabine Becker (Heidelberg: Universitätsverlag Winter, 2007), 8. Also see Michèle Godau, *Wirkliche Wirklichkeit: Mythos und Ritual bei Adalbert Stifter und Hans Henny Jahnn* (Würzburg: Königshausen und Neumann, 2005); Alice Bolterauer, *Ritual und Ritualität bei Adalbert Stifter* (Vienna: Praesens, 2005), 130–142, 394–406.

are to the closed fixedness of the past, and are thus reflective of the particular habit of collecting that predominates many of Stifter's tales.[54] How might we understand the nature of the pastor's sacrifices vis-à-vis this opposition between moral habit and transgressive repetition?

The answer may lie in the temporal structure of the pastor's sacrificial gestures that we identified earlier. On one level his sacrifices have as their object the future well-being of the children, yet on another level these future-oriented sacrifices ultimately emerge as retrospective attempts to redress a past transgression—one that is kept alive within the pastor's attachment to this past's material manifestation (the linen). The dual movement of the pastor's acts of devotion that outwardly project into the future even as they secretly attend to the past offers a felicitous illustration of "repetition" in Kierkegaard's own terms: *gjentagelsen*. Like the German *Wiederholung*, the Danish word does not denote an identical iteration of a finished event, but instead literally means a "taking anew" of the past *in* the present instant such that this instant swells with potentiality and change. As a result, the temporal emphasis of repetition for Kierkegaard paradoxically falls not so much on the past as on the futurity that is inherent to any action undertaken with an eye to reconstituting the past. Returning to *Limestone*, then, we can see how the pastor's future-oriented sacrifices are simultaneously "retakings" of the past in an attempt to dissolve its tenacious grip upon the present.

Opus Operatum

With this in mind, there is a final question to ask: How do both of these temporal underpinnings of sacrifice in *Limestone*—that is, the devotion to the future well-being of the other that is at the same time an expiatory "taking again" of one's own past—relate to Stifter's categories of law? Though in one sense the natural law occupies the

---

54. See Samuel Frederick, *The Redemption of Things: Collecting and Dispersal in German Realism and Modernism* (Ithaca, NY: Cornell University Press, 2022), 69–100.

foreground of the novella insofar as the violent storm and the resultant flood most immediately determine the key moments of the plot, moral law is the true focal point of its embedded narrative about the pastor's actions and their unspoken, unseen roots. Let us therefore examine the ethical implications of his sacrifices vis-à-vis Stifter's theoretical system of an underlying, universal, "gentle" law.

The pastor's commitment to the children's safety clearly fulfills a key principle of the moral law by standing in opposition to one-sidedness or self-interest. His physical act of protecting them from unseen "pits and hollows" beneath the surface of the water can be viewed as a representative image of his self-sacrificial *habitus*, including his financial and physical self-denial for the sake of funding a new schoolhouse whose location would keep the children out of harm's way. However, he will eventually confess that these acts are at least partially undertaken as a means of atoning for his inability to give up the white linen he has hoarded all these years. It must be emphasized that according to the theological paradigm that the pastor explicitly espouses, the linen, like the Augustinian motif of fruit evoked by the peaches that he had left for the widow's daughter to find, does not correspond *qua* object to concrete sinful acts (that is, youthful lust and the subsequent, idolatrous commemoration of this lust), but instead stands for the very condition of sinfulness. In other words, it is not as an object of sin but as an objective correlative of sinfulness per se that the linen warrants repentance.[55] As we have seen, in Stifter's poetics of natural and moral lawfulness, condition and cause possess a higher degree of significance than singularity and effect. Insofar as this poetics can be said to inform the character of the pastor, the condition of sinfulness

---

55. In my view, the linen and the memories associated with it neatly illustrate T. S. Eliot's concept of "a set of objects, a situation, a chain of events" that become a "formula" of a "*particular* emotion; such that when the external facts, which must terminate in sensory experience, are given, the emotion is immediately evoked." However, an important distinction is that in *Limestone* the linen correlates, not simply to emotion, but instead to the recognition of an entire state of being that generates the emotions in question. Eliot, "Hamlet and His Problems," in *The Sacred Wood: Essays on Poetry and Criticism* (London: Methuen, 1960), 100.

therefore demands atonement more than any singular sinful deeds that have been committed as an effect of this condition.

Thus, like the vision of the pastor wading through the currents of the flooded river, his sacrificial gestures also pertain to Kierkegaard's dialectic of observable "fruits" of kenotic charity and the unseen ground out of which they grow. Should we regard these sacrifices for the benefit of the other as being nevertheless at odds with the moral law outlined in Stifter's preface, given that the motivation for them is at least partly rooted in a torsion of conscience? Or, to ask in a reformulation of Kierkegaard's metaphor, would the moral law of reciprocal love correspond more to the invisible *roots* of a tree of sacrifice or to its visible and knowable *fruits* (that is, in sacrificial works and acts)?[56]

If the narrative itself can be said to offer any answer, it is that in addition to being ingrained in the border between unseen conditions and seen effects, sacrifice also rests upon a temporal movement whereby the futurity of intention and the retrospection of conscience nimbly fall together in a single instant of ethical decision that transpires as habit. According to the preface, the ethical substance of human actions, sacrificial or otherwise, is determined by the degree to which the ramifications of these actions contribute to universality as opposed to singularity: "It is always in people's ordinary everyday infinitely recurring actions that this law most surely forms the fulcrum, for these actions are the lasting the underlying ones, like the millions of fibrils of the tree of life" (7). Paradoxically, it is precisely because the pastor's acts fail to qualify as truly *kenotic* self-sacrifice due to their hidden impetus—that is, because they "retake" an individual past in order to do penance for it by means of the children's future good—that the cyclicity, constancy, and collectivity of the moral law is finally achieved. To frame the matter in more Kantian terms, although the pastor's sacrificial impulses may have their source as much (or somewhat more) in conscience than

---

56. A striking echo of this occurs in a line from one of Stifter's earlier stories, *Der Hagestolz* (*The Bachelors*, 1844/1845), in which the protagonist's uncle declares: "I'd even say that devoting oneself to others—even unto death—is nothing less than the flower of a man's life, bursting open in its finest form." Stifter, *The Bachelors*, trans. David Bryer (London: Pushkin Press, 2008), 133.

in a wholly duty-bound "will to good," that very source conditions the specific temporal character of his actual sacrifices, and this temporal character ultimately comes forth as the guarantor of the moral law (in Stifter's conception) on a structural level; it is because of the pastor's *acts*, and not the concealed motivations behind them, that the children will continue to be kept safe even after he is no longer there. Exceptions of law become part *of* law, like an invisible chink in the "chain of flowers" from *Abdias* that from a certain angle suddenly becomes visible, if only as shadow.

To a certain degree, this reading evokes Freud's hypothesis, advanced first in *Totem and Taboo* (1913) and then in a revised form in *Moses and Monotheism* (1939), that sacrifice emerges within human culture as a response to a collective, unconscious sense of guilt over a foundational act of violence. More particularly, Freud suggests that cultural systems of morality, ethics, and law are the results of this primordial guilt having insinuated itself first into religious rituals of sacrifice, and from thence into societal mores of restraint (and even repression). However, even though the pastor's moral obsessiveness has a certain neurotic structure insofar as it is compulsive and responds to a past event, the process by which his guilt is transposed into a spiritual, moral, *and* ethical praxis is conscious and individual, rather than unconscious and collective.[57] He knows guilt to be the source of his actions, and he also knows the source of this guilt. Consequently, the pastor's sacrificiality manifests a superegoic aspect of morality rather than an unconscious one. This also might have to do with how sacrifice's function within the life of the pastor reflects its function within Stifter's schema of law as well: because it is not an *unconscious* propitiatory response to a violent

---

57. Compare Elsbeth Dangel-Pelloquin, "Weiße Wäsche: Zur Synthese von Reinheit und Erotik bei Keller und Stifter," in *Die Dinge und die Zeichen: Dimensionen des Realistischen in der Erzählliteratur des 19. Jahrhunderts*, ed. Sabine Schneider and Barbara Hunfeld (Würzburg: Königshausen und Neumann, 2008), 143–156; Katharina Grätz, "Erzählte Rituale—ritualisiertes Erzählen: Literarische Sinngebung bei Adalbert Stifter," in Becker, *Ordnung—Raum—Ritual*, 164–171; Nitschke, "Chaos und Form," 561–564; Isolde Schiffermüller, "Rhetorik des Schweigens: *Kalkstein*," in *Buchstäblichkeit und Bildlichkeit bei Adalbert Stifter: Dekonstruktive Lektüren* (Vienna: Studien, 1996), 187–217.

act, sacrifice here constitutes a denial of the self (albeit one that is not fully kenotic) rather than the violent expurgation of a substitutive object (such as the linen). Self-sacrifice is the manifestation of a particular kind of guilt, in other words, making apparent what was initially invisible to the narrator just like the pastor's body signals the underwater hazards of the riverbed to our view above the surface.

In the final passages of the story, we learn that the empirical objective of a new schoolhouse is finally attained after the community, moved by the revelation of the pastor's ceaseless pursuit of their children's safety, collectively donates the necessary outstanding funds.[58] In *Limestone*, acts of sacrifice put the moral law into effect even if the motivation behind these acts is not grounded in a Kantian sense of duty fully conditioned by and oriented toward the idea of the good. In this respect, more can be explicated about Stifter's novella if one looks not to Enlightenment ethics but instead to the much older theological distinction between a rite whose validity rests upon the moral purity of the officiant (*ex opere operantis*) and a rite whose sacramental value is tied solely to the fact and event of the rite's performance (*ex opere operato*).[59] The pastor's works of love, as a cumulative *opus operatum* rather than an *opus operantis*, manage to uphold the gentle law by virtue of their effects, even if the hidden cause of the work diverges from some of this law's tenets.

Moreover, just as the preface suggested that it is possible for the moral and natural laws to be unsynchronized, the priest of the Corrie shows that an internal, Hegelian duality of ethics (*Sittlichkeit*) and morality (*Moralität*) is possible within a single category of law.[60] The gentle law can be ethically in effect (that is, it can have

---

58. The tearful remark made by the pastor's tenant following this realization is significant: "Oh, how I misjudged the man, I almost took him for a miser" (90).

59. *The Catholic Encyclopedia*, s.v. "Sacraments," vol. 13, ed. Charles George Herbermann et al. (New York: Appleton, 1913), 295–305. Given the centrality of water symbolism for our reading, it is interesting to note that this distinction was first drawn in third- and fourth-century debates (most famously between Augustine and the Donatists), specifically about the sacrament of baptism.

60. "The ethical [*sittliche*] world, disrupted into the this-worldly present and the other-worldly beyond, and the moral [*moralische*] worldview are thus the spirits whose movement and whose return into spirit's simple self existing-for-itself develop themselves, and, as their goal and result, the actual self-consciousness of absolute

formally "purposive" [*zweckmäßige*] consequences according to Stifter's *Sittengesetz*) by way of sacrificial acts even if the moral grounding of these acts is not entirely "unmotivated" (*zwecklos*)—that is, kenotic. This particular text thus allows a space in which Stifter's poetics can unfold fully, for in the arc of the pastor's life—along with the variety of actions that give it its shape—we can find both an imprint and an itinerary of the laws that are said to give the world its shape in turn.

Thus, the pastor's sacrificiality inverts the two key terms of the gentle law: effects are now "higher" than their causes. Yet even in spite of this inversion, by all appearances the gentle law is very much in effect at the end of the novella. In the same way that sacrifice had illuminated the jointure of law's interrupted effects and its uninterrupted cause in *The Solar Eclipse*, in *Limestone* it carries out an internal movement by which law—in the form of the gentle law—can be simultaneously in suspension and in effect. This movement is not miraculous, as in *The Solar Eclipse*, but has been incorporated into the very concept of law itself; and it has also brought us from the light to the water, where subsequent German Realist narratives will tend to remain, as we shall see over the course of this book.

"As if an Ocean of Light Had Been Given to Us"

If one were to take Benjamin's cue and search Stifter's work for traces of a "demonic shadow" in its visually determined poetics, one would find that the motif of disrupted vision exemplifies both a figurative and, in certain texts, a literal "darkening" (*Verfinsterung*) of cosmic law.[61] The forms of nonvisibility that herald nature's disturbances of its own regularity are tied in varyingly explicit ways to characters' impressions of fate's operation within nature. In many of Stifter's most iconic tales, moments of uncanny privation—or, alternatively,

---

spirit steps forward." G. W. F. Hegel, "VI: Spirit," in *The Phenomenology of Spirit*, ed./trans. Terry Pinkard (Cambridge: Cambridge University Press, 2018), 255. / "VI: Der Geist," in *Phänomenologie des Geistes*, in *Werke*, vol. 3, ed. Eva Moldenhauer and Karl Markus Michel (Frankfurt am Main: Suhrkamp, 1976), 327.

61. Benjamin, "Stifter," 608.

excess—of light register as suspensions in the natural order.[62] Whether in the 1842 eclipse, the inexplicable circumstances and ramifications of lightning in *Abdias*, or the sublimely frightening suffusions of snow and luminescence within a "white darkness" in *Rock Crystal* and *From the Bavarian Forest*, light blinds through its presence as well as its absence.[63]

In the "chain of flowers" principle from *Abdias* and in novellas such as *Limestone* and *Cat-Silver*, by comparison, water and the threat of drowning it poses to children constitute a "gap" or, to borrow Benjmain's term, a "shadowy nocturnal side" of the gentle law. The topos of the river is no stranger to philosophical discourse on lawfulness, for with its simultaneously constant and protean quality, it has often served as a preferred metaphor for cosmic *physis* and human *nomos* throughout Western thought. Deleuze, for instance, evokes these Heraclitian tropes in order to illustrate law's dual components of normative generality and a mutability that allows this generality to perdure: "Law unites the change of the water and the permanence of the river," he writes.[64]

In *Limestone*, the river that has overrun its banks and threatens the safety of the local children would seem at first glance to move away from this model, presenting instead the aftermath of a compromised (if not injured) gentle law. Yet this apparent disruption of the law in nature is soon countered by the narrator's perception of it as a scene of selfless devotion. At the same time, the priest's physical mediation of the seen and unseen spheres of the water literalizes the contingency of third-person observation, for the narrator and reader subsequently learn that both the witnessed instant in

---

62. This motif reflects a broader dimension of Stifter's oeuvre—namely, the recurrent evocation of Aristotelian topics. (Admittedly, in this specific instance Stifter's poetics diverges somewhat from Aristotle by underscoring *disjunction* in the order of things, whereas Aristotle uses the same example of blindness—as the result of an excess of either light or darkness—in order to emphasize the *coherence* of subject and object, and to do so in support of the larger argument that "the activity of the object of perception and of that which can perceive is one"). Aristotle, *De Anima*, trans. D. W. Hamlyn (Oxford: Oxford University Press, 1993), 49 (III.2, 426a15–27); compare 27 (II.7, 418b3–13).

63. See Schiffermüller, "'Jenes Ding . . . das Licht,'" 30–33.

64. Deleuze, *Difference and Repetition*, 2.

which the pastor delivers the children from danger as well as his ongoing dedication to their future safety have an additional, secret impetus. In other words, the acts and gestures that are glimpsed by a Blumenbergian spectator from the "shore" as unprovoked works of love and self-sacrifice simultaneously correspond with the clandestine atonement for guilt and truths hidden "beneath the surface." To a similar degree, the pastor's asceticism eventually slides into focus at the end of the tale, weaving the earlier image of him in the river into a contextual fabric of sacrifice.

Water, then, as a symbol and setting of the pastor's sacrifices, is the focal point of lawfulness in *Limestone*. Both that novella and *The Solar Eclipse* invoke sacrifice in connection with scenes of disrupted law, staged alongside abnormal manifestations of light and water. The latter text directly associates Christ's crucifixion with the liminal instant between the disappearance and reemergence of the sun (whereby, for Stifter, it seemed "as if an ocean of light had been given to us"), while in the former the priest's presence in the river marks a simultaneous deviation from the moral law and a fulfillment of it.[65] The theme of drowning further adds to the symbolic resonances of water, for if in Stifter's writing water and light can embody the often-unnoticed effects of law's operation in nature, then drowning embodies the potential for this hidden order to become unexpectedly visible. However, rather than evincing a miraculous suspension of law by the divine, as the eclipse had, a child's drowning would constitute an unveiling of a graver sort; not to the "physical eyes" of simple perception, nor to the "mental eyes" of reason, but instead to the "eyes of the heart."[66] And through those eyes, such an event would cause any question of lawful order—hidden or not—to become suddenly, terribly beside the point.

As we leave the realm of Stifter's early prose and turn to subsequent texts of German Realism, we will encounter different paradigms of

---

65. Stifter, "The Solar Eclipse," 257.
66. Stifter distinguishes between "physical" and "mental" eyes in the preface (4); and in *Abdias* the narrator drew a distinction between "the eye of the soul" (in the foreword) as well as "bodily eyes" and "eyes of the heart" (in the story itself).

law, sacrifice, and ethics. By the time of Stifter's death, the more optimistic, selfless modes of sacrifice introduced by *The Solar Eclipse* and developed in *Limestone* will have given way to post-Biedermeier anxieties and pessimisms linked to water rather than to light, as in various works by Gustav Freytag, Ferdinand von Saar, Theodor Fontane, Marie von Ebner-Eschenbach (as we have already seen), Gottfried Keller, and Theodor Storm—and specifically the drowning scenes central to their plots. Stifter's work anticipates these themes in notable ways, showing how the solace that one might derive from the consistency of sunlight's disappearance and return is countered by water's preclusion of figural and temporal predictability. Whether in his fictional settings such as the Corrie, whose humble parish priest attempts to redress his past and to protect the children from the river, or in the factual instance of Stifter's own foster-daughter committing suicide by drowning in the spring of 1859, what water reveals—or, perhaps better, reflects—in his work and life is a Benjaminian "shadowy nocturnal side" of Heraclitus's most famous axiom, in which the sole certainty one can cling to is uncertainty.[67]

Nowhere does Stifter's writing intimate this more hauntingly than in the autobiographical fragment *Mein Leben* (*My Life*), which he worked on slowly from 1866 until October 1868, three months before he took his own life.[68] At one point in the text, as he strains to reach back to the first glimmer of his conscious memory as a young child, he offers this impression: "Then I was swimming in something undulating, I swam back and forth, and it grew softer and softer inside of me; then it was as though I were drunk, and then there was nothing more."[69]

---

67. The body of Juliane Mohaupt had been discovered in the Danube on April 18, 1859. See Wolfgang Matz, *Adalbert Stifter oder "Diese fürchterliche Wendung der Dinge"* (Munich: Hanser, 1995), 304.

68. Hermann Augustin, *Adalbert Stifters Krankheit und Tod: Eine biographische Quellenstudie* (Basel: Schwabe, 1964), 116–126.

69. Stifter, "Mein Leben [Nachlaßblätter]," in *Gesammelte Werke in vierzehn Bänden*, vol. 14, ed. Konrad Steffen (Basel: Birkhäuser, 1972), 117.

3

FLUMEN PUBLICUM

The Imitation of Right and the Recognition of Rite in Keller's A Village Romeo and Juliet

> It was late, late in the evening
> The lovers they were gone;
> The clocks had ceased their chiming
> And the deep river ran on.
> —W. H. AUDEN, "AS I WALKED OUT ONE EVENING"

Gottfried Keller had only been engaged to Christina Luise Scheidegger for a number of weeks when, on the morning July 13, 1866 (a Friday), her body was found in the shallow pond of her garden in Herzogenbuchsee.[1] Keller left behind almost no records of the effect

---

Epigraph: W. H. Auden, *Selected Poems: Expanded Edition*, ed. Edward Mendelson (New York: Vintage International, 2007), 68.

1. Emil Ermatinger, *Gottfried Kellers Leben, Briefe und Tagebüche*, vol. 1 (Stuttgart: J. G. Cotta, 1924), 425; Walter Baumann, *Gottfried Keller: Leben, Werk, Zeit* (Zurich: Artemis, 1986), 139–146; Hans Wysling, ed., *Gottfried Keller, 1819–1890* (Zurich: Artemis, 1990), 240–245.

that his fiancée's death had on him; as a consequence, we cannot know if he ever reflected upon how eerily this tragic event echoed the conclusion of a novella he had written ten years earlier.[2] In the final scene of *Romeo und Julia auf dem Dorfe* (*A Village Romeo and Juliet*, 1856), the two protagonists, having been barred from a sanctioned marriage in their community, conduct a private wedding ceremony on the banks of a river.[3] Then, shortly after recognizing each other as husband and wife, they drown themselves.

Whether or not this macabre imitation of art by life ever occupied Keller's thoughts, one can certainly regard the underlying motivation of scholarship on *A Village Romeo and Juliet* as an attempt to identify the ultimate cause of the story's tragic climax and dénouement. The answers have been myriad, ranging from the necessary effects of capital, to bourgeois mores and normative ideals, to the interior frameworks of subjectivity itself. All of these approaches, whatever their nuances and differences, ultimately assume an overarching causality of transgression and consequence in the plot.[4] The reasons for this are understandable enough; Keller's tale follows the short lives of Sali and Vrenchen, whose fathers set in motion a series of events and actions that condemn their children to shame in the eyes of the community. It is this social stigma that ultimately impedes Sali and Vrenchen's ideal existence in the village as a respectable married couple, and in the end they sacrifice their lives in exchange for a brief taste of this ideal, though only by way of simulation.

---

2. Walter Baumann and Hans Wysling both speculate that Keller destroyed all such materials himself, possibly with the subsequent assistance of his literary executor (Baumann, *Gottfried Keller*, 139; Wysling, *Gottfried Keller*, 240).

3. Quotations from the novella refer to the following translation: *A Village Romeo and Juliet*, trans. Ronald Taylor (Richmond, VA: Alma Classics, 2015), unless otherwise noted. Any references to the original German will be included in parenthetical citation, with respective page numbers preceded by the abbreviation *RuJ*, and are drawn from the following edition: *Romeo und Julia auf dem Dorfe*, in *Sämtliche Werke: Historisch-kritische Ausgabe*, vol. 4, ed. Walter Morgenthaler (Frankfurt am Main: Stroemfeld, 1996), 74–159.

4. Walter Benjamin's own comments on the novella established these as key points of interpretive interest. See Benjamin, "Gottfried Keller: Zu Ehren einer kritischen Ausgabe seiner Werke," in *Gesammelte Schriften*, vol. 2.1, *Aufsätze, Essays, Vorträge*, ed. Rolf Tiedemann and Hermann Schweppenhäuser (Frankfurt am Main: Suhrkamp, 1991), 283–295.

In this chapter I examine how both the stage and the choreography of Keller's text consist of a single, key pattern: throughout the novella, particular sorts of infractions against particular forms of law result in the necessity for particular modes of sacrifice.[5] In the first part of the story, the young protagonists ritualistically bury a doll that they have mutilated and adorned together. This motif then repeats itself in their fathers' surreptitious seizure of land they privately believe already to be owned, only to obscure this secret deed by publicly bidding for legal ownership over a small triangular corner of the soil. The sacrificial mode of burial introduced by the children's game thus reflects an impulse that the adults also share vis-à-vis the law: namely, to hide from view something taboo. In the second half of the story, by contrast, the protagonists pretend to be a married couple out of the desire precisely *for* recognition within the gaze of their community. Their imitation of a particular legal status is driven by the wish to be misrecognized—to be seen not as who and what they are, but as something they want to be—and this imitation of lawful recognizability per se ultimately constitutes their transgression against it. Appropriately, their second sacrificial rite takes place in water rather than earth, because it aims not so much to transform and conceal, but to renew and reveal. Rather than ceremonially immolating an object or a creature, Sali and Vrenchen's last rite offers up their own lives in order to hold fast to a desired model of life. We can conceptualize

---

5. Derek Hillard and Winfried Menninghaus have thus far provided the most perceptive accounts of sacrificiality in the novella, and although my own analysis takes cues from several of their observations, I will ultimately offer a different reading. For Menninghaus, the protagonists' suicide functions as an attempt to redress infractions against lawful order by mythic means of violent self-sacrifice. Hillard is similarly interested in the issue of myth's preservation within the material and social order as a result of sacrifice, but focuses upon the burial of the doll, rather than the drowning, as support for his thesis that the main function of sacrifice in the tale is to instantiate a secret, "cryptic" space where presocial forms of myth—embodied in play—can survive within (or beneath) society. Menninghaus, "*Romeo und Julia auf dem Dorfe*: Eine Interpretation im Anschluß an Walter Benjamin," in *Artistische Schrift: Studien zur Kompositionskunst Gottfried Kellers* (Frankfurt am Main: Suhrkamp, 1982), 91–159; Hillard, "Violence, Ritual and Community: On Sacrifice in Keller's *Romeo und Julia auf dem Dorfe* and Storm's *Der Schimmelreiter*," *Monatshefte* 101, no. 3 (2009): 361–381.

this in terms of the Aristotelian distinction described by Giorgio Agamben that we also saw (in chapter 1) to be at issue in Marie von Ebner-Eschenbach's *Beyond Atonement*: in the drowning scene, the protagonists offer their lives (*zoè*) to the water in exchange for being able to fully "live out"—to experience as both real and true—their fantasy of a particular *form of life* (*bios*).[6]

Such themes of community, reciprocation, mimesis, and sacrifice immediately bring to mind the theory of René Girard, and aspects of his work will indeed prove useful for reading *A Village Romeo and Juliet* (as they have for other works of Keller's as well).[7] A good point of entry in this regard is Girard's basic premise that sacrifice (as a solution to widespread, mimetic vengeance in ancient society) precedes modern judiciary systems (as limited, formalized exercises of vengeance), though both share the same essential function: namely, to prevent communal violence.[8] By contrast, Keller's novella offers a portrait of sacrifice's autonomous subsistence *within* the bounds of nineteenth-century Swiss bourgeois society—that is, within a quintessential embodiment of lawfulness. By the end of the story, we will have seen a paradigm of sacrifice emerge that can be found in all of the works under examination in this book and that challenges many conceptions of sacrifice familiar to us from twentieth-century theorists: in German Realism, sacrifice is not something that simply prefigures, symbolizes, or subverts law, but is instead a vessel of human desires that have lawfulness itself as their very object.

---

6. Agamben, *Homo Sacer: Sovereign Power and Bare Life*, trans. Daniel Heller-Roazen (Stanford, CA: Stanford University Press, 1998), 1–2.

7. Similar interweavings of sacrificiality and sociality within the setting of nonurban bourgeois community can be found not only elsewhere in the *Seldwyla* cycle (one thinks especially of *Dietegen*) but also in separate projects, such as *Der grüne Heinrich*. For instance, Joachim Pfeiffer reads Anna's death in that novel along Girardian lines as a latent instance of the mythic *pharmakos* paradigm. Pfeiffer, *Tod und Erzählen: Wege der literarischen Moderne um 1900* (Tübingen: Max Niemeyer, 1997), 56–62.

8. René Girard, *Violence and the Sacred*, trans. Patrick Gregory (Baltimore: Johns Hopkins University Press, 1977), 18–22, 297–299.

I.

The Empty Field

Much like Stifter's stories, the setting in which Keller's tale begins is a serene landscape of gentle order and proportion. The breadth of the land that the narrative eye gradually descends upon extends between the river and the horizon, immediately suggesting water and soil as the spatial and thematic poles of the story that is to follow. Little seems to be hidden from view as the description homes in on three parallel fields, the middle one of which "appeared to have lain fallow for many years, for it was full of stones and tall weeds, and a myriad of creatures winged their untroubled way across its rustling grasses" (3). The wildness of this middle space belies the cultivated symmetry of the outer two fields, which are being languidly plowed by two farmers who seem to be both visual and rhythmic mirrors of each another:[9] "Thus the two men worked peacefully on, affording a pleasant aspect in the stillness of the golden autumn landscape as they passed each other silently at the top of the slope, drew further and further apart again and finally vanished behind the ridge like two setting stars only to appear again a short while later" (4–5). What this introductory sequence establishes before all else is a relationship between the tranquility of agrarian order and a visual access to that order as it operates. This association is at its clearest when the farmers' gradual and symmetrical progress through the parallel fields is compared with the cosmic movement of celestial bodies ("like two setting stars"), whose regular disappearance and reappearance bespeak rhythmic equilibrium. (Keller's use of this particular metaphor to describe the synchronized course of the plows is lyrical in multiple senses; after all, as Seamus Heaney notes, a *versus*, from which "verse" derives, was the Latin word both for a poetic line as well as

---

9. Compare Alexander Honold, "Vermittlung und Verwilderung: Gottfried Kellers 'Romeo und Julia auf dem Dorfe,'" *DVjs* 78, no. 3 (2004): 463; and Hans Dietrich Irmscher, "Konfiguration und Spiegelung in Gottfried Kellers Erzählungen," *Euphorion* 65 (1971): 319–333.

for "the turn that a ploughman made at the head of the field as he finished one furrow and faced back into another.")[10]

The two fathers pause their work with the arrival of their young children (a boy, Sali, and a girl, Vrenchen), leaving their plows in the half-finished furrows and greeting each other as they settle down to their midday meal. They begin to discuss the legal status of the abandoned field lying between their respective properties, and it is only at this point that we learn their names: Manz (the father of Sali) and Marti (the father of Vrenchen). Manz remarks: "Still, it is a pity to see good ground left in this state. For almost twenty years nobody has troubled about it" (7). This brings both of them to reflect on the fact that none of their neighbors possess a legal claim to the land, and that the whereabouts of the rightful inheritors— "the children of that wastrel, the Trumpeter"—are unknown. Marti continues this line of thought: "Whenever I look at the Black Fiddler, who spends half his time with gypsies [*Heimatlosen*] and the other half playing for village dances, I could almost swear that he is one of the Trumpeter's grandchildren. Of course, he does not know that he owns the field, but what would he do with it?" (7/ *RuJ* 78). Here Marti hints at the legal ambiguity of physiognomy, for the Black Fiddler—a spectral outsider of the community whose skin has been darkened by his trades of tinkering, burning coal, and boiling pitch—visually resembles the last known owner of the land. This implicit suggestion of unwritten rights (*Recht*) immediately provokes Manz to counter with a reference to the bureaucracy of written documentation: "'And it might have unpleasant consequences,' rejoined Manz. 'We've already got enough on hand to dispute this wretched Fiddler's right of residence [*Heimatrecht*] in our community.... How in Heaven's name are we expected to know that he is the Trumpeter's grandson? Even if his swarthy face does remind me of the Trumpeter, I tell myself that no man is infallible, and the smallest scrap of paper, a mere fragment of a birth certificate, would satisfy my conscience better than a dozen wicked

---

10. Seamus Heaney, "The Makings of a Music: Reflections on Wordsworth and Yeats," in *Preoccupations: Selected Prose, 1968–1978* (New York: Farrar, Straus and Giroux, 1980), 65.

faces!'" (8/*RuJ* 78, translation modified). Manz insistently casts doubt on the validity of the Fiddler's appearance with respect to his possible claim to the field, aligning this visual mode of identification first and foremost with the human tendency for misrecognition. Faces, as well as the eyes that regard them, are more prone to error than to accuracy, he suggests. Alternatively, a physical document such as a baptism or birth certificate would dispel all ambiguity regarding the Fiddler's lineage, and thus secure (or, alternatively, controvert) his hereditary claim to the land.

However, because such documentation does not exist, ownership cannot be legally proven or disproven. As a result, the very appearance of a human body becomes capable of replacing law's usual objective manifestation (that is, text).[11] While it may not be possible to prove or disprove the Fiddler's *legal* claim to the field because he does not possess the necessary documents to do so, his physical features nonetheless perform a textlike role in insinuating the possibility of his *rightful* claim to it by virtue of a filial relationship. The roots of this visual and somatic state of exception spring from the space between law (*Gesetz*; Lat. *lex*) and right (*Recht*; Lat. *ius*), and it is within this space that Manz and Marti will eventually carry out their gradual infraction of land theft.

Before moving forward, it is worth identifying two legal concepts—one ancient and one specific to nineteenth-century Switzerland—invoked by this brief scene. First, the question of possession that the empty field brings into the foreground is also one that Roman jurists devoted thought to. The precept of *nullius res occupanti cedit* held that when a potentially claimable object or terrain is unowned or unoccupied—that is, when it is literally "nobody's thing" (*res*

---

11. According to Cornelia Vismann, the relation between visuality and textuality is integral to the origins of law. While many legal histories focus on the spoken and written word (for instance, the provenance of Roman *lex* as a textual documentation and transmission of the *ius* that originally was proclaimed vocally), Vismann underscores the role of spectatorship—and theatricality in particular—in the development of juristic forms. As Aeschylus's *Eumenides* demonstrates, the filiation between law and tragedy centers every bit as much upon what is *seen* as upon what is heard and read. Vismann, *Medien der Rechtsprechung* (Frankfurt am Main: Fischer, 2011), esp. 29–37, 72–96. On the relationship between *lex* and *ius*, see Peter Stein, *Roman Law in European History* (Cambridge: Cambridge University Press, 1999), 4ff.

nullius)—it properly belongs to whomever seizes it first.[12] This directly concerns the question of whether the Black Fiddler is in fact an extant claimant to the land given his possible relation to the only established owner; in other words, the question of whether or not the field is a true *res nullius*.[13]

These ancient Roman parameters for land acquisition lead us to a second legal issue broached by the scene that is contemporaneous with Keller himself. Manz refers to an ongoing process in the village of contesting the Fiddler's right of residence (*Heimatrecht*), which if successfully carried through would result in the official designation of him as homeless (*Heimatlos*) and thereby ineligible to own or inherit property.[14] As Theodor Mügge described in an 1847 account, nineteenth-century Swiss communal assemblies (*Gemeindeversammlungen*) had the authority either to include or exclude persons from the community's "citizen book" (*Bürgerbuch*), which determined whether or not they were allowed to enjoy rights of residence.[15] It is therefore important to note the present tense of Manz's remark, which implies that the Fiddler has not yet been formally stripped of

---

12. Gaius's *Institutes* (161 CE) cite this precept as follows: "But it is not only by delivery that we acquire things as a matter of natural reason; this applies also to things which we get by first taking and which become ours because previously they belonged to no one" (§66). Gaius, *Institutes*, trans. W. M. Gordon and O. F. Robinson (Ithaca, NY: Cornell University Press, 1988), 152–153, 144–145.

13. With the establishment of the autonomous *Eidgenossenschaft* in the late Middle Ages, each Swiss canton had its own independently functioning law codes, a scenario that lasted until the first centralized constitution was implemented in 1848. With respect specifically to laws of land use and ownership (*Grundeigentum*), western Switzerland and Bern adopted Roman *usucapio* guidelines, but eastern and central Switzerland did not. See Louis Carlen, *Rechtsgeschichte der Schweiz: Eine Einführung* (Bern: Francke, 1978), 9–30, 50.

14. Regula Argast, *Staatsbürgerschaft und Nation: Ausschliessung und Integration in der Schweiz, 1848–1933* (Göttingen: Vandenhoeck und Ruprecht, 2007), 118; Thomas Meier and Rolf Wolfensberger, *"Eine Heimat und doch keine": Heimatlose und Nicht-Sesshafte in der Schweiz (16.–19. Jahrhundert)* (Zurich: Chronos, 1998), 68–82.

15. Theodor Mügge, *Die Schweiz und ihre Zustände: Reiseerinnerungen*, vol. 1 (Hannover: C. F. Kius, 1847), 270–273. Quoted and cited by Jürgen Hein, *"Romeo und Julia auf dem Dorfe": Erläuterungen und Dokumente* (Stuttgart: Reclam, 1971), 77–78. Compare Edgar Hein, *Gottfried Keller: "Romeo und Julia auf dem Dorfe"—Interpretation* (Munich: Oldenbourg, 1988), 30–31.

his citizenship rights ("we already have enough on hand [*Wir haben so genug zu tun*] to dispute this wretched Fiddler's right of residence in our community"). This grammatical detail, along with the absence of any written confirmation of the Fiddler's birth or baptism, make the question of visual recognition all the more salient. After all, regardless of whether or not there is any ambiguity surrounding the Fiddler's legal claim to the land at the time that this conversation between Manz and Marti takes place, his physiognomy has nonetheless established itself in both men's minds as the primary scale by which to determine both the weight and the classification of transgression that would result from seizing the field.[16] As a consequence, what seems to weigh upon them most is an unspoken but shared sense that acknowledging the Fiddler's visual resemblance of the "that wastrel, the Trumpeter" (that is, *Erkennung*) might somehow lay the groundwork for a symbolic recognition (that is, *Anerkennung*) of his rightful inheritance of the field apart from the bureaucratic institution of pro forma identification.

Years later the Fiddler himself will address this very opposition between legal documentation and the unwritten laws of recognition and conscience. Speaking to Sali and Vrenchen, who have encountered him by chance in the same middle field while out walking

---

16. Edgar Hein, by contrast, opines that the legal matter has already been settled in the village by the time that this scene takes place. This would mean that the Fiddler is not registered in the *Bürgerbuch*, and therefore legally not a member of the community. In this case, Manz and Marti, by seizing the field, would be transgressing, not against the formal *Gemeinderecht*, but instead against a universal (but uncodified) moral precept. This localized authority of village councils was curtailed by the Swiss *Heimatlosengesetz* of 1850 (three years after Theodor Mügge's account), Article 1 of which decreed that being deprived of one's communal *Gemeinderecht* did not automatically qualify one as legally homeless (and thereby ineligible to inherit or own property), as this was only the case if cantonal citizenship had been officially revoked: "According to this regulation, those who possess Cantonal rights of citizenship [*Kantonsbürgerrecht*] but not communal ones [*Gemeindsbürgerrecht*] are not homeless; however, these persons are not to be confused with those who do not possess Cantonal rights of citizenship and are instead granted mere 'toleration' [*Duldung*] or affiliation." Schweizerischer Bundesrat, "Bericht des Bundesrathes an die Bundesversammlung über das Gesetz, betreffend die Heimathlosigkeit, vom 30. September 1850," *Schweizerisches Bundesblatt*, year II, vol. 3, no. 46 (1850): 125–126; E. Hein, *Gottfried Keller*, 30–31.

together, the Fiddler confirms that he was denied inheritance of the land because he possessed neither a baptismal certificate nor written proof of his familial origin. "Look at me!" he exclaims, "your fathers know me well, and all the villagers recognize me as soon as they see my nose. . . . I begged your fathers to confirm my claim, for their conscience must have told them I was the true heir" (48). The Fiddler's reference to his own facial features parallels the issue of the middle field itself, for both are distinct, visible, empirical objects that nevertheless pertain to an opaque zone of ambiguity within the law.

This latter point becomes especially important when we recall that Keller's text began by suggesting a close relationship between order and visibility; that is, with the unimpeded ability of the gaze to perceive and interpret objects both far away and nearby. Interestingly, while a general sense of equilibrium was conveyed by this open field of vision, allusions in the text to actual ordinances regarding ownership and citizenship have revealed that the process of visual recognition in fact seems to pose a challenge to the authority of written law. This opposition between formal recognition "in the eyes of the law" by way of civic documentation, and extrajudicial recognition solely by means of the naked eye, will prove highly important in the remainder of the tale.

The Burial

Given that Keller's text has established such a relation between lawfulness and visibility, one can reasonably expect that it will portray transgression against the law in similar terms of vision and sight. This is borne out by the scene that follows, in which Sali and Vrenchen ceremonially dress, mutilate, and then bury a doll so that it is hidden from view. In looking more closely at what exactly this rite depicts and consists in, three issues will be of foremost importance: First, the scene establishes imitation as a key element of transgression. Second, the ritual activity consists both in an imitation that is transgressive and in this transgression's concealment, which occurs as part of the sacrifice of a living creature (an entombed fly). Lastly, the setting for the burial—the middle field—at this point in the story has no fixed legal status; it lies at the center of the community and its laws and, simultaneously, outside of them. The sacrificial burial's setting both within and beyond the law—literally on the "land," the soil itself—provides the context for understanding the drowning at the end of Keller's novella contrastively as an act of sacrifice that occurs, not in order to hide a transgression, but instead out of a desire *for* lawfulness that has itself become transgressive.

After Manz and Marti resume their work, the two children wander into the empty field together. After exploring the wild and overgrown space, they decide to sit down near a thistle bush, and Vrenchen begins to dress her doll using the nearby vegetation at her disposal, fashioning a miniature dress out of weeds and a bonnet from a red poppy flower: "Now the little person looked like a sorceress, and even more so when it was given a necklace and little girdle of red berries. Setting it on top of the bush, they both regarded it for a while. Then the boy, tired of looking at it, knocked it down with a stone and disarranged its clothes" (9/*RuJ* 79, translation modified). This brief passage introduces two parallel levels of imitation. On one level, Vrenchen simulates the parental act of dressing a small child, and on another level the doll takes on the appearance of a "little person." Furthermore, the doll also assumes a subtle but laden function as the object of a shared gaze, placed carefully in the thistle like a makeshift idol. This sequence of imitation and observation quickly becomes a leitmotif, for once Sali has broken the momentary vigil by hurling a stone at the small figure, Vrenchen immediately begins to undress it so that she can adorn it once again (9/*RuJ* 79). Sali's own impulse for repetition intercedes, however, as he quickly snatches the doll away, flinging it about as Vrenchen vainly attempts to retrieve it. He then tears at the little woven body with his fingernails. Having finally had his fill, he tosses the doll to the ground, and Vrenchen reverts once again to an emulation of parenthood, throwing herself over the limp form and weeping as she cradles it in the folds of her apron.

At this point the first dramatic turn (or "verse") occurs in the empty field: guilt slowly seeps into Sali following his rampage, and he stands "repentant and uneasy." As soon as Vrenchen notices this internal shift, she suddenly undergoes a role reversal and begins to attack her former tormenter, beating Sali with the doll. In his response, Sali mimics the doll more than Vrenchen: "She suddenly hit him several times with the doll, whereupon he cried out 'Ouch! Ouch!' and pretended to be hurt. So realistically did he do this, that she was appeased, and proceeded to help him dismember and destroy the doll" (10). In the instant when Sali feigns suffering comparable to what the doll is imagined to have endured, Vrenchen in turn experiences a degree of satisfaction that moves her to become a fellow aggressor in the scene of violence that now repeats itself. Together the children disembowel the doll of its pollard stuffing before setting upon the martyrial "battered body" (*Marterleib*) once again, dismembering it in a fashion akin to the Bacchic rite of *sparagmos*, until only its head remains intact. Then, seeming to act almost from a sense of methodical obligation, they carefully decapitate it.

Then comes the next "turn." Sali spots a fly hovering nearby and, with Vrenchen's assistance, traps it inside the hollow head. The doll's quotidian capacity to imitate life is now transposed into a new, sinister register as the children install it in an elevated post just as Vrenchen had initially done at the beginning of the scene. This time, however, they seem to go about their task in full awareness that they have moved from the innocent realm of playful simulation to that of purposeful *ritual*:

> They held it to their ears and then stood it solemnly [*feierlich*] on a stone.... The modicum of life in the pitiful little image aroused the children's cruel instincts [*menschliche Grausamkeit*], and they resolved to bury it alive. So they dug a hole and, without asking the insect's permission, put the head in it and solemnly erected a cairn of stones at the head of the grave. But then they began to shudder [*da empfanden sie einiges Grauen*] at the thought that they had buried a real living creature, and they moved some distance away from the eerie spot [*unheimlichen Stätte*]. (11/*RuJ* 81)

On a strictly formal level, this final vignette simply echoes the previous sequences of imitation, transgression, and subsequent repetition in the scene. However, this specific iteration also indicates a pivotal "turn" in the psychology of Sali and Vrenchen: when they ceremoniously place the head with its trapped occupant on top of the stone, it suggests that they are consciously invoking their preceding abuses of the doll. The *Grauen* (horror) that suddenly fills them at the sight of the uncannily alive totemic visage is concomitant with a mutual recognition of their transgressive actions. This acknowledgment, instigated by their shared view of the doll, is subsequently projected back from the macabre face in front of them. Having externalized the awareness of their guilt through this visual exchange with the effigy, they promptly put it out of sight in a ceremonial act of burial. More specifically, this act, which occurs outside the periphery of their fathers' vision, is itself obscured from outside view.[17]

A brief word is clearly due on the resonances of the foregoing scene with modern theories of sacrifice, and with Girard's thought in particular. Though the motif of a surrogate victim's destruction at the hands of a collective agent can certainly be found here, I believe that the mimetic character Girard attributes to sacrifice per se allows for a richer understanding of sacrifice as it appears in Keller's text.[18] This is to say that here and later in the story, Sali and Vrenchen enact ceremonies that are essentially *automimetic* insofar as they not only imitate an original transgression but also replicate their very own operativity as imitative, ritualistic acts. Girard claims that sacrifice consists of a reenactment of an original crisis of mimetic vengeance "that was resolved by means of a spontane-

---

[17]. Peter C. Pfeiffer suggests that as the doll gradually ceases to resemble a human being, its mimetic function shifts into a symbolic one, culminating in the substitution of the body itself with the *Denkmal* of stones—"Representation via abstract signs replaces mimetic representation." In this way, the gravesite evinces a certain problematic of the written word, of the semiological "burial" of the thing beneath its *sema*. See Pfeiffer, "'Den Tod aus dem Bereich des Romans fernhalten': Zur ästhetischen Funktion des Todes in der Literatur des bürgerlichen Realismus," *Germanic Review* 70 (1995): 20.

[18]. One of Girard's key antecedents, Freud's *Totem und Tabu* (1913), similarly proposes that collective sacrificial punishment for a transgression often constitutes a *reciprocation* of the transgression itself. Sigmund Freud, *Totem und Tabu: Einige Übereinstimmungen im Seelenleben der Wilden und der Neurotiker*, in *Gesammelte Werke*, vol. 9, ed. Anna Freud, Edward Bibring, and Ernst Kris (Frankfurt am Main: Fischer, 1986), 6–7, 89, 169–170, 182.

ously unanimous victimization."[19] However, on this point the burial scene resists a strictly Girardian analysis, for while Girard asserts an original act of violence to be the implicit referent of any such rite, the focus of Sali's and Vrenchen's activity originates as a simulation of behaviors inherent to lawful social existence, not primeval violence. We must remember that the scene begins with Vrenchen dressing the doll to outwardly resemble a human child, *after* which violence erupts. This is followed by their desire for the doll to simulate biological life, a standard childhood impulse that is then fulfilled by gruesome means when they imprison the living fly inside the lifeless doll's head. In spite of this difference, though, Girard's theory offers a path for understanding how the ritual *intention* of the burial was not the imitation of an original act of violence carried out in order to establish or maintain law, for the ritualized violence and final interment—themselves repetitions of imitations—only occurred after the children's initial imitations of lawful behavior. Let's now trace how this logic of the sacrificial burial repeats itself in the scene that immediately follows.

The Field of Vision

While the children have been digging, their fathers have been plowing. As soon as the doll has been buried, both farmers complete their day's work; suddenly, one of them—the text does not specify which—turns back his plow and cuts a rigid strip of earth from the adjacent balk of the middle field, thereby increasing the area of his own.[20] He continues this unsanctioned course, and the calm order from earlier in the day seems to reassert itself as the breeze begins to lightly tousle the tip of his cap as it had done in the opening passage of the text. Yet this apparent return of rhythmic normalcy in fact accompanies mutual infraction, for the other farmer has also swerved his plow in order to hew his own new furrow from the op-

---

19. Girard, *Violence and the Sacred*, 94.
20. E. Hein, *Gottfried Keller*, 33. The original text refers to the unnamed farmer only as "Der Meister" as he commands his "Knecht" to continue with another "verse" of the plow, thus sounding a Hegelian note in anticipation of the contract scene that soon follows (see below).

posite side of the thicket. The sense of symmetrical infringement in this moment is marked, not in the physical comportment of either farmer, nor in the altered topography of the land, but instead in each man's uncommented—that is to say, concealed—recognition of the other in the midst of the shared deed: "Each saw clearly through what the other was doing, and yet neither of them seemed to see it [*aber keiner schien es zu sehen*]. Passing each other without a word, they went their separate ways like two constellations setting beneath the horizon" (13/*RuJ* 83, translation modified). As in the children's ornamentation and mutilation of the doll, here too the chief characteristic of the fathers' transgression is its foundational reenactment of lawful and orderly behavior—namely, the plowing that was accompanied by neighborly goodwill, moral equilibrium, and an unhindered view of the surrounding *paysage moralisé*.[21] This is indicated by the recurrence of the wind and star topoi that had been used to characterize both men's rhythmic—and nontransgressive—movements across their respective fields earlier in the day.

In many respects the greater portion of Manz and Marti's shared guilt derives not so much from their act of literal "transgression" in allowing their plows to cross beyond previously accepted boundaries in the soil, nor even from their intuition about the Black Fiddler's undocumented claim to the land, but more primarily from the mutual recognition of their complicity that remains mutually buried.

---

21. This term was coined by Erwin Panofsky while describing the artistic technique of figurally representing a moral quandary by means of "the device, common in late-mediaeval and Renaissance painting, of dividing the landscape background into two halves of symbolically contrasting character," as when "the antithesis between Virtue and Pleasure is symbolized by the contrast between an easy road winding through beautiful country and a steep, stony path leading up to a forbidding rock." Equally resonant with Keller's tale, however, is the opening stanza of an untitled 1933 poem by W. H. Auden that was re-published in 1945 as "Paysage Moralisé": "Hearing of harvests rotting in the valleys, / Seeing at end of street the barren mountains, / Round corners coming suddenly on water, / . . . / We honour founders of these starving cities / Whose honour is the image of our sorrow" (lines 1–6). See Erwin Panofsky, "The Early History of Man in Two Cycles of Paintings by Piero di Cosimo," in *Studies in Iconology: Humanistic Themes in the Art of the Renaissance* (New York: Routledge, 2018; orig. Oxford University Press, 1939), 64; Patricia Emison, "The *Paysage Moralisé*," *Artibus et Historiae* 16, no. 31 (1995): 125–137.

This shared affront that is "seen yet not seen" continues unabated for the next several harvests, "neither man even seemed to see what wrong he was doing [ohne daß ein Menschenauge den Frevel zu sehen schien]" (13/RuJ 83, translation modified). Years later, the incrementally shrunken middle field is at last due to be sold by public auction, and Manz ultimately outbids Marti and is awarded ownership of the land.

Only after this intercession of civic legality do both men openly address the issue of ownership and transgression with each other, though neither makes direct reference to their original misdeed. Instead, after the onlookers have dispersed, Manz accuses Marti of having surreptitiously cut a small triangular section out of the field that now legally belongs to him. Marti denies the claim, pointing out that the land is in exactly the same state as it had been in before the auction, and furthermore that they had inspected it together beforehand. Manz then exclaims, "As it now belongs to me, you will realize that I cannot have a crooked edge like that in it, so you can hardly object if I straighten it again . . . a thing has to be properly settled [alles muß zuletzt eine ordentliche grade Art haben]. Right from the beginning these two fields have been dead straight [grade]. What strange quirk is it that makes you want to introduce such an ugly shape? What sort of reputation would we get if we left it crooked? The odd corner simply has to go!" (16). What is interesting about this exchange is the way in which it openly addresses the issue of infringed property rights while simultaneously alluding to the threat posed by the communal gaze. Both topics invoke the original transgression, but only in veiled terms, for although Manz speaks freely of offended boundary lines, it is not in reference to his and Marti's shared act from years before. Instead, he forcefully raises the question of the soil's proper appearance, while the issue of whether or not the field may have rightfully belonged to the Black Fiddler to begin with remains conspicuously unvoiced.

In essence, then, the recognition of a transgression against conscience that had taken place in the visual exchange between both men continues to hover in suspension (one might say in "Aufhebung") through the successive seasons. Manz's pointed concern with the land's visual distribution following the auction—rather than with the question of how it originally came to possess its configuration in the time leading up to the auction—is a figurative burial. Until this official intervention of communal law in the fate of the middle field, Manz and Marti simply continue "not to see" what they had first recognized in each other on that September evening. Once the land has attained the status of property by virtue of the auction and sale, however, they effectively make this recognition more lastingly "unseen" by hiding it beneath the field in its new conceptual form. In other words, by openly broaching a *new* transgression against the *legally* designated boundaries of the soil, they retroactively obscure and replace the original one against its unwritten, *rightful* boundaries.

This process of "burying" an ethical transgression beneath legal formality is grounded in the concept of the contract, whereby something that is *possessed* as material is transformed into something that is *owned* as property. Here, Hegel's account of the emergence of property in human society proves to be a useful point of reference. In his *Philosophie des Rechts* (*Philosophy of Right*) of 1820, Hegel ascribes particular importance to the issue of ownership, arguing that an individual's wish to possess an object in the world marks the first phase of free will's formation (§44). For Hegel, the primal gesture of seizing a desired thing is also a preliminary stage in the development of law, for the object can become truly *owned* only when the conceptual form of property is projected onto it (§§55–56). At the core of this transition from possession to ownership by way of the contract we find a familiar leitmotif from throughout Hegel's writings: "Contract presupposes that the contracting parties *recognize* [*anerkennen*] each other as persons and owners of property; and since it is a relationship of objective spirit, the moment of recognition [*Anerkennung*] is already contained and presupposed within it" (§71).[22] The teleological significance of the contract rests in its presupposition of mutual recognition between subject and other, not

---

22. G. W. F Hegel, *Elements of the Philosophy of Right*, trans. H. B. Nisbet (Cambridge: Cambridge University Press, 1991), 103. / Hegel, *Grundlinien der Philosophie des Rechts*, in *Werke*, vol. 7, ed. Eva Moldenhauer and Karl Markus Michel (Frankfurt am Main: Suhrkamp, 1979), 152 (emphasis in the original).

only as legal actors ("owners of property"), but as "persons." The instant of law's emergence into human relations in the form of the contract thus mirrors the original instant of human relation per se, insofar as both pivot upon reciprocal recognition.[23]

This Hegelian schema dovetails nicely with what we have observed in the two preceding scenes: the children's burial involves the literal removal of a recognized transgression from view, whereas their fathers' "burial" consists in their "seeing yet not seeing" a shared transgression. Both burials incite a series of events that ultimately culminate at the end of the story in the protagonists' drowning. In these early scenes of the novella, the motif of burial establishes being "seen" by law as something to be avoided; in the second half of the novella, by contrast, what Sali and Vrenchen desire is precisely *to be "seen"* by law. Ironically, this very desire will lead to their transgressing against the law by imitating it.

Now that we have observed how the "ritual logic" of the children's burial rite recurs in the transgression committed by their fathers, it becomes possible to see how and why there is also a "sacrificial logic" of this burial rite that is decisive for what takes place in the second half of the narrative. In order to see this clearly, however, we must first ask what makes the burial sacrificial—what is sacrificed, in what way is it sacrificed, and for what purpose? On a basic level, the burial is sacrificial in what Jean-Luc Marion refers to as the "common sense" insofar as its ritual work consists first and foremost of removing an object from the normal domain of human experience and use.[24] That is to say, it is a *sacrificium* that has been distilled down to its etymological root of "*sacrum facere*," of mak-

---

23. This reciprocal acknowledgment is fundamental not only to the relationship between freedom and law but also to Hegel's concept of ethos and ethics more generally. See Axel Honneth, *Der Kampf um Anerkennung: Zur moralischen Grammatik sozialer Konflikte* (Frankfurt am Main: Suhrkamp, 1994), 174–211; William E. Conklin, *Hegel's Laws: The Legitimacy of a Modern Legal Order* (Stanford, CA: Stanford University Press, 2008), 162–187.

24. Jean-Luc Marion, "Sketch of a Phenomenological Concept of Sacrifice," in *The Reason of the Gift*, trans. Stephen E. Lewis (Charlottesville: University of Virginia Press, 2011), 70–72. Compare Georges Bataille, *The Accursed Share: An Essay on General Economy*, vol. 1, trans. Robert Hurley (New York: Zone Books, 1993), 55–61.

ing something *sacred* solely by making it no longer "profane"—making it no longer *usual* by rendering it no longer *usable*.²⁵

There is more to it than this, though. The burial ritual is first and foremost a ritualization of simulative behavior, which in that scene involved enactments of everyday reality (such as dressing and fearing for a child), and also of decidedly irregular acts of violence (such as dismemberment and living interment). Imitation here underlies both innocent and transgressive activities, but most crucial is the temporal mechanism that underlies imitation itself: repetition. The most immediate objective of the burial is to hide the product of the children's imitative behavior, but the very act of burying in fact reinstantiates the transgression that the ritual seeks to hide in the first place. In other words, that which is intended to be banished from view and immured in the past is in fact made newly visible and present by way of its very concealment; the burial in essence rematerializes what is being buried in that very same instant. In this respect the children's rite inadvertently assumes one of the most ancient symbolic functions of sacrificial ceremony: it ensures a future repetition of its own performance as well as the conditions of this performance.²⁶

However, there is a third way in which the burial constitutes an act of sacrifice rather than merely a ritualistic concealment of transgressive behavior: a life is given (or rather, taken) for the sake of fantasy. That is to say, the fly is killed in the service of simulating life within the doll and then hiding this grotesque simulation from sight. Concomitantly, the act of imitation has become an act of transgression. *This* is what will be at the core of the drowning as well, which will also consist in an offering up of life for the sake of fantasy, but

---

25. The association of utility (from the Latin *usus*) with the profane has deep roots in the Western tradition. In a Christian (and specifically Augustinian) context, for instance, the category of *usus* is restricted to temporal existence and transitory objects. In a characteristically Neoplatonist gesture, Augustine opposes this earthly mode of use to the spiritual mode of "enjoyment" (*fruitio*), which he reserves for that which is both "eternal" and "true"—namely, the divine, and the Trinity in particular. Augustine, *On Christian Doctrine*, trans. J. F. Shaw, in *A Select Library of Nicene and Post-Nicene Fathers of the Christian Church*, vol. 2, ed. Philip Schaff (New York: Scribner, 1907), 523–524 (I.3–5).

26. Henri Hubert and Marcel Mauss, *Sacrifice: Its Nature and Function*, trans. W. D. Halls (Chicago: University of Chicago Press, 1981), 89.

in a way that is very distinct from the burial: while the burial sacrifices a life in Marion's "common sense" of destroying it, of making it *"sacer"* simply by removing it from the quotidian realm in order to prevent its transgressive mimesis from being discovered, the drowning sacrifices life in exchange for remaining simultaneously *within* the realm of fantasy *and* in the sight of law. Whereas the protagonists' first sacrifice is a burial that removes an illicit object from view, their second sacrifice will offer up their own lives and future in exchange for the momentary fantasy of being what they wish to be seen as. The medium of their final sacrifice will therefore be not concealment in the earth but submergence in the water that borders the community. Within a private *Augenblick*, the two lovers briefly disappear from public view, only to reemerge into it in the end.

II.

The River

Appropriately, in the second half of the narrative Sali and Vrenchen develop an awareness of their vulnerable exposure to the gaze of their community. This new awareness is most marked in the scene of their reunion on the public riverbank after years of separation during Manz and Marti's estrangement. Given that the text's dialectic of lawfulness and sacrificiality will develop in correspondence with visual recognition between the private and communal spheres, it is worth considering the sequence in some detail.

As the feud between the two families intensifies, Manz and Marti both pour all of their money into lawsuits and counterclaims over the small corner of soil, and Sali and Vrenchen make efforts to avoid seeing one another. This situation endures for several years but is brought to an abrupt end when both fathers and their children unexpectedly meet at the river, for the vitriol of their legal entrenchment (along with routine gambling) has bled Manz and Marti dry financially, and they must resort to fishing in order to provide for their families. The banks of the river are populated with others who have also found themselves compelled to make their living outside of the community. The scene is rich with foreshadowings of Sali's and Vrenchen's climactic drowning in the very same river that will in part respond to this state of socioeconomic exigency brought about by their fathers' monetary "runoff" (*Geldabfluß*). The hapless figures scattered along the shore drape feet, limbs, and angling rods into the water; one man stands on a stone in the shallows, "but although standing in the water, he had such dirty feet that it looked as if he still had his boots on," an image that suggests nature's inability to wash completely clean every stain of capitalistic plight (33).[27]

In fact, the river as a topos can even be said to embody an ancient exception to laws regarding personal possessions and property, for the Roman legal tradition established that no flowing bodies of water (*aqua profluens*) could ever be subject to ownership.[28] The river in *A Village Romeo and Juliet* exemplifies this legal status of *flumen publicum*, reappearing throughout the remainder of the narrative as a counterpoint to various forms of societal privation: both

---

27. Diana Schilling observes that in Keller's novella, the topos of the river loses the classic metaphorical value that is still to be found in contemporary *Dorfgeschichten* of the nineteenth century: "Those who return to the river are ones for whom life no longer has any movement." This differs substantially from more symbolist readings such as Jürgen Rothenberg's, according to which the flowing river (whether in this particular story or as a broader leitmotif in Keller's prose) represents the linear openness of diachrony and Heraclitian "Wechseldauer." Schilling, *Kellers Prosa* (Frankfurt am Main: Peter Lang, 1998), 119; Rothenberg, *Gottfried Keller: Symbolgehalt und Realitätserfassung seines Erzählens* (Heidelberg: Universitätsverlag Winter, 1976), 62, 99.

28. This is most explicitly codified by Justinian's *Institutes* (II.1): "Thus by natural law these things are common for all: air, flowing water, the sea and its shores" (§1); "Rivers and ports are also public for all: thus it is also a common right to fish in ports and in rivers" (§2) (*Et quidem naturali iure communia sunt omnium haec: aer et aqua profluens et mare et per hoc litora maris . . . Flumina autem omnia et portus publica sunt: ideoque ius piscandi omnibus commune est in portubus fluminibusque*). Justinian, *Institutes*, in *Corpus Iuris Civilis*, vol. 1, ed. Paul Krueger (Hildesheim: Weidmann, 1993), 10 (translation mine). Friedrich Carl von Savigny would carry this ancient idea into German law at the beginning of the nineteenth century with the following image: "Thus the boatman owns his ship but not the water he sails upon, even though he makes use of both for his purposes." Savigny, *Das Recht des Besitzes: Eine Civilistische Abhandlung* (Gießen: Heyer, 1803), 2. Compare Hans W. Baade, "Springs, Creeks and Groundwater in Nineteenth-Century German Roman-Law Jurisprudence with a Twentieth-Century Postscript," in *Comparative and Private International Law*, ed. David S. Clark (Berlin: Duncker und Humblot, 1990), 66.

the derelict townsfolk as well as Sali and Vrenchen, whose ideal future together in the community is eventually occluded, are drawn to the unclaimable river.[29]

Against this backdrop the two embittered farmers encounter one another on opposite banks. As Manz and Marti begin to shout slurs and accusations, Sali attempts to glimpse Vrenchen, who, consistent with her habit of the previous few years, avoids his gaze and stares at the ground. Manz and Marti suddenly run to a narrow bridge spanning the water, colliding in the middle with a cascade of fists and curses. As the two children rush toward the mêlée, Vrenchen finally casts a glance at Sali, whose attention is focused on freeing his father from Marti's grip. This network of missed gazes between the protagonists finally coheres within a dramatic instant of visual exchange: "At that moment [*Augenblicke*] a ray of sunlight glinted through a gap in the clouds, and Sali saw before him the face that he had known so well but which had since taken on a fresh beauty. [In this moment] Vrenchen also saw his astonishment, and gave him a fleeting smile through her tears" (38/*RuJ* 103, translation modified). This mutual recognition by the water is then followed by a prefiguration of Sali's and Vrenchen's death, for as Manz and Marti at last cease their struggle and turn away from each other, their children "[barely breathed] and were silent [as death], but as the two groups parted, [the children] quickly clasped each other's hands, cold and wet from the water and the fish, [unseen by] their parents" (38/*RuJ* 104, translation modified).

In this moment, the recurring motif of a shared recognition is set against the gaze of others (the fathers, in this case) that can either witness or overlook the meaning produced in the private exchange. The setting and context of this scene provide an interesting variation on the classical trope of the *locus amoenus*, for the enclosure of the riverbed in which Sali and Vrenchen share a fleeting glance,

---

29. One might juxtapose the *flumen publicum*, as something that cannot be owned, with the middle field in the beginning of the novella as a *res nullius*, as something that *could* be owned but simply isn't. Critics have pointed out that the field and river mirror one another as settings, but the fact that they also correspond with these opposing categories of law shows them to serve as poles of the narrative in more than just a topographical sense.

"unseen by their parents," is nevertheless at the center of public attention and concern. Keller's depiction of this pastoral *Augenblick*, a small vestige of the antique idyll planted in the somber soil of a contemporary landscape, at once brings to mind the seventh Canto of Goethe's *Hermann und Dorothea* (1798), in which the eponymous protagonists meet at a well that lies outside the edge of the community. At one point they both lean over a spring "and they saw reflected their image in the heaven's blue," and then, as they begin to set off toward town, "both looked back once more / into the well, and sweet longing seized them."[30]

Sadly, the chain of events that stretches out from Sali and Vrenchen's auspicious *Augenblick* does not mirror that of Goethe's poem. In the remainder of Keller's tale there are a number of confrontations between the gazes of the private and public spheres prefigured by the river scene, but one of these in particular contains the greatest significance for the relation between law, transgression, and sacrifice. Most importantly, it provides the impetus for the culminative drowning scene.

The Sunday Walk

In the weeks that follow, Sali and Vrenchen's love and misfortune grow in equal measure. After visiting each other secretly the day after their fathers' altercation at the river, the two are discovered by Marti, who attacks his daughter in a rage and whom Sali in turn strikes on the head with a stone.[31] The injury turns out to have permanently affected Marti's cognitive capacities, and he is eventually institutionalized. For Sali and Vrenchen, all possibility of a respectable marriage in their community at once seems irretrievably lost: "We could never have the peace of mind to build a

---

30. Johann Wolfgang Goethe, *Hermann und Dorothea*, in *Werke: Hamburger Ausgabe in 14 Bänden*, vol. 2, *Gedichte und Epen II*, ed. Erich Trunz (Munich: C. H. Beck, 1982), 492, 494 (VII, lines 41, 106–107).

31. For an analysis of domestic violence within the context of German Realism (including this scene from Keller's novella), see Barbara N. Nagel, *Ambiguous Aggression in German Realism and Beyond: Flirtation, Passive Aggression, Domestic Violence* (New York: Bloomsbury, 2019), 99–101.

life on this foundation," Vrenchen laments (61). They resign themselves to the necessity of leaving the village in order to find work and livelihoods apart from each other. In the face of this unhappy reality, they decide to spend one last day together in which they can live out their fantasy of happiness and repletion as a young, newlywed couple. This fantasy begins within—and is constituted by—their appearance to the collective gaze of society. Sali sells his pocket watch in order to buy new shoes for Vrenchen, who wishes to dance with him at the parish fair the next day, and the following morning both dress in their Sunday best (or their closest possible approximations thereof).

This visual simulation of an ideal reality promptly crosses over into active deception, for a neighbor drops by and, catching sight of the two, expresses surprise and curiosity over their changed appearance. Without hesitating, Vrenchen, "in a friendly, almost condescending tone," says that Sali is her fiancé, and furthermore that the bitter rift between the two families has ebbed (71). Before the neighbor can respond to this dramatic statement, Vrenchen's prevarication picks up momentum and she goes on to assert that Sali has won the lottery, allowing them to purchase a home and plan a wedding. The neighbor three separate times questions the truth of this story before finally accepting it. But with this initial fabrication, Sali and Vrenchen effectively commit to transforming their private fantasy of being seen into an actual public charade. This transition into the full view of the community is initiated by the neighbor, who, moved by Vrenchen's tale of unexpected fortune, lists and extols the paradigmatically bourgeois virtues she (now) seems to evince, exclaiming: "Happiness will surely come your way, or there is no justice in the world! You are beautiful and intelligent, and gifted in all manner of ways. I know no finer or nobler person anywhere, and the man that wins you will feel he is living in paradise" (73).

Paradise on earth indeed seems to be what Sali and Vrenchen are bound for as they set out into the resplendent September morning, making their way across bucolic meadows toward the neighboring village where they can be seen together without being recognized, and instead be taken simply for "a couple who were made for each other [*die sich von Rechts wegen angehören*]" (76/*RuJ* 135). As I will discuss in greater detail shortly, this invocation in the original German to *Recht* (right)—as opposed, crucially, to *Gesetz* (law)—not only limns the object of their shared desire, but also constitutes the ethical framework that will designate their behavior as transgressive. After all, it is the vision of being "made for each other" not only *by right* (*von Rechts wegen*) but also by way of a *lawful* status of marriage, which the two fervently wish for and in turn imitate for each other and for strangers, and yet their public simulation sacrifices the very quality of lawfulness intrinsic to the condition they desired. This is not yet at hand, however, and as they arrive at the next village and are seated at an inn, their spirits are high, because "the landlord's wife obviously considered them to be honest [*rechtliche*] young folk who deserved to be treated with respect" (77/*RuJ* 136).

After a meal that leaves them content from hearty food as well as from the fond attention the innkeepers bestow on them, Sali ceremoniously signals that the time has come to leave, "and although their poverty could not be disguised, they had displayed a perfect demeanor, and the host bade them a friendly farewell. Courteously the young couple took their leave and walked out into the sunshine" (77–78). Even after they have left the town and wander alone, they maintain this respectable comportment and "thus they passed for a pleasant, respectable young couple out for a walk" (80). As they enter another inn, their mimicry once again meets with a believing audience as the hostess greets them: "Are you not a young couple on your way to the town to get married? . . . You are an attractive and honest-looking pair, so you need not be ashamed. A decent [*ordentliche*] couple can make a success of life if they start young, and work hard, and are faithful to each other. . . . I was so pleased to see such a happy couple" (81/*RuJ* 139). Like in the previous tavern, Sali and Vrenchen's performance is substantiated by the recognition and praise of the impression it seeks to effect in others. They therefore continue to play their parts, and the spectators' validation of the spectacle only redoubles their conviction. They move on to the market square, where, when the other is not looking, they both secretly procure rings to give the other when the time finally comes to part.

Here, however, their simulation is brought to an abrupt end. As they stand absorbed in their gifts and in each other, passers-by begin to take notice and, as a number of them hail from Sali and Vrenchen's home village, they quickly recognize the two. Whispers slowly course through the growing group of onlookers, and when Sali and Vrenchen finally look up and see the ring of observers watching them, "they saw nothing but staring faces on all sides" (88, translation modified).

Vrenchen is suddenly overcome with anxiety at the many staring faces and becomes feverish and pale, so Sali quickly leads her away. This is pointedly due to the preceding instant of reciprocal recognition between them and the community, for at this moment the nature of Sali and Vrenchen's naive imitation was transformed from make-believe into disgrace. Though the two have freely indulged in their own illusion throughout the day, they nevertheless have not reached the point of mistaking it for reality in the same way that their successive audiences have. It is not until they see themselves being seen *in flagrante imitatione* that their charade retroactively assumes a transgressive quality. This transition seems to be simultaneous with their self-recognition within the "staring" gaze of the collective, as signaled by the swift onset of Vrenchen's feverishness and pallor. Ironically, it is in the instant of being *accurately* recognized by members of their own community that Sali and Vrenchen cease to belong to it. Sali voices this sentiment plainly: "Let's go and join the poor folk; that's where we really belong, and they won't look down on us there" (80).

The discomfort and shame that fill Sali and Vrenchen in this exchange have two immediate sources. On the one hand, the stigma of their fathers' bitter feud that culminated in Sali's violence against Marti is once again thrown into the harsh and unsparing light of public apprehension. On the other hand, an additional locus of guilt can be traced to the protagonists' sustained act of imitation, whose true referent is also laid bare in this instant of recognition. Key to this is the theme of desire's intrinsic connection to law, which operates in *A Village Romeo and Juliet* within two distinct paradigms: first, in the early scene of Manz and Marti's theft of the middle field, one can identify the Pauline concept of individual desire emerging in reaction to—and inspiration by—specific prohibitions, a dialectical relation in which, as Jacques Lacan puts it, "the Law causes our desire to flare up only in relation to the Law."[32]

In the second half of the story, by comparison, this causal diptych closes in upon itself, for what Sali and Vrenchen desire *is* the edifice of law itself as represented by the bourgeois paradigm of an official marriage that is recognized by society. Moreover, the assumed implausibility of this latter element—the communal validation—underscores it for them as a *sine qua non*. This logical bind leads them to yet another one, for they decide to imitate a married couple and thereby elicit a specific outward recognition (*Erkennung*) from others that they so desperately long for. Yet according to their own moral parameters, the state of lawful marriage, which they are imitating, is itself predicated upon a conceptual, formal recognition (*Anerkennung*) having already taken place.

Thus, when an authentic recognition finally *does* occur in the town square, the anxiety and discomfort it induces is not due simply to the fact that Sali and Vrenchen have pretended to be something that they are not. More particularly, it is due to the fact that what they have consciously simulated up to this point is the very appearance of decency, orderliness, honesty, and respectability as such (73, 76, 77, 80). That is, the ethical categories that they imitate are in essence adverse to behaviors such as imitation. Consequently, the double process of knowingly mimicking lawfulness, morality, and honorability—*and* of these imitations being misrecognized as genuine and real by others—is concomitant with an external disturbance of, and an internal contradiction in, the constitutive terms of those ethical categories. Even though assuming the likeness of a respectably married couple does not bespeak a legal impediment to marriage at some future point in time, the more complex act of outwardly invoking a social category of lawful order per se—and being recognized as having

---

32. Jacques Lacan, *The Ethics of Psychoanalysis: The Seminar of Jacques Lacan, Book VII*, ed. Jacques-Alain Miller, trans. Dennis Porter (London: Routledge, 1992), 83–84. In allusion to the Pauline notion of this relationship between law, desire, and transgression, Lacan cites the Epistle to the Romans 7:7–8: "Nay, I had not known sin, but by the law. . . . But sin, taking occasion by the commandment, wrought in me all manner of concupiscence. For without the law sin was dead."

done so—instigates Sali and Vrenchen's moral exclusion from that order. *Erkennung* has occluded *Anerkennung*. As with their abuse of the doll, and as with Manz and Marti's illicit plowing of the middle field at the beginning of the story, the transgressive status of the act is concretized within an interpersonal and reciprocal gaze that first transfixes them and then impels them to flee.

III.

The Little Garden of Paradise

The "poor folk" to whom Sali and Vrenchen feel they now belong is made up of fellow outcasts from proper society, such as debtors and the homeless. Their address is a formerly well-kept tavern in the countryside that has since fallen into disrepair and disrepute, though it has retained its original name: "The Little Garden of Paradise" (*das Paradiesgärtlein*). The establishment's explicit invocation of Eden clearly mirrors the novella's setting and events, for both the building itself and its current patrons constitute a postlapsarian ruin of the world that Sali and Vrenchen have felt compelled to abandon. The interior of this fallen Eden is covered with Rococo images and effigies of airborne angels and cherubim; however, the once-gilded details and lively hues have become faded by time and exposure to the elements, and although the space is filled with music and energetically dancing guests, which might at first seem to echo the cheery ornamentation above, the wildness of the tune and the intoxication of the undulating figures belies the once cozy and respectable atmosphere. The distance separating heaven and earth is underscored precisely by the spatial proximity between their respective representatives in this "little garden of paradise." In fact, the two spheres even meet: Vrenchen, whose heavy spirits are suddenly lifted by the opportunity at last to dance, climbs with Sali onto a raised platform where the revelry is underway and the two fall in with the "ragged folk from Seldwyla" (90).

The *Paradiesgärtlein* thus functions as the venue not only for a simulation but a perversion of the bourgeois paradigm within which Sali and Vrenchen have wished to take their place. Moreover, by incorporating themselves into this debased vision of their desired (and lost) paradise in a final attempt to experience some form of it, however decrepit, they in effect reinstantiate the conditions of their transgressive imitations from throughout the day. This is first marked in a sequence of mutual recognition that functions as a striking inversion of the one that occurred only shortly beforehand in the village square. After the dance comes to an end, Sali and Vrenchen look around and are frightened when they suddenly spot "the sinister figure of the Black Fiddler ... who, however, greeted them cordially ... and they were glad to have a friend there; indeed, they almost felt as though they were under the Fiddler's special care and attention" (91). It is worth noting the significance of the fact that this recognition—which is both an empirical *Erkennung* and a symbolic *Anerkennung*—is enacted by the Fiddler himself, whose own physiognomic recognizability had overshadowed Manz and Marti's surreptitious theft of his field. As such, it operates simultaneously as the negative reflection and the completion of the trajectory inaugurated by the opening scenes of Keller's tale.

Having arrived at the end of this ring structure, Sali and Vrenchen feel despair over their original resolution to part ways. That very morning they had accepted the reality of a life apart in exchange for remaining faithful to their shared ideal.[33] But this ideal now seems to them to be more out of reach and frail than ever before, and they at last stagger beneath the weight of their own imperative: "They both knew that they could find true happiness only by becoming

---

33. It is unclear whether there are implied legal barriers to the possibility of Sali and Vrenchen relocating to a different community altogether and marrying there instead. After all, Swiss laws of *Niederlassungsfreiheit*, which would have allowed them to move wherever they pleased, were introduced by the *Bundesverfassung* in 1848 (Art. 41) and subsequently developed between 1866 and 1874. Regardless of this context, however, the story makes clear that their ideal existence is linked to their *own* village's recognition of them, not solely to the legal category of marriage— it is *Recht, Erkennung,* and *Anerkennung* rather than *Gesetz* alone that are at issue in the fantasy. On the above-mentioned laws of relocation, see Andreas Heusler, *Schweizerische Verfassungsgeschichte* (Aalen: Scientia, 1968), 377; Hans-Peter Bärtschi, *Industrialisierung, Eisenbahnschlachten und Städtebau: Die Entwicklung des Zürcher Industrie- und Arbeiterstadtteils Aussersihl; Ein vergleichender Beitrag zur Architektur- und Technikgeschichte* (Basel: Birkhäuser, 1983), 239.

man and wife. Lonely and abandoned as they were, this thought was the last flicker of that flame of honor that had burned in their families in times gone by.... [T]he happiness they craved had to have a firm foundation, and though their blood throbbed in their veins and longed to flow together, that foundation seemed to be ever beyond their grasp" (94–95/*RuJ* 150, translation modified). Wracked with sadness and indecision, the two are suddenly happened upon by the Fiddler, who proposes a simple solution to their woes, suggesting that they join him and his compatriots in the wilderness, where they can finally live together and eschew the society, laws, and mores that have already eschewed them. However, Vrenchen rejects the possibility of comparable happiness within this parallel dimension of lawlessness, moral unaccountability, and lack of consequence: "I do not want to live where things like this go on" (97).

As soon as Sali and Vrenchen rejoin the company inside the tavern, a bizarre scene ensues. The Fiddler officiates a ritualistic simulation of a wedding, mounting an irreverent yet nakedly faithful staging of the protagonists' original fantasy of a formal marriage recognized by the community:

> "Here come the bride and groom!" cried the Fiddler.... They allowed themselves to be led to a table, happy of a chance to be able to be with other people for a moment [*Augenblick*].... Sali and Vrenchen sat there without speaking, clasped in each other's arms. Then suddenly the Fiddler called for order and performed a mock ceremony that was meant to represent a wedding. He made them take each other's hands, then bade the assembled company rise and come up one by one to congratulate the young couple and welcome them to the fraternity. They submitted in silence, taking it as a jest, but at the same time overcome with chilled and flushed trembling. (98/*RuJ* 152–153, translation modified)

The integral role of imitation and conscience in this mock ceremony once again brings Girard to mind, particularly his anthropological account of how in certain societies the law forbids imitative behavior due to its capacity to create a simulacrum of its object that could be used for malevolent rituals.[34] In such communities, imita-

---

34. Girard, *Things Hidden since the Foundation of the World*, trans. Stephen Bann and Michael Metteer (Stanford, CA: Stanford University Press, 1987), 10–11.

tion not only stands in opposition to law but is something that law must actively combat in order to protect society's cohesion. According to Girard, there are two ways in which mimetic behavior might threaten this cohesion: First, it impedes a general ability to distinguish between authentic and replicated material (that is, it poses the same hazard that Plato ascribes to mimetic art in *The Republic*). Second, the creation of such simulacra makes it possible for socially unsanctioned rituals (such as sympathetic magic) to be performed. Because law's purpose (at least in this context) is to regulate official rituals of social life, it therefore also exists in order to prevent *unofficial* rituals.[35] In Girard's reading, then, imitation is a thorn in the flesh of the law.

A similar dynamic seems to be at the core of the fake wedding that has just taken place in the *Paradiesgärtlein*. From the perspective of both the protagonists and the assembly, the parodic ceremony simultaneously theatricalizes and supplants Sali's and Vrenchen's bourgeois ideal, embodied as it has been throughout the novella by the title and sacrament of marriage.[36] Although the Fiddler's ritual announces the possibility of a life together within an inversion of *Bürgertum*, and although Sali and Vrenchen on the surface regard the entire pageantry merely as "jest," on a deeper and unspoken level something inside of them begins to writhe. It is almost as if the earlier public recognition in town that had flooded them with unease recurs in a new form, as evidenced by their visceral reaction to the mimicked substitution of proper marriage ("with chilled and flushed trembling"), which echoes Vrenchen's symptoms from the market square (where she "trembled and turned pale and red," 88, translation modified).

Crucially, however, this time the recognition originates, not from the external "staring faces" of the community, but instead from within Sali and Vrenchen themselves. The Fiddler's ceremonial mim-

---

35. Girard, *Things Hidden*, 14–15.
36. Interestingly, the aforementioned *Heimatlosengesetz* insinuates a correlation between homelessness and cohabitation that occurs outside the bounds of legal marriage (*Konkubinatsverhältnisse*). See Schweizerischer Bundesrat, "Bericht des Bundesrathes," 135. Compare Meier and Wolfensberger, *"Eine Heimat und doch keine,"* 39–61.

icry both culminates and perverts their own imitations, and by virtue of the assembled company's enthusiastic validation of the rite—their *Anerkennung* of Sali and Vrenchen as newlyweds—the formal coordinates of the fantasy are simultaneously fulfilled and distorted. Just as when they were children they had been stricken and "began to shudder" with *Grauen* once the mangled doll literalized its mimetic function to simulate life by suddenly having an actual living creature trapped inside of it, here too the actualization of their desire to be taken for a "bride and groom" ultimately unmasks them before an interior gaze of conscience.

It is crucial to notice that these unmaskings occur not merely because imitative behavior is inwardly recognized as such (after all, during both the burial scene and the Sunday walk Sali and Vrenchen had contentedly carried on with their simulations). Rather, the unmasking occurs only when the *product* of imitative behavior is outwardly recognized as such and treated nevertheless as a functional substitute for the real. Or, to use the terms of Girard's model, law (and therefore conscience) rears up as soon as ritual becomes possible; and ritual becomes possible as soon as a simulacrum is willingly employed in lieu of the real thing it simulates. It is at the moment that the Fiddler and his companions make Sali and Vrenchen the object of their imitative ritual that the two suddenly register guilt rather than shame, just like the sounds of the entombed fly from within the doll had suddenly awakened in them a jarring sense of transgression. Encircled by the homeless band in the derelict tavern, Sali and Vrenchen seem at once to register that their capacity to subsist upon simulation and make-believe has not outlasted the day, leaving them to confront the somber possibility that neither their fantasy of a respectable village existence nor its grotesque reflection in the Saturnalian Little Garden of Paradise can suffice as hiding places from self-recognition.

The final scene of the novella stages a sacrifice consisting in a double negation, for Sali and Vrenchen's last moments are devoted to a *second* imitated wedding ceremony that, in reimagining their original fantasy of marriage, aims to replace the Fiddler's pasquinade of it while at the same time solidifying their own guilt. Keller's poetic genius was to set this concluding instance of ceremonial repetition, reflection, and transformation on the banks of the river, and from there into the water itself.

Last Rites

The company rises and, led by the Fiddler's playing and the influence of drink, moves out into the night, making its way through the countryside in a nocturnal counterpoint to the protagonists' walk earlier that day. They eventually find themselves on the hill abutting the three parallel fields where the novella began, and the party lingers for a while before continuing on, but Sali and Vrenchen remain behind. Finally left to confront their decision to flout the Fiddler's proposition and instead hold fast to their original fantasy, they are once again enveloped by sorrow at the thought of their impending separation.

Hearing the gentle rushing of the river's currents nearby, they walk down to the shore and exchange the rings they had secretly bought for each other at the fair that afternoon. Vrenchen completes the ceremony in her pronouncement: "Now we are really betrothed—you are my husband and I am your wife! Just let's pretend it's really true for a minute [*Augenblick*]" (101/*RuJ* 155). In this *Augenblick* the simple but earnest performance of a nuptial vow activates all the structural and thematic mechanisms of ritual that have been observed in the story thus far. An inner change overcomes Sali, who, up to this instant, we are now told, has not regarded the question of marrying Vrenchen as "the inescapable decision between life and death" to the same degree that she, "with passionate decisiveness," has.[37] However, as they embrace, he instantaneously shares in her inner state:

> But now at last he saw a light, and what was womanly feeling in the young girl forthwith became in him a wild and hot desire, and a bright glow [*glühende Klarheit*] lighted up his senses. Vehemently as he had embraced and caressed [Vrenchen] before, he now did it in a different and

---

37. Here and in the quoted passage that follows, I use Paul Bernard Thomas's translation due to its more felicitous and accurate rendering of the original text, as found in *A Village Romeo and Juliet* (New York: Frederick Ungar, 1955), 93 (*RuJ* 156).

more tempestuous way, overwhelming her with kisses. In spite of her own intense feeling [Vrenchen] noticed this change at once, and a violent trembling thrilled her entire being; but before the streak of cloud had crossed the moon she too was convulsed by passion. With impetuous caresses and struggles their ring-adorned hands met and clasped each other tightly, as if celebrating a wedding on their own account, without the command of a will.[38]

In this passage, two structural and recurring aspects of the entire tale intersect with one another as the reciprocal dynamics of sight and thought shed a harsh light upon the equally prevalent gendering of those dynamics—the male and female protagonists share an *Augenblick* of gazing into each other's eyes, but it must be said that Keller does not have them do so from an equal *Augenhöhe*.[39] The account we receive is of "womanly feeling in the young girl" being transposed into a more forceful, sexual desire within Sali that is nevertheless accompanied by a wholly noetic event of realization and clarity (*glühende Klarheit*), whereas Vrenchen's "own intense feeling" merely progresses into more intensely physical reactions to this same event ("violent trembling"; "convulsed by passion"). Only in Sali, that is, do we witness hallmarks of *logos* accompanying those of *eros* with masculinized overtones that are almost Winckelmannian in pitch.

Indeed, this is perhaps the most acute point at which issues of gender are addressed by the text in direct connection with the imminent act that both characters are about to undertake, though in ways that are probably more complicated and ambiguous than the parochialism of this scene might lead us to expect. On the one hand, the *Augenblick* of mutual recognition has prepared us for the imminent drowning to invoke the stereotypically gendered tropes of suicide (especially in water) and of sacrifice, tropes that Keller himself employs in other works.[40] On the other hand, though, it is not

---

38. *A Village Romeo and Juliet*, trans. Thomas, 93 (*RuJ* 156).

39. For a thorough discussion of gender problematics in Keller's work, see Antje Harnisch, *Keller, Raabe, Fontane: Geschlecht, Sexualität und Familie im bürgerlichen Realismus* (Frankfurt am Main: Peter Lang, 1994), 29–78.

40. On several such instances of "'Vergeschlechtlichung' des Todes," see Stefan Voß, *Männlichkeit und soziale Ordnung bei Gottfried Keller: Studien zu Geschlecht und Realismus* (Berlin: De Gruyter, 2019), 379–382.

just Vrenchen but Sali too who will commit suicide, thus disrupting the standardized nineteenth-century motif of the solitary, stoic, yet suffering woman who slips quietly out of view and of life.[41] It is precisely from out of their shared, futile desire to assume the both archetypical and stereotypical roles of bourgeois husband and wife that *both* protagonists submit themselves to the depths. So, let us at last turn to this impending, climactic scene.

As soon as the two foregoing moments of exchange—first of rings and then of feeling and conviction—have taken place, Sali resolves upon a sacrificial culmination of the rite: "This must be our wedding hour—then we must leave the world behind. Over there is the river—where no one can part us. We will have been together—whether for a short time or a long time can be all the same to us" (102/*RuJ* 155, translation modified). With this statement, he names the objective of their imminent drowning as actualizing and then preserving, through death, a singular instant of shared experience. In a further echo and variation of rituality in Keller's story, this moment centers upon a reciprocal recognition between subject and other to an almost mystical degree and remains unseen by other characters. However, the culmination of this union will also occur outside even the reader's view: the two make for an anchored hay barge floating near the shore, and as Sali carries Vrenchen through the shallows toward the vessel, she is suddenly reminded of that day at the river, recalling aloud how cold and wet their hands had been when they had secretly clasped them together, "unseen" by their feuding fathers. They embark, and as the boat drifts into the current the reader is, for the first time, restricted access to a private moment between the protagonists. We are permitted only to follow the ship's winding and gradual progress along the river from afar, thus allowing the consummation to remain wholly "unseen." As day

---

41. As, for example, in the tale *Regine* from his later *Sinngedicht* cycle of 1881, in which the eponymous protagonist is caught in a web of rumors about her potential marital infidelity and takes her own life in what Voß describes as both a "final elusion in the surrender of all hope" and an "emancipatory act," albeit one which "nevertheless does not liberate the 'ill-fated woman' from her cooptation as a collective projection screen." Voß, *Männlichkeit und soziale Ordnung*, 363–364.

begins to break, the brief voyage comes to an end: "As [the boat] approached the town, two pale figures rose in the chill of the September morning and slipped from the dark hull into the cold waters below, clasped in each other's arms" (105). The drowning that goes unwitnessed by fellow characters thus signals a final sacrifice of Sali and Vrenchen's wish to see themselves as, and be seen as, bona fide members of the community.

"Whether for a Short Time or a Long Time"

In order to come away with a complete account of *A Village Romeo and Juliet*, we must dwell a while longer on the question of what significance the drowning bears for the narrative as a whole. On a simple level, it fulfills a structural function of sacrifice insofar as it stages an ultimate relinquishment of a desired end. Moreover, the implicit transgression vis-à-vis their society's mores (that is, their sexual intercourse outside of *legal*, not simply simulated, wedlock) precludes a realization of the married life together that it is traditionally meant to symbolically inaugurate.[42] As a consequence, disappearing from the above-surface sphere of observability into the underwater sphere of nonvisibility and nondifferentiation is an especially fitting mode of sacrifice. If we regard the scene of drowning as a kind of culmination of the wedding rite—corresponding in spatial terms with a movement from the banks of the river to its unbounded depths—one is necessarily brought to reflect upon the events preceding both linked instants. The most pivotal of these, as suggested already, is Sali and Vrenchen's mutual *Erkennung* on the shore during their fathers' confrontation. This diptych of scenes near and in the water points to a trajectory of the protagonists' brief time together that is structured around instants of reciprocal visual exchange and that reaches its completion within the moment of ceremonial *Anerkennung* (on the shore, once again). The subsequent act of drowning thus highlights a sacrifice of the future fulfillment

---

42. See Karin Tebben, *Von der Unsterblichkeit des Eros und den Wirklichkeiten der Liebe: Geschlechterbeziehungen—Realismus—Erzählkunst* (Heidelberg: Universitätsverlag Winter, 2011), 167.

of an ideal in exchange for indulgence in a fleeting, present approximation of that fulfillment.[43]

What is offered up is therefore not simply a desired status and moral framework, but also the temporal structure that underpins both. In this regard, the setting of the river once again invokes classical antiquity, though this time in a poetic rather than legal context. Like the souls that Aeneas observes pressing forward to the banks of the Lethe in the sixth book of the *Aeneid*, Sali and Vrenchen come to their own shore in order to wash away memory.[44] However, whereas the teeming shades in Virgil's underworld are waiting to drink from the river so that they will forget their past lives and thereby be able to re-enter the world above as new, unhaunted subjects, Keller's young protagonists are arguably more akin to Dante's Pilgrim in the *Purgatorio*, who is bathed in these same Lethic currents in order to forget his sins before at last being reunited with his lost love, Beatrice. Similarly, Sali and Vrenchen go into the water in order to "lay aside the seed of weeping."[45] And as in Dante's Purgatory, the riverbank becomes a site not just of forgetting but even of narrative omission and paralipsis.[46]

---

43. The final section of the text has an interesting publication history that seems to bespeak vacillations in Keller's moralistic intentions for the narrative. The 1856 version had an extended epilogue that bewailed the "corruption and wilding of the passions" evidenced by the motivation behind the protagonists' suicide. However, Paul Heyse deleted this epilogue for the version that appeared in the 1870 volume of his *Deutscher Novellenschatz*, choosing to have the story end abruptly with the drowning itself (in other words, with an overt emphasis of precisely that which Keller sought to discourage). Keller subsequently came up with a third solution for the second edition of *Die Leute von Seldwyla* in 1876 (the one quoted here), allowing the boat to come to rest in a what Rolf Selbmann calls a "peaceful image of the everyday world" that remains "unspoilt." See Rolf Selbmann, *Gottfried Keller: Romane und Erzählungen* (Berlin: Erich Schmidt, 2001), 64–65; Erika Swales, *The Poetics of Skepticism: Gottfried Keller and "Die Leute von Seldwyla"* (Oxford: Berg, 1994), 86; Michael Titzmann, "'Natur' vs. 'Kultur': Kellers 'Romeo und Julia auf dem Dorfe' im KOntext der Konstituierung des frühen Realismus," in *Zwischen Goethezeit und Realismus* (Tübingen: Niemeyer, 2002), 456.

44. Compare Paul Ricoeur, *Memory, History, Forgetting*, trans. Kathleen Blamey and David Pellauer (Chicago: University of Chicago Press, 2004), 27.

45. Dante Alighieri, *The Divine Comedy of Dante Alighieri*, vol. 2, *Purgatorio*, trans. Robert M. Durling (Oxford: Oxford University Press, 2000), 533 (XXXI, line 46).

46. "When I drew near the blessed shore, '*Asperges / me*' was heard so sweetly that I cannot remember, / let alone write it." Dante Alighieri, *The Divine Comedy*,

Like the living burial of the fly that the protagonists performed as children, the drowning is also a sacrifice of life for the sake of fantasy and imitation. Their fantasy consists precisely in being seen by their community and "recognized" by law, but as something that the community will never be able authentically to see. What they exchange their lives for is the ability to fully and completely invest in an instant of fantasy—in an imitation that can be experienced as true by not being tempered with an implicit expectation of experiencing anything afterward that might militate against the lived fantasy. This is tied to the fact that the tragic dilemma of *A Village Romeo and Juliet* is one of temporal consciousness, for Sali and Vrenchen's declared inability either to live together in matrimony or to exist apart is due to their awareness of past events as well as future inevitabilities. The sole alternative is therefore to give up diachrony for the sake of synchrony, to experience a moment only once and never again in order to insulate it from a past that might tarnish it and a future that might eclipse it ("We will have been together—whether for a short time or a long time can be all the same to us," Sali says).

The temporal logic of his remark is central to the sacrificial logic of the drowning, and we should consider it carefully. A helpful cue for our analysis can be taken from Augustine's theory of subjective or "distended" time. This concept of *distentio* famously presents our consciousness as something split in two directions, reaching simultaneously into the memory of things past and into the expectation of things to come. However, Augustine notices that he cannot hold onto the present instant as a distinct phenomenon; and yet the present instant surely exists, for time as such is made up of a flowing sequence of "presents," which he is able to experience only as a bifurcation of the past and the future. Where, then, can the present instant be said to take place, given that it always evades our psyche's grip?

According to Augustine, the locus of the present *Augenblick* is the *attentio*, a "threshold" in our consciousness positioned between expectation and memory, which Andrea Nightingale describes as "a passive point of transit—it marks the present moment where ex-

---

535 (lines 97–99). Comparatively, it is after the pointed narrative omission aboard the hay barge that Sali and Vrenchen are submerged in the river.

pected future events move into memories of the past."[47] But where is *attentio* itself rooted, if it cannot be perceived by us in itself, but is nevertheless central to our perception of temporality per se? Nightingale's solution to this paradox is elegantly simple: we cannot perceive the present instant of *attentio*'s operation because this operation is grounded not in our minds, but in our bodies.

This notion of an "embodied" rather than a purely psychic present is made most clear in the analogy that Augustine himself chooses to illustrate *distentio*—namely, the act of reciting a hymn: "The life of this act of mine is stretched two ways, into my memory because of the words I have already said and into my expectation because of those which I am about to say. But my attention [*attentio*] is on what is present: by that [= *attentionem meam*] the future is transferred to become the past."[48] As Augustine begins to sing, his *expectation* reaches *into his memory* to find the known words in preparation for reciting them anew. Yet as soon as the words are sung, they have already become part of his memory again; the present instant of articulation is either expected or recalled, but can never be grasped in the moment as it takes place. *Attentio* therefore constitutes the *Augenblick*, grounded in the *bodily* present of natural diachrony (here, in the human voice as it sings).[49] However, this *Augenblick* of embodied *attentio* cannot be experienced consciously because it is the very fulcrum against which *distentio* splits our consciousness in order to stretch it apart in the opposite directions of memory and expectation.

How might Augustine's account of *distentio* help us to better understand Sali and Vrenchen's drowning as a sacrificial exchange of life—that is, of diachrony—for the synchronic *Augenblick*? Keller's stark imagery of intertwined bodies slipping into water certainly

---

47. Andrea Nightingale, *Once Out of Nature: Augustine on Time and the Body* (Chicago: University of Chicago Press, 2011), 89.

48. Augustine, *Confessions*, trans. Henry Chadwick (Oxford: Oxford University Press, 2008), 243. / Augustine, *Confessiones: Bibliotheca Sanctorum Patrum et Scriptorum ecclesiasticorum Theologiae et christianarum Litterarum cultoribus accommodata*, ser. 6, vol. 2, ed. Felice Ramorino (Rome: Bibliotheca Ss. Patrum, 1909), 341 [11.xxviii.38].

49. Nightingale, *Once Out of Nature*, 92.

underscores a spatial and particularly bodily understanding of "the instant" that Sali and Vrenchen wish to preserve from expectation and memory. Comparatively, for Augustine, to be human is to exist according to the two frameworks of temporal experience described above: the linear flow of natural time (the "bodily present") and the distention of our minds by the past and the future. However, Augustine claims in line with Christian teaching that in the afterlife we will receive spiritual bodies, but without being subject to the kind of embodiment that had characterized our mortal lives; "leaving behind the old days," we will be "gathered to follow the One, 'forgetting the past' and moving not toward those future things which are transitory but to 'the things which are before' me, not stretched out in distraction [*distentus*] but extended in reach [*extentus*]."[50] Augustine suggests that with a body that is immortal and a mind that is not distended, our temporal experience of life on earth will be succeeded by "the things that are before [*in ea quae ante sunt*]." But what are these "things," and what is "before" supposed to designate? Nightingale suggests that by this, "Augustine is referring to a time before time existed. He longs to forget the past and transcend *all* temporal befores. He looks forward to an escape from time—to the eternity that is before time.... What is 'before' time is the eternity of God."[51] The mode of this longing for an eternity prior to time is articulated in terms of *extension*; of reaching toward the (future) eternal present and away from our (present) temporal embodiment—in short, it is articulated in terms of being extended rather than distended (*non distentus, sed "extentus"*).

This, however, is the point at which the logic behind Keller's drowning scene diverges from that of Augustine's eschatological hope: whereas Augustine aims precisely to extend "further up and further in" (to slightly reappropriate C. S. Lewis) from the human body's anchorage within the here and now and the mind's imbrication within *distentio* in order to become "gathered" into an eter-

---

50. Augustine, *Confessions*, trans. Chadwick, 244; Augustine, *Confessiones*, 342 [11.xxix.39].

51. Nightingale, *Once Out of Nature*, 97.

nity of the divine, Sali and Vrenchen wish to extend "inward" into an unending *attentio*. Put another way, they desire not the "resurrective" eternity of a heavenly hereafter, but the "embodied" atemporality of an eternally preserved *Augenblick*. In this regard, a basic but salient aspect of the drowning is the image of their bodies' concrete localization within the underwater space—which is counter to any possible image of distention in linear time.

This commitment to inward "attention" in the present rather than upward and outward "extension" into eternity is further deepened by a final distinctive aspect of the drowning that sets it apart from the burial: namely, the issue of sacrificial intention. Though the essential operation is still a removal of the "ritual content" from view, as in the burial, the ends to which this is carried out are certainly more ambiguous than was the case in the empty field at the beginning of the story. Before Sali and Vrenchen climb aboard the hay ship, Vrenchen asks, "What are you doing? Do you mean to steal the farmers' hay barge?" Sali's reply is blunt and full of implication: "They will find their property down by the weir, which is where they would take it in any case, and they will never know what happened" (104). This prediction is duly fulfilled, for after the lovers' bodies slip into the frigid currents, the ship comes to rest near a bridge and, as we are told in the final paragraph, eventually drifts back to town and makes land, just as the drowned bodies are later discovered "below the town" (105), thus aligning Sali and Vrenchen with the vessel as "property" of the community that ultimately does get retrieved from the *flumen publicum*.

Sali's suggestive juxtaposition of his and Vrenchen's imminent drowning with the notion of property invites, by way of conclusion, a consideration of how water, extra-peripherality, and sacrifice are related to community, visibility, and lawful order. With respect to the symbolism of seeing, there is a clear link between the burial and the drowning as operations that remove a specific object from public view, but this very similarity also reveals a crucial point of contrast. Whereas the burial of the doll seemed to correspond with an urge to eliminate the imitative product of the ritual, the drowning ultimately results in a darkly ironic realization of Sali and Vrenchen's original wish to be seen, insofar as it reinscribes them into the existing order. The differing status of visibility in both acts is in tune with these differing patterns of objective and effect: the buried doll can no longer be seen, whereas the drowned protagonists initially disappear from view on the outer edges of the community but ultimately come back to the surface and are found.

Drowning thus underwrites Sali and Vrenchen's exit into the "off-stage" (Grk. *obskené*) domain of "obscene" ritual and their return to the visible "stage" of society and its paradigms, though not in their originally desired form of a properly married young couple. Instead, they are preserved within the bourgeois, communal imaginary as a transmutation of this fantasy by being described in the newspaper reports of the event as celebrants of a "desperate and God-forsaken wedding" (*RuJ* 159, my translation). The drowning, as opposed to the burial, therefore bespeaks a tacit expectation to reemerge into view eventually. On a structural level, what Sali and Vrenchen sacrifice is a particular mode of temporal experience in exchange for a different one; that is, they give up the hope of an impossible future event of communal recognition and its effects in order to live out a singular recognition between themselves. By drowning themselves immediately afterward, they seal the impossibility of ever remembering this moment from a future, retrospective vantage point in time. Nor can they proleptically look forward from this singular moment of private recognition of each other as husband and wife in even hypothetical anticipation of a reciprocal recognition of this status from the side of the community. One could therefore suggest that the fundamental insight of Keller's outwardly simple tale is to be found, not in its lyrical portrait of star-crossed love, nor in its critique of bourgeois ideology and false consciousness, but instead in the thought that sacrifice, insofar as it is essentially a rite of recognition, is at heart the offering in and of time.

Among the few surviving documents in which Keller refers to his fiancée's drowning is a two-line letter he wrote to her uncle, in whose house he had first met her that very winter. The second (and final) line of the note reads: "The dead woman looked at me for an instant [*Augenblick*], and then continued along her lonely way without knowing what she was moving past."⁵² One cannot help but ruminate on the fact that ten years before writing these words, Keller had chosen to portray a drowning, not as incomprehensible or tragic, but as sacrificial, rooting it in the offering up of desire for a future form of life in exchange for a fleeting reflection of it in the present instant. Within a single movement, Sali and Vrenchen immolate their wish for a moment that might ramify into the future and therefore also be woven into their memory. In place of this wish, they offer each other the moment itself; a both rapturous and resigned "blink of an eye" that is wholly lived, and then given quietly to the water. And in doing so, they also, finally, offer a modern answer to an ancient question: "Who will lay hold on the human heart to make it still, so that it can see how eternity, in which there is neither future nor past, stands still?"⁵³

---

52. Gottfried Keller, letter to Karl Gottlieb Wegmann (July 28, 1866), in *Gesammelte Briefe*, vol. 4, ed. Carl Helbling (Bern: Benteli, 1954), 128; cited in Werner Staub, "Christina Luise Scheidegger (1843–1866): Die Braut von Gottfried Keller," *Jahrbuch des Oberaargaus* 25 (1982): 176. The other known document by Keller that alludes to Scheidegger's drowning is an untitled memorial poem, dated August 8, 1866. The lines address a "Sweet dead one, . . . who in quiet shoes in the early morning / sought her peace and took away mine [*die Ruh' gesucht und mir die Unruh' gab*], / . . . Vanished good, oh heart filled with rare goodness, / if you would only arise and shake off your wet hair!," (lines 2, 5–6, 9–10).
53. Augustine, *Confessions*, trans. Chadwick, 229.

4

A Faint Wake

Atonement and Afterward in Storm's Late Works

> ... But it is the sea
> That takes and gives remembrance,
> And love no less keeps eyes
> attentively fixed,
> But what is lasting the poets
> provide.
>
> —Friedrich Hölderlin, "Andenken"
> (Remembrance)

At one time the land and fields of North Frisia, Theodor Storm's home for nearly his entire life, lay beneath the sea. Over a period of centuries, the water had been gradually pushed back, the shoreline

---

Epigraph: Friedrich Hölderlin, "Andenken" (Remembrance) (1803), lines 56–59, in *Selected Poems and Fragments*, trans. Michael Hamburger (New York: Penguin, 1998), 253.

extended ever farther out, until the sand could be cultivated into fertile marshland.[1] From a young age, Storm seemed to share in a local consciousness of living on stolen ground, with the sea always eager (yet patient) to reclaim what had been taken from it. Among the North Frisian legends and folklore that Storm and two university friends recorded and compiled in the early 1840s, we read at one point that "there is an old belief that where water once was, water can return."[2] This staid awareness of the past's ability to wash onto the present like the tide onto inhabited land is also implicit throughout Storm's writing; however, it is most palpable in his later novellas (written between 1872 and 1888, the year of his death), in which the salience of memory is complemented by a ubiquity of drowning scenes. In this chapter I explore how and why the two may be linked.

To that end, I will focus upon two exemplary texts from Storm's late period, *Aquis Submersus* (1876) and *Der Schimmelreiter* (*The Rider on the White Horse*) (1888), though I will also make briefer reference to other important works from within this time frame. Ultimately I argue that drowning occurs so frequently in these stories because of what water conveys for Storm: namely, a particular threshold inherent to memory. The symbolically rich opposition between water's surface and its depths is employed in Storm's writing in order to portray remembrance as a constant oscillation between retrieval and loss. A second important aspect of memory in this late period of Storm's work is its enmeshment with ethics, and more specifically with the questions (faced by his characters time and again) not only of how one will be remembered, but also of how one should remember others. In the novellas examined below, this ethical aspect of memory is bound up with the theme of desire to atone for past transgressions, which in turn is bound up with the concept of sacrifice. As we shall see, the various acts of sacrifice that occur in these stories either react to an infraction against some form of law

---

1. David Blackbourn, *The Conquest of Nature: Water, Landscape and the Making of Modern Germany* (London: Jonathan Cape, 2006), 116–124.
2. Theodor Storm, "Woher die großen Fluthen kommen," in *Sagen, Märchen und Lieder der Herzogthümer Schleswig, Holstein und Lauenburg*, ed. Karl Müllenhoff (Kiel: Schwersche Buchhandlung, 1845), 129.

or themselves constitute such an infraction. In each of them, memory depends upon a trace to which it can attach itself, but it also seems that the trace is produced by memory in the first place.

That ambiguous boundary between being here and being gone is the common thread joining the imagery of drowning with the themes of memory and penitence. After all, Storm's late fiction is filled with characters who drown and with characters who negotiate their own memories, but also with characters who wonder about the implications of being here *again* in the form of another person's memory. Water is always the site where the contingency of human action confronts the inexorability of time; yet water, like memory, is simultaneously ever-present and unstill.³ Consequently, the various chronicles of law, sacrifice, and penitence that we encounter in these narratives are ones that were not merely entrusted to a narrator's memory and subsequently put to paper, but inscribed in other surfaces as well—most significantly, the natural landscape itself—in the hope of leaving a trace.

I.

In many ways Storm's final phase of writing can be seen as an organic extension of a theme that had appeared in much of his work up to the 1870s. This theme—which in chapter 3 we saw Keller pursue at length—concerns the tension between the desire to attain an idealized existence within bourgeois society and the many obstacles to realizing this desire that economic instability presents. Novellas such as *Auf dem Staatshof* (*In the Great Hall*, 1859), *Auf der Universität* (*At the University*, 1863), and *Draußen im Heidedorf* (*The Village on the Moor*, 1872) introduce two developments that

---

3. Hildegard Lorenz has perceived several topological resonances of water in Storm's work that will be helpful to keep in mind throughout this chapter. Foremost among these is death: "As a result of its physical characteristics, water is endlessly expandable and minimally hemmable; it is therefore texturally suited to manifesting indeterminate exteriors as well as closely bounded interiors, both of which can represent death." Lorenz, *Varianz und Invarianz: Theodor Storms Erzählungen; Figurenkonstellationen und Handlungsmuster* (Bonn: Bouvier, 1985), 103, 109, 201.

become central components of Storm's later works: the temporal characteristics of inheritance and debt gradually become associated with different forms of law, and the narratives begin increasingly to center upon the tension between these forms of law and the individuals who must navigate them.

In the Great Hall is one of the earliest examples of this plot type; here the primary concern is the necessity of marriage for securing a familial legacy and estate. Notably, the instances of drowning that occur Storm's novellas between 1860 and 1870 are often suicides that are the desperate reactions of characters who have violated the law or otherwise feel crushed beneath its strictures. Some critics have suggested that in this phase of Storm's work, portrayals of drowning as a "return to nature" ultimately point to the lack of recourse for characters who have been ostracized by their community, with death in water on the periphery of the town figuring as a symbolically rich and culturally established means of escape.[4] In *At the University*, too, we find the theme of failure to realize an ideal existence in society. This tale recounts the hidden torment of a young woman who is beset by external societal constraints and expectations, and eventually internalizes them. As a consequence of this, her drowning seems to simultaneously negate and legitimate these constraints and expectations insofar as it renounces the prospect of life in the social order, yet nonetheless it signals a desperate reaction to the unattainability of this very order.[5] In light of water's signature features of ambivalence and flux, the drowning scenes in novellas such as *In the Great Hall* and *At the University* can be read as spatial representations of this zone in which the negation and legitimation of societal desiderata coalesce.

The Village on the Moor carries this theme forward, although the dynamics are altered slightly. The story revolves around the disappearance of a young man from his remote community, and we learn

---

4. David A. Jackson, *Theodor Storm: The Life and Works of a Democratic Humanitarian* (New York: Berg, 1992), 115; Malte Stein, *"Sein Geliebtestes zu töten": Literaturpsychologische Studien zum Geschlechter- und Generationskonflikt im erzählerischen Werk Theodor Storms* (Berlin: Erich Schmidt, 2006), 58–59.
5. Karin Tebben, "'Wo keine Göttinnen sind, da walten Gespenster': Dämoninnen und Philister im Werk Theodor Storms," *Germanic Review* 79, no. 1 (2004): 20.

of his obsession with a mysterious newcomer to the village, on whom he lavished gifts paid for by the dowry of a neighboring farmer's daughter he has recently married. It is eventually discovered that on the night of his disappearance he had attempted to convince the young woman to leave with him, and that upon her refusal he had pulled out gold earned from selling his horses and thrown it into a nearby well before vanishing into the night. This literal "liquidation" of capital turns out to have foreshadowed his own end, for his drowned remains are found in the marshes soon thereafter. In a parallel process, after the young woman disappears from the village without a trace, the gold is retrieved from the well. The narrator notes that she is said to have eventually settled in "a large city, I am not certain which one . . . and there she slipped away in the floods of humanity."[6] The novella therefore ends with a tripartite metaphor: the image of money being submerged in the well, followed by that of the man drowning out of despair over his futile passion and self-wrought financial ruin, are both juxtaposed with the woman's "submergence" in the tides of mass society.

In addition to the standard realist fare of material conditions and capital, in these texts one also finds equally prevalent themes of sexual politics and gender relations, though in this regard Storm's social criticism (to the extent that his writing engages in it) could hardly be said to push many envelopes.[7] Nonetheless, commentators have explored how water in Storm's writing often becomes a vehicle for communicating narrative aspects of gender, most particularly in the contrastive ways in which male and female bodies relate to bodies of water. Irmgard Roebling nominates *Psyche* (1875) as an exemplary text in this regard because it gathers together multiple strands of gendered water motifs—the nymphic "water-woman" (*Wasserfrau*) above all—that

---

6. Theodor Storm, *Draußen im Heidedorf*, in *Sämtliche Werke in vier Bänden*, vol. 2, ed. Karl Ernst Laage and Dieter Lohmeier (Frankfurt am Main: Deutscher Klassiker, 1987), 101 (hereafter cited as *SW*).

7. Recent scholarship has begun to return to this topic, however, and question whether it is not more complex and layered than previously assessed. See Kathryn Ambrose, "Women in Theodor Storm: The Opposition of Conformity and 'Otherness,'" in *The Woman Question in Nineteenth-Century English, German and Russian Literature* (Leiden: Brill Rodopi, 2016), 93–116.

can be found not only throughout much of Storm's own corpus but across the nineteenth-century literary and cultural milieu.[8] The opening scene of the novella has all of this on full display: on a stormy summer's day, two women (one elderly, one "a mere bud of a girl") part ways on the shore, the former watching anxiously after the latter, who has insisted on a swim despite the dangerous conditions: "The path to the swimming dock was entirely underwater, such that the wooden hut rocking back and forth appeared to be deprived of all connection to the land. The green, heaving surface of the water stretched far into the distance; the foreshore beyond was so heavily flooded that her eyes could only vaguely distinguish the green edge of the bank."[9]

The perspectival "back and forth" play with the waterscape in this scene begins on what is described as the "women's dock" (*Frauenfloß*) side of the water, and figurally encodes themes of helplessness and passivity: the elder's gaze is emphasized for its inability to distinguish the shore in the distance, and the flooding tide has severed connections between spaces of safety by overrunning the earth, rendering uncertain the movements and autonomy of the two women. Things look decidedly different from the other side of the "women's dock," where the male protagonist commands an unhindered vantage of the churning sea. He soon catches sight of "a woman!—a child! ... but not an Oceanid" and teichoscopically narrates in precise detail her distress and "vain" struggle against the waves, which he is soon parting with his "powerful arms," moving resolutely forward through the natural element in imitation of his "bright gaze," which has been fixed upon its goal from the outset as he "flies over the foaming waters" (321–323).

These issues of age, gender, and agency have much to do with the pathos of an individual's relation to the community that is such

---

8. Irmgard Roebling, "Wasserfrauen zwischen Fließen und Festschreibung: Storms Darstellung von Geschlechterverhältnissen am Beispiel seiner Novelle *Psyche*," in *Theodor Storms ästhetische Heimat: Studien zur Lyrik und zum Erzählwerk Storms* (Würzburg: Königshausen und Neumann, 2012), 275. Compare Malte Stein, "Grenzgänge: Zur Bedeutung des Wasserfrau-Motivs in Storms Erzählung *Auf der Universität* und *Der Schimmelreiter*," *Storm-Blätter aus Heiligenstadt* 11 (2005): 19–32.

9. Theodor Storm, *Psyche*, in *SW*, 2:318–319.

a core theme of Storm's fiction (and indeed of German Realism as a whole), though it is by no means particular to the nineteenth-century cultural imaginary. Giambattista Vico opined in his *New Science* (1744) that even before formal domains of law were first established, there existed an innate collective yearning for one's place in both the landscape and the family unit to be extended forward in time. As a consequence, he proposes, the three foundational institutions of human culture—religion, matrimony, and burial of the dead—were developed due to their capacity to establish "plots" in the earth and in communal memory that might endure, outlasting their inhabitants in order to be inherited and tended to by subsequent generations.[10] (Significantly for our purposes, Vico assigns primary importance to sacrificial practice as an outgrowth of divination, which he identifies as one of the most primordial religious impulses that preceded formalized institutions.) In this way, the underlying impetus of ceremonial acts is mirrored in that of the laws that subsequently emerged within the "grounded" community as extensions and codifications of these foundational ritual forms of social existence. After all, Vico suggests, the root of "laws"—*leges*—names above all a basic human will to gather (*legere*) and bind (*ligare*), to cull particular elements from a greater, chaotic whole such that they can be sought and found in a single place, and with a unity of purpose, through time.[11]

In Storm's work this central element of inheritance identified by Vico informs the dialectical relation between law and penitence, for they both center upon the activity of memory, though from opposite directions: while law in a sense extends out of the past and into the present, atonement involves a reaching back into the past from out of the present. Even more specifically, though, they both involve an essential investment in *trace*, which for Storm is necessary for memory in the first place. And as we shall now see, in his late works the most legible traces are those left by acts of sacrifice.

---

10. Giambattista Vico, *The New Science (Third Edition of 1744)*, trans. Thomas Bergin and Max Fisch (Ithaca, NY: Cornell University Press, 1984), 7–10 (§§8–15), 97 (§333).

11. Vico, *The New Science*, 78 (§240).

II.

Sema and Submergence—*Aquis Submersus*

Often regarded as the text that marks the beginning of Storm's late period, *Aquis Submersus* (1876) boasts a plenitude of well-explored themes, from guilt, fate, and tragedy within the innermost narrative frame to art, memory, and temporal perception within the outermost one. Although any reading of *Aquis Submersus* will necessarily happen upon these well-trod paths, I hope to cover new ground by deepening our understanding of how the symbolism of drowning functions in the text—not merely as its thematic centerpiece, but as a determining component of its narrative logic and structure. First I will explore how law is associated with the temporality of inheritance insofar as its different manifestations take the form of generational atavism and supernatural revenance, both of which involve a resurgent "force" from the past that acts upon the present. Then I will explore how the climactic scene—a drowning—forms the root of the plot's second temporal underpinning: penitent retrospection. Ultimately, I will suggest that this scene takes place as a narrative instant poised between the "inheritant" force of law and the retrospective activity of penitence, a schema that becomes intrinsic to the function of sacrifice in Storm's late work overall.

The first narrative frame wastes little time in bringing us to the site of the novella's central, titular event. The narrator guides us through his memories of childhood, conjuring the setting of a palace garden and a dried fishpond near an embankment, from which one can see a distant church tower rising up from the otherwise uninterrupted horizontality of the heath. He then turns to the primary objects of his childhood fixation inside the church itself, whose walls are adorned with depictions of the Passion and other scenes surrounding the crucifixion. However, the narrator's attention is captured most by an image of a very different sort:

> Among all these strange and eerie things there hung in the nave of the church the innocent painting of a dead child, a beautiful boy of about five lying on a cushion with lace decoration, holding a white water lily

in his small pale hand. The delicate face, as though beseeching help, still carried the last sweet trace of life beside the horror of death; and an irresistible feeling of compassion came over me when I stood before this painting. But it was not hanging here alone; close by was a grim, dark-bearded man in clerical collar . . . according to my friend this was the father of the beautiful child; who, it is said even to this day, met his death in the pond in our pastor's enclosure.[12]

The noteworthy juxtaposition between the sacred and the secular images in the church invites us to compare them, most immediately in terms of their shared themes of innocence and death. The narrator's "irresistible feeling of compassion" seems to be less for the actual death of the unknown boy than for the young body's palpable contingency; the faint hint of life perceptible just beneath its form underscores the fact that things might have been otherwise. Storm is believed to have based this fictional portrait upon an actual painting he saw in the parish church of Drelsdorf some years prior to 1876.[13] The image in question constitutes part of the seventeenth-century Bonnix family epitaph, and shows the young son Heinrich, set against an indistinct, somber background and glancing pointedly out at the viewer with a red thistle suspended between his thumb and forefinger. The inscription beneath his portrait informs the viewer that he "drowned due to the carelessness of a servant" on May 7, 1656, at ten years of age (*Henricus Bonnix aquis incuria servi submersus obyt Ao 1656 7 May Aetatis 10*). If one contrasts the Drelsdorf portrait with the narrator's description of the painting in *Aquis Submersus*, it is almost as though the still-living visage of Heinrich Bonnix stirs beneath the lifeless one of the unnamed boy in the novella and lends it the "last sweet trace of life," to which the narrator reacts.

The narrator remembers how on one such visit to the church as a young man, he discovered a detail in the portrait that had hitherto escaped his notice: in the lower corner, four letters are inscribed

---

12. Theodor Storm, *A Doppelgänger—Aquis Submersus*, trans. Denis Jackson (London: Angel Books, 2015), 34.
13. Karl Friedrich Boll, "Das Bonnixsche Epitaph in Drelsdorf und die Kirchenbilder in Theodor Storms Erzählung *Aquis Submersus*," *Schriften der Theodor-Storm-Gesellschaft* 14 (1965): 24–38.

Figure 1. Bonnix family epitaph, 1656–1657, Evangelisch-lutherische Kirchengemeinde Drelsdorf. Courtesy of the Landesamt für Denkmalpflege Schleswig-Holstein.

in red paint: "C.P.A.S." Upon asking the pastor what they mean, the narrator is told that according to local legend, the latter two letters stand for "aquis submersus" (sunk in water), but that the significance of the first two are unknown. As we gradually learn, both the image and the inscription in the painting refer to an event of drowning, and by doing so indirectly rather than explicitly, they also convey a key significance of drowning symbolism in Storm's late work: like the division between surface and depths, both the image and the inscription imply that the relationship between signs and their referents relies upon memory as much as memory relies upon signs. As such, they also convey the fragility of this relationship, for the possibility of misinterpreting signs is mirrored by the uncertainty of remembering properly, or at all.

The frame narrative has in fact already introduced a connection between water and memory, for the narrator began his account at a

Figure 2. Bonnix family epitaph (detail, Heinrich Bonnix), 1656–1657, Evangelisch-lutherische Kirchengemeinde Drelsdorf. Courtesy of the Landesamt für Denkmalpflege Schleswig-Holstein.

dried-up fishpond before proceeding north to the pond outside the rectory where the boy in the painting is rumored to have drowned. The physical site of the water in the landscape is here linked with the image of the mysterious painted letters as things to which meaning and context must be assigned at a later point in time by means of remembrance. This correlation is made clearer as the narrator's account continues. He recalls standing before the portrait with the pastor and attempting to infer the first half of the inscription. The pastor notes that "casu periculoso" ("in a calamitous accident") had been suggested as a possibility, but the narrator's instinct points in a different direction:

"It could equally well be *Culpa?*"

"*Culpa?*" replied the pastor. "'Through guilt'?—but whose guilt?"

The grim picture of the old preacher then came into my mind, and without a moment's thought I said aloud: "Why not: *Culpa patris* [through guilt of the father]?" (35)

The pastor swiftly rejects this interpretation, pointing out that, were the father indeed responsible, he hardly would have wanted this fact to be immortalized alongside his own likeness. The narrator, at a loss once again, gives up. However, his uncanny intuition for the hidden significance of the inscription is vindicated several years later while he is visiting relatives in the nearby village. In an upstairs room he discovers another painting that "portrayed an elderly, serious-looking man. . . . [T]he painter had laid a pale boy in his arm who held a white water lily in his small, limp hand which hung down—and I recognized this boy from old. Here too it must have been death that had closed his eyes" (37). As had been the case with the first painting of the child, and like the pond he is said to have drowned in, here too the images correspond with a meaning that remains always just out of the narrator's reach. Both of the fictional Baroque portraits, which share a single referent, somehow "implant" a significance into the mind of the narrator that is not explicitly communicated by the content of the image. In this respect, they fulfill a central tenet of post-Reformation image making.[14] More importantly, though, their semantic and narrative functions effectively mirror those of the rectory's pond from the beginning of the frame narration. Each of these objects first emerges in the text as a signifier devoid of a signified; only through the course of the narrative can their secret meanings be retroactively ascribed to them.

The paintings' connection to the child's drowning thus extends beyond the context of the images themselves, for drowning, as such, deftly symbolizes the contingency of signs: when something disappears from the world above into the depths below, it reaffirms

---

14. Joseph Leo Koerner, *Reformation of the Image* (Chicago: University of Chicago Press, 2004), 105, 160–161.

the impossibility of leaving any trace on water.[15] To be "aquis submersus" is necessarily to be memorialized and thereby remembered in a different place and through a different medium than the water (in contrast to the scenario of being buried in the earth, for instance). Therefore the essentially semiotic nature of remembrance is emblematized not so much in the painting and its inscription as in the uninscribable water itself. The portrait in the church and its cryptic inscription are connected to the pond nearby, though not merely because both of them pertain to the same event of drowning. As narrative topoi that are also physical markers of a lost meaning and an extinguished life, both the portrait and the pond can be construed as *signs* in line with the ancient etymology of *sema*, which could also mean "tomb."[16] This dual sense deepens when the narrator discovers a testament written by the artist responsible for both images. The journal begins in the year 1661 as the painter Johannes (who is also the intradiegetic narrator of the novella's inner frame) is returning to North Frisia after his years of apprenticeship in Amsterdam. Johannes arrives at his destination, only to learn that his beloved patron, Gerhardus, has died. He then encounters Gerhardus's beautiful daughter Katharina, whom Johannes had known as a child and "in whom, as fate would later have it, all my life's happiness and misfortune and also all my nagging penance would be decided, now and for all time" (40). The grounds for this "penance" are first insinuated by the fact that Katharina has been promised in marriage to a local man by her bellicose and domineering brother, Wulf. Johannes, who promptly falls in love with Katharina after their years apart, is hired to paint her engagement portrait.

He sets about his work and soon develops the habit of spending his breaks in the family gallery, studying the faces of Katharina's

---

15. See Elisabeth Bronfen, "Leichenhafte Bilder—bildhafte Leichen: Zu dem Verhältnis von Bild und Referenz in Theodor Storms Novelle *Aquis Submersus*," in *Die Trauben des Zeuxis: Formen künstlerischer Wirklichkeitsaneignung*, ed. Hans Körner et al. (Hildesheim: G. Olms, 1990), 305–334; Claus-Michael Ort, *Zeichen und Zeit: Probleme des literarischen Realismus* (Tübingen: Niemeyer, 1998), 53–91, esp. 83–90.

16. See Gregory Nagy, "Sêma and Nóesis: The Hero's Tomb and the 'Reading' of Symbols in Homer and Hesiod," in *Greek Mythology and Poetics* (Ithaca, NY: Cornell University Press, 1992), 202–222.

forbears in search of her features. He finds these at once in the visages of her parents, but notes the curious fact that they bear no discernible resemblance to her brother. Rather, it is in a portrait from several generations earlier that he recognizes Wulf in the countenance of a sinister old woman: "I shuddered slightly at the soul that had departed this life so long ago; and I said to myself 'This is the one, here! What mysterious routes Nature takes! Sometimes, for a century and more, running as though hidden under cover through the blood of generations, then, long forgotten, suddenly resurfacing again to trouble the living'" (53). Crucially, the association of heredity with the rhythms of nature's laws is expressed using the language of submergence and resurfacing. The image Johannes describes is that of nature's claim to two dialectical movements: one upward and into the visible realm of physiognomy, lived history, and recognition, and another that dips back down beneath the surface, remaining hidden from sight and knowledge until the process repeats itself. This portrayal of genetic inheritance as a kind of continuous oscillation between surfaces and depths that extends forward through time is then elaborated upon: Katharina explains that the woman in the portrait—known as the Ancestress—had been the spouse of her father's ancestor more than a century before. According to local lore, her daughter had been in love with a man beneath her station and drowned herself out of despair after the match was forbidden and cursed by the Ancestress, whose ghost is rumored to haunt the property still.

It is interesting to notice that the narrative quickly moves from considering the natural laws of heredity to the human laws of matriarchal command and links the two together by the spectral "law" of the curse—all expressions of law's roots in the act of binding (*ligare*). Equally implicit are law's etymological bonds with the notion of "legacy" as a "legible" product of "gathering" (*legere*). However, all these valences of law that converge within the legacy of the Ancestress are simultaneously counterposed by the imagery of submergence—of dissolution and disappearance—invoked throughout the passage: first in the conceptualization of nature's dialectical movement between the surface and depths of the "blood of generations," and then in the legend of the Ancestress and her daughter's drowning. There is a central association between imperative and the determination of the family line—that is, an association between law and inheritance in a broad sense. Yet, in slight contrast to how this association appeared in *The Village on the Moor*, here it does so not only in the economic context of inheritance, but also in the natural context of generational progression, and ultimately in the supernatural context of continuation (haunting).

Much has been written about how the Ancestress's atavistic will seems to become an actual, baleful agent in Johannes and Katharina's love story.[17] But what I wish to emphasize on this point is simply how the logic of inheritance central to the Ancestress's interdiction is countered by her child's death in water. This interdiction goes on to take the form of a curse, becoming a "force" from the past that weighs upon the present; the daughter's drowning signals an individual act of decision that moves against her mother's command, and in so doing pushes back against the insistent diachrony of law. Water becomes the topos of law's halted progress, for it not only flouts the content of the command, but also cuts short the forward march of time intrinsic to it by ending a life (and with it a bloodline). If we recall Johannes's earlier description of the natural order's manifestation within the inherited characteristics of offspring as a "coming to the surface," then the daughter's drowning assumes quite a subtle significance: the act of sinking underwater not only moves against the Ancestress's imperative of obligation (*ob-ligare*) to the family line, but also on a figurative level moves against the upward and forward-moving current of nature's "mysterious routes."

Within this short scene, then, the act of drowning stands in opposition to maternal law and natural order as forces of continuation. At this point in the text the motif of drowning is tied to the active choice of a free agent (the daughter) to take her own life in reaction to her mother's prohibition. However, the central scene of

---

17. For two recent examples, see Christian Begemann, "Figuren der Wiederkehr: Erinnerung, Tradition, Vererbung und andere Gespenster der Vergangenheit bei Theodor Storm," and Elisabeth Strowick, "'Eine andere Zeit': Storms Rahmentechnik des Zeitsprungs," both in *Wirklichkeit und Wahrnehmung: Neue Perspektive auf Theodor Storm*, ed. Elisabeth Strowick and Ulrike Vedder (Bern: Peter Lang, 2013), 13–37, 55–72.

drowning around which *Aquis Submersus* revolves (that of the boy in the painting) has been designated from the outset as an unwilled event in which paternal guilt rather than filial decision is the principal cause. In the last section of the novella, the temporal opposition between drowning (synchrony) and law (diachrony) will be complemented by the retrospective acts of memorialization and penitence that return to the moment of drowning from later points in time. As we shall see, these acts are instigated by Johannes's realization that the drowning constitutes a tragic sacrifice for which he himself bears responsibility.

The preceding scene foreshadows how events will unfold, given the fact that Katharina's brother Wulf has forced her into an engagement to a man she does not love, and that she and Johannes harbor feelings for one another. One summer evening (the feast of St. John, to be precise), Wulf and Johannes have an altercation in the village tavern, and Wulf sets his two hunting dogs upon Johannes, who is forced to flee back to the house.[18] He takes refuge in Katharina's bedroom, narrowly escaping the hounds after she helps him climb through her window. Their long-awaited night of passion at last occurs, and the following morning Johannes sets off for Amsterdam in the hopes of securing a home and livelihood to which he can one day escape with Katharina. When he is finally able to return for her several years later, however, she is nowhere to be found. Johannes soon receives a commission to paint the portrait of a pastor from a nearby village, and so he makes his way north.

He arrives at the parish rectory and meets the pastor, who is accompanied by his son, a young, pale boy of about four. As the days pass, Johannes finds himself inexplicably drawn to the child, and after a time finally discerns the root of his fixation: "the eyes of the handsome pale boy—they were *her* eyes!" (86). In the same instant that he recognizes Katharina in the boy's physiognomy, he also realizes that she must be the pastor's wife. An even more dramatic recog-

---

18. On the numerous symbolic resonances between the folk rituals associated with *Johannisnacht* and Storm's novella, with particular attention to the traditional practice of sacrificial drowning, see Gerhard Kaiser, "Aquis Submersus—versunkene Kindheit: Ein Literaturpsychologischer Versuch über Theodor Storm," *Euphorion* 73 (1979): 413, 415, 430–431.

nition soon takes place in the rectory's garden, however. In the story's climactic scene, Johannes returns from a walk on the moor and notices an enclosure of willows framing a small pond, behind which he discovers Katharina playing with the child. Unaware of Johannes's presence, Katharina at one point moves toward him and kneels down: "she let her head sink onto her breast, and it was as if, unseen by the child, she wanted to rest in her sorrow" (91).

This outwardly simple vignette in fact plays out a tragic disparity of intent and outcome, for in desiring not to be seen by her son for a brief moment, Katharina unwittingly lays the path for his death, which will occur while *he* is unseen for a fatal span of moments. The division between visibility and hiddenness anticipates the drowning scene (and indeed the figural dimensions of water itself), which will divide the text between the "stage" of the adults' encounter, to which the reader is given access, and the unseen, "offstage" (*obskené*) space mere feet away in which the child perishes. The seen "scene" (*skené*) of action comprises classical dramatic moments of recognition, as well as a struggle between moral duty and erotic impulse, with Katharina and Johannes respectively embodying each. Johannes pulls Katharina from her crouched position and confronts her about her marriage to the pastor during his absence in Amsterdam; Katharina defends herself with the revelation that the pastor "got this post because of it . . . and your child [got] an honorable name" (92).

The emotional force of this revelation that the boy is Johannes's son is coupled with a tension between two forms of loyalty—parental obligation to the child's social legitimacy and romantic fidelity to the child's biological father—that incites a feverish dialogue. Johannes, initially in shock, expresses desperation and anger at the prospect of being separated from his lover and child by mere custom, while Katharina displays both resignation and relief over the societal and moral equilibrium that this custom ensures. The narration notes, "At this moment a faint singing came to us. 'The child,' she said. 'I must go to him; he could come to harm!' But my senses were fixed entirely on the woman I desired" (92–93). As the child's voice carries through the willows, Katharina makes to leave with a final appeal to moral obligation: "I am another man's wife;

don't forget that." But Johannes's journal recounts that "these words filled me with a wild anger"; passion and piety collide, and the former proves to be stronger, for Johannes pulls Katharina back to him, and they embrace fervently. The text does not specify for how long, nor does it indicate when precisely the child's song falls silent. This distended instant coincides with what Johannes will subsequently realize to be the sacrifice of his son to erotic passion—not *casu periculoso*, but *culpa patris*.

The two lovers finally part when they hear the pastor's voice cutting through the now quiet autumn air, calling for Katharina. Johannes returns to the house but is not there long before a scream—Katharina's—rings out from the direction of the pond. After hurrying back to the enclosure of willows, Johannes finds "only turbid water and traces of wet mud" (94). He then encounters the pastor, who reveals that Katharina has confessed the child's illicit origin. A graver report follows, however: "His parents have let him drown!" The pastor enjoins Johannes immediately to capture his dead son's likeness in paint so that the portrait can be placed in the church. Johannes accepts, but before he begins work, he has a critical moment of realization that "suddenly lift[ed] my life's guilt and repentance out of the darkness like a stroke of lightning, such that I saw the whole chain of it, link by link, light up before me" (95).

Johannes sets about immortalizing the remains of his son that have been retrieved from the water, copying down the small, supine form on his canvas. When he comes to the hands, he suddenly takes artistic license and adds "a white water lily to the portrait, held in his hand as though he had fallen asleep while playing with it" (97). Precisely by virtue of its arbitrary introduction into the image, the water lily, shown to be held as though in sleep, becomes an allegory for more than the jointure of innocence, death, and water.[19] The portrait

---

19. Interestingly, the white lily is also one of the main instances of the narrative's deviation from the Bonnix portrait, in which the young subject holds a red thistle (figure 2). Even more interestingly, it was this very detail of the painting that Storm himself could not recall from his visit to Drelsdorf, according to his letter to Paul Heyse from June 20, 1876: "A couple of years ago during a visit to the North Frisian village of Drelsdorf, which lies two miles from [Husum], I saw in the old church some poorly done portraits of a pastor's family from the area. The boy was

as a whole converges upon this small detail of the flower that derives not from the real world but instead from the artist's imagination, and as such stands for Johannes's recognition of guilt for his son's drowning; by an act of independent will similar to that of artistic invention, Johannes acknowledges his removal of the child from the real world by inserting a new image into the painted one. This acknowledgment continues to unfold dramatically: after leaving the room for a short pause in his labor, Johannes reenters and notices that

> it appeared that the eyelids in the small face had opened a little. Then I bent over in the delusion that I might once again win my child's glance, but as the cold eyes lay before me, I was filled with dread; it was as though I was looking at the eyes of that family's Ancestress, as though she wanted to announce from the dead face of our child: "So my curse has caught up with you both!" But at the same time . . . I wrapped my arms round the small pale corpse and gathered it up to my breast and amid bitter tears hugged my child for the first time. "No, no, my poor child, your soul . . . did not look out of such eyes; it is death alone that looks out here. Nothing has arisen out of the depths of the terrible past; nothing but your father's guilt; it has plunged us all into the dark flood." . . . Then I dipped my brush in a dark red and wrote below in the shadow of the picture the letters: *C.P.A.S.*, which was to mean: *CULPA PATRIS AQUIS SUBMERSUS.* "Drowned through the fault of the father." (97–98)

Johannes thus articulates a sacrificial consciousness similar to that of Goethe's Ottilie, whose contrition in *Elective Affinities* pertained precisely to her awareness of the fact that *she* lost the child to the water as a consequence of choice—as opposed to fate, destiny, or a curse having *taken* the child as some sort of propitiatory victim. In both texts, drowning constitutes the terrible cost of such choice and thereby illuminates a distinct sense of sacrifice.[20] Moreover, it pre-

---

painted again as a corpse, but I do not remember whether he had a flower (or what kind)." In Storm, *Der Briefwechsel zwischen Paul Heyse und Theodor Storm*, vol. 1, ed. Georg Plotke (Munich: J. F. Lehmann, 1917), 125–126.

20. Helga Bleckwenn also offers a comparative reading of these two drowning scenes, but emphasizes the theme of discontinuation rather than sacrifice, arguing that the children in both texts represent hope and future possibilities that are foiled. Bleckwenn, "Aquis Submersus: das Motiv des ertrinkenden Kindes in Storms Novelle und in Goethes *Die Wahlverwandtschaften*," *Schriften der Theodor-Storm-Gesellschaft* 52 (2003): 75–83.

cipitates an inward transition from the psychological context of impulsive *Wahl* to one of reflective decision; like Ottilie, after acknowledging his personal guilt Johannes is filled with penitent resolve and he decides to add two visible *semata* of this guilt to the portrait: a pictorial allegory (the water lily) as well as the written cipher. This sequence invites us to recall the other painting associated with drowning in the novella—namely, that of the Ancestress—along with the other valence of "parental law" that was tied to the natural order of generational inheritance. The image that Johannes paints, by comparison, stands for the retroactive acknowledgment of a past transgression that cannot be undone. In looking from one image to the other, therefore, we also witness one law of inheritance being replaced by another: the curse that preys upon the individual in the present against their will has been substituted by the willed remembrance of something that one would likely wish to forget but chooses *not to* in a gesture of penitence.

Whether Storm consciously intended it or not, the painted lily's subtle concatenation of guilt and confession with the element of water invokes an established paradigm of atonement that subtends the juxtapositions of drowning and baptismal motifs in *Aquis Submersus*. Foucault neatly explicates the connection between confession (and penitence more broadly) and water in his lectures on Tertullian and the origins of baptism as a sacrament. He first traces the Christian concept of repentance to the Platonic notion of *metanoia*, which is "the change of the soul ... the movement by which it turns away from what until then it had been looking for, and to which it was attached."[21] Tertullian would go on to argue that repentance—not to be confused with penitence, which involves *acts* of contrition, penance, and ultimately atonement, as opposed to mere remorse—was innately linked to the figure of John the Baptist, whose practice consisted first and foremost in "*baptimus paenitentiae*, the baptism of repentance ... that is to say nothing more than men's *regret* for

---

21. Michel Foucault, *On the Government of the Living (Lectures at the Collège de France, 1979–1980)*, ed. Michel Senellart, trans. Graham Burchell (New York: Palgrave Macmillan, 2014), 128. Compare William L. Cunningham, "Wassersymbolik in *Aquis Submersus*," *Schriften der Theodor-Storm-Gesellschaft* 27 (1978): 43; Kaiser, "Aquis Submersus—versunkene Kindheit," 415.

their own sins."[22] If we consider the conjoined symbolism of baptism and drowning that Storm associates with Johannes, a similar progression is noticeable: first is the tragically literal submergence of his son that incites Johannes's sorrowful recognition of guilt (repentance), followed by his subsequent documentations of penitence and confession (the portrait and the journal).

While *Aquis Submersus* is sometimes read as a story about the inability of art to transcend finitude, in many ways it is more a story about how the decision to embrace this inability might lay the foundation for atonement.[23] At the beginning of this chapter, we saw how Storm's writing up to 1870 had begun to link law to the concept of inheritance (primarily in conventional terms of property and capital). This model of law is also at work in *Aquis Submersus*, where it takes the form of both natural and supernatural continuations of the past within the present. However, we also observed a second temporal motif emerge—namely, the retrospectivity of memory and penitence; indeed, the entire frame narration turns out to be a confession of the guilt that was only cryptically acknowledged in the painting. As both the point within which Johannes can visually localize his guilt (reinforced by the inscription) and the *Ansatzpunkt* (point of departure) for the frame narrator's own memory of how he gradually pieced together the rectory's tragic past,[24] the image becomes a kind of portal: Johannes projects his representation of paternal guilt and filial innocence into the future *through* the image, while the frame narrator in a sense returns the gaze from his

---

22. Foucault, *Government of the Living*, 129, 154 (emphasis added).

23. Compare Sven-Aage Jørgensen, "Vergangenheit und Vergänglichkeit: Zur Funktion des Erinnerns in Theodor Storms Novellen," *Schriften der Theodor-Storm-Gesellschaft* 35 (1986): 11–12.

24. Here I'm employing the term *Ansatzpunkt* in the hermeneutical sense outlined by Erich Auerbach when he describes "the following methodological principle: in order to accomplish a major work of synthesis it is imperative to locate a point of departure [*Ansatzpunkt*], a handle, as it were, by which the subject can be seized. The point of departure must be the election of a firmly circumscribed, easily comprehensible set of phenomena whose interpretation is a radiation out from them and which orders and interprets a greater region than they themselves occupy." Auerbach, "Philology and *Weltliteratur*," trans. Maire and Edward Said, *The Centennial Review* 13, no. 1 (1969): 13–14.

present, looking back through the painting and into the past.[25] This aspect of the portrait anticipates similar dimensions of what Walter Benjamin would later describe as the dialectical image:

> Every present is determined by the images that are synchronic with it: each "now" is the now of a particular recognizability. In it, truth is charged to the bursting point with time.... It is not that what is past casts its light on what is present, or what is present its light on what is past; rather, image is that wherein what has been comes together in a flash with the now to form a constellation.... The image that is read—which is to say, the image in the now of its recognizability—bears to the highest degree the imprint of the perilous critical moment on which all reading is founded.[26]

The image that Johannes paints contains a similarly "perilous" moment that is shared by both narrative frames (as well as by the gazes of their respective narrators). The moment of image-reading is precarious because it is challenged to house a flash of proper understanding in which the "now" and the "has been" simultaneously condition *each other*. Storm's novella literalizes this precarity of the read image, not merely by structuring the tale around a portrait and inscription whose veiled meanings must be interpreted, but by positioning the very act of viewing as an instant that conjugates two distinct narrative times. Within these narrative times, two distinct processes of meaning-making take place, one commemorative and the other hermeneutic. As we shall see, this "perilous moment" is a trope that Storm would return to more than once in subsequent works.

---

25. Christiane Arndt, "Die Überschreitung des Rahmens—Theodor Storms *Aquis Submersus*," in *Abschied von der Wirklichkeit: Probleme bei der Darstellung von der Realität im deutschsprachigen literarischen Realismus* (Freiburg im Breisgau: Rombach, 2009), 193–223; Tove Holmes, "Literary Images: Viewing and Visuality in German Realism" (PhD diss., Johns Hopkins University, 2011), 149–180; Franziska A. Irsigler, *Beschriebene Gesichter: Ekphrastische Porträts in der Erzählkunst des Poetischen Realismus* (Bielefeld: Aisthesis, 2012), 410–411.

26. Walter Benjamin, *The Arcades Project*, trans. Howard Eiland and Kevin McLaughlin (Cambridge, MA: Harvard University Press, 2002), 462–463 (translation modified) / Benjamin, *Das Passagen-Werk*, in *Gesammelte Schriften*, vol. 5.1, ed. Rolf Tiedemann (Frankfurt am Main: Suhrkamp, 1982), 578 (N 3,1).

III.

In the final decade of his life, Storm produced numerous texts that carry forward as well as develop the core themes of transgression, guilt, and inheritance brought so vividly to the foreground in *Aquis Submersus*. Themes such as these are familiar hallmarks of the "Chroniknovelle" genre for which Storm's late writing is well known, yet one feels compelled to reiterate their close association with drowning scenes in his writing. *Carsten Curator* (1877), *Renate* (1878), *Hans and Heinz Kirch* (1882), *John Riew'* (1885), *Bötjer Basch* (1886), and *Ein Doppelgänger* (1887) all feature actual, implied, or narrowly averted deaths in water that occur in constellation with one or several of these themes. However, the specific issues of sacrifice and atonement receive their most complex and poetic treatment in Storm's very last novella.

"Time of Leaden Inheritance"—*The Rider on the White Horse*

As befits a final work (and, for many critics, a magnum opus), *The Rider on the White Horse* (1888) draws together the leitmotifs from the novellas that precede it: the climax of the tale—portrayed through three separate levels of narrated memory—comprises a self-sacrificial drowning that aims to atone for transgressed laws.

As in *Aquis Submersus*, the outermost narrative frame takes the form of remembrance—specifically, the narrator's memory of reading a chronicle as a child. We are promptly inserted into this account (the middle frame), whose narrator recalls riding along the austere North Frisian coast during a violent storm one October night around 1830.[27] The first crucial aspect of the account's mise en scène, in contrast to that of *Aquis Submersus*, is that the narrator's vision of the landscape is almost completely impeded. The sea and sky to his

---

27. On Storm's sources of inspiration for the setting and plot, see Gerd Eversberg, *Der echte Schimmelreiter: So (er)fand Storm seinen Hauke Haien* (Heide: Boyens, 2010). Compare Karl Ernst Laage's commentary in *SW*, 3:1064–1082.

right coalesce within an indistinguishable swarm of darkness and water. This impaired visibility results in a general sense of blurred boundaries that at once foreshadows spectral phenomena; and, as if on cue, something emerges from out of the gloom ahead of the narrator: "I heard nothing, but ever more clearly as the light of the half-moon grew sharper, I thought I could make out a dark shape, and soon, as it came nearer, I saw it. It sat on a horse, a high-boned, haggard white horse. A dark mantle fluttered across the figure's shoulders, and as he flew past, two burning eyes stared at me out of a pale face."[28] This passage establishes a dramatic contrast between the swirling darkness of the coast and the detail of the apparition; soon, however, these supernatural forms are swallowed up by the natural environment: "I saw [the horse and rider], farther and farther away; then it suddenly seemed as though I could see their shadows riding along the inner side of the dike, facing the land.... When I reached the place where they had vanished, I saw gleaming under me, in a marsh close to the dike, the water of a large hollow.... Even taking the protective dike into account, the water was conspicuously unruffled. The rider could not have troubled it; I saw nothing more of him" (185–186).

The remainder of the novella comprises the biography of the ghostly rider, Hauke Haien, and the events that lead to the instant of descent and disappearance whose spectral repetition the narrator has just witnessed. The teller of this tale is yet another frame narrator, the schoolmaster from the nearby village. He begins the story of Hauke Haien (which forms the innermost frame), born in the local village toward the middle of the previous century and obsessed from his earliest years with finding a solution to the ancient threat posed to the community by the sea. A great deal has been written about the qualities and implications of Hauke's *Bildung*, so let it suffice here simply to mention the most important points. Though the son of a modest farmer, Hauke teaches himself geometry at a young age and soon combines his prodigious mathematical gifts with his fascination for the sea, spending whole days staring out at the water. He

---

28. Theodor Storm, *The Rider on the White Horse and Selected Stories*, trans. James Wright (New York: NYRB Classics, 1964), 185.

recognizes that the walls of the dike have been constructed at too steep an angle, resulting in increased force and erosion from the breaking waves, and so he resolves to design and build a new one. Filled with ambition not only to assert control over nature but also to gain respect and admiration from the village, Hauke sets out to marry the local dikereeve's daughter, Elke, and eventually to become dikereeve himself.

The elemental conflict at the core of Hauke's confrontation with the sea is the one around which the other dialectical relationships that pervade the story converge (for instance, rationality versus superstition, Enlightenment versus myth, and culture versus nature), all of which could be argued to derive from the classical relationship between *techne* and *physis*. For the purposes of this chapter, I wish to begin with a relatively small component of this much larger network of themes—namely, the opposition between the physical longevity of the natural landscape and the "spectral" immateriality of human memory. While Hauke's innovative dike and the sea remain, Hauke's very being becomes an object of local superstition, the last instants of his life and decision calcified within a ghostly repetition.

In what follows, I explore how these variant "spatializations" of memory—the permanence of material and natural memorials, on the one hand, and the shadowy spectrality of revenance and legend, on the other—relate to Hauke's drowning. This will enable us to observe how, in his last story, Storm once again conceptualizes inheritance and retrospection in terms of law and atonement and portrays the liminal threshold between them as an instant of sacrifice.

Sacrifice Deferred

As a point of entry, it warrants mentioning that Theodor Adorno regarded the representation of memory (and temporality more generally) in spatial terms as Storm's primary narrative trademark. So central did Adorno find this spatialization of time and its traces to be in Storm's writing that he suggested that it was intelligible even in the typographical form of the texts themselves. In what he terms

"Storm's solemn hyphen," for instance, Adorno not only sees a visual ligament joining past events to the subsequent recollection of them like "wrinkles on the forehead of the text." More significantly, he identifies in them a delineation of a "time of leaden inheritance" that seems to contain "something of nature's baleful contiguity.... This is how discreetly Myth conceals itself in the nineteenth century; it finds a hiding place within typography."[29]

This mythic element, which Adorno links to the portrayal of time and memory, is ubiquitous in the story. However, the component that is most relevant to the present discussion of Hauke's trajectory, culminating in his dramatic final act, is the confrontation between two different paradigms of law. The first of these is found in the ancient Frisian practice of sacrificing a living creature in order to ensure the longevity of a new human structure (in this case, Hauke's new dike). This primeval, cultic requirement clashes starkly with the second mode of law, the rationalist codes and imperatives of morality that Hauke upholds and eventually transgresses. As we will see, the collision of these differing modes of lawfulness—one actualized in rituals of sacrificial offering and the other in the repudiation of such practices—establishes the conditions for Hauke's suicidal drowning, which he himself ultimately designates as a sacrificial offering.

The first paradigm of "cultic law" is introduced shortly after Hauke, recently instated as dikereeve, is inspired to construct a new dike that will both redouble security against flooding and integrate a new swath of fertile marshland into the territory already protected by the current wall. Elke (now his wife) cautions him not to be hasty, noting that the villagers will most likely resist the project, citing a local belief that the tidal streams ramifying inland across the vast shore should not be obstructed. "Why not?" Hauke replies. "That's just an excuse for laziness!" (232). Elke goes on to recount a gruesome rite that she remembers overhearing the household servants

---

29. Theodor Adorno, "Satzzeichen," in *Noten zur Literatur: Gesammelte Schriften*, vol. 11, ed. Rolf Tiedemann (Frankfurt am Main: Suhrkamp, 1974), 108, 109.

discussing when she was a child. "They said there was only one way to build a dam out there: to bury something alive in it while it was being built" (232–233). Hauke again dismisses this archaic imperative as inane superstition, but the practice is soon enough revealed to exercise as strong a hold over the local imagination as ever. When the construction of the new dike is nearly complete, Hauke discovers his workers furtively trying to bury a stray dog in the earthen wall. He commands them to stop, declaring, "I won't allow any sacrilege in our work!" The language of "sacrilege" immediately establishes a framework of lawfulness that is divided down the middle: Hauke, disgusted by the "heathen nonsense" of his workers, forbids them from performing the blood sacrifice that they believe to be necessary for guaranteeing the community's protection from the sea. The moralistic mode of imperative invoked by Hauke proves not to be as easily observed, however.

Later in the story Hauke is conducting his usual inspections of the dike. At the point where the original wall meets his newly constructed one, he makes a disturbing discovery: the older structure bears the signs of erosion and instability at the precise spot where the tidal streams once flowed inland. Hauke is overcome with panic, recognizing in an instant that this vulnerable section of the dike could spell the doom of the entire village if it were ever exposed to a sufficiently violent storm. In the same instant, he realizes that the only way to protect the village would be to sacrifice the recently won moorland to the sea by puncturing the wall of his new dike and reverting to the original boundary line in order to alleviate the potential force of the waves.

Having infringed upon the ancient laws of sacrifice by depriving the new dike of a living offering, Hauke will now transgress against his own moral framework by carrying out a burial of a figurative sort. Desperate over the choice between either undoing the years of vision that had been devoted to his new dike or investing the additional labor and expense that would be necessary for reinforcing the original structure, Hauke allows a simple, dangerous thought to take hold of him: perhaps the damage is not as grave as appearances might suggest. He says nothing to Elke of what he has discovered, though she senses an unspoken burden, and the following morning he returns to the site. At first cannot find the damaged spot:

> But then, shading his eyes with one hand, he saw it. He must have been deceived by the shadows of the twilight, yesterday. The bed of the current seemed shallower now.... "So it wasn't really so terrible," said Hauke to himself with a sigh of relief.... The year wore on, but the older it grew, the more plainly the new grass forced through the covering of straw, and whenever Hauke walked or rode past the unsettling [*unheimliche*] spot, his anxiety grew accordingly. Sometimes he averted his eyes; sometimes he rode closer along the inside of the dike; several times he simply had his horse, already saddled, led back to the stable. But then he would slip away from home and hurry back out to the dike; even during these clandestine expeditions, he sometimes turned back, unable to trust his own eyes to examine the place again ... for the dike was like a wound in his conscience that had taken on external form before him ... and there was no one to whom he could speak about it, not even his wife. (271)

The intriguing association that occurs in this passage between Hauke's emotional interior and the physical landscape around him calls to mind several core themes of contemporary eco-phenomenology that it is worth pausing to consider. Gernot Böhme, for instance, has devoted much attention to the epistemological as well as ecological implications of the perceiving human body's coextension with the natural world. Böhme borrows the Husserlian term *Leib* as a label for this interpenetration of our inside and outside, and describes it as the means and mode by which we are part of nature as understood in the ancient sense of *physis* (that is, everything that participates in Being). *Physis* is "given" to us in a phenomenological process of encounter with the *Leib* in which we find ourselves, and yet it is simultaneously already part of us (as are we of it) in that same *Leib* within which it too is always already rooted.[30] According to Böhme, this comprehensive "lived body" is not to be conceived in strictly medical or biologi-

---

30. Gernot Böhme, *Leib: Die Natur, die wir selbst sind* (Frankfurt am Main: Suhrkamp, 2019), 31. Compare David Abram, "Philosophy on the Way to Ecology," in *The Spell of the Sensuous: Perception and Language in a More-Than-Human World* (New York: Pantheon Books, 1996), 31–72.

cal terms in the same way as one's empirical body (*Körper*) is—"by *Leib* I mean much more the primary way of Being-in-the-World and the foundation of self-consciousness within self-sensation."[31]

In Storm's description above, and along similar lines as Freud's analysis of the uncanny some thirty years later (1919), the primacy of the "unsettling" *Unheimlichkeit* that Hauke experiences in relation to the dike wall derives from the fact that something interior and hidden (*heimlich*) to him—the "wound in his conscience"—has become unconcealed (*unheimlich*) and "taken on external form before him." This both anticipates and inverts the structure of what Böhme has called an "ecological aesthetics of nature," which springs, not from "suffering at the hands of society, but rather from suffering at the hands of nature insofar as the human begins to feel in and with his own body [*am eigenen Leibe*] that which he has inflicted upon nature."[32] The great tragedy of Storm's novella, however, is that Hauke will not come to experience the repercussions of his actions within his own *Leib* alone; rather, as a direct consequence of them, he in fact will unilaterally incorporate the coastline and its inhabitants—human and nonhuman alike—into a collective *Leib* that will not merely "feel" but ultimately be destroyed by "that which he has inflicted upon nature."

In the final scene of the schoolmaster's narration, Hauke is given one last chance to remedy his concealed recognition of the compromised dike wall and the disaster it portends. A torrential storm unlike any before lashes the coast, and Hauke frantically patrols the wall's perimeter. Suddenly he notices local men attempting to perforate the new dike, which he had privately recognized before as the only means of saving the village from a flood. But in this moment, Hauke, blinded by fury, forbids them; seconds later, at the point where the old and new walls converge at the "*unheimliche* spot*,*" the sea breaks through. "'It's your fault, Dikereeve!' a voice cried from the company. 'Your fault! You'll have to answer to God for this!'" (279).

---

31. Gernot Böhme, *Für eine ökologische Naturästhethik* (Frankfurt am Main: Suhrkamp, 1989), 33.

32. Böhme, *Für eine ökologische Naturästhethik*, 24.

Before turning to the final moment of Hauke's story—the very moment witnessed by the frame narrator as a spectral replay at the beginning of the text—we must briefly consider how its sacrificial implications have been sown. In particular, I want to examine several senses in which Hauke's concealment of the truth (both from Elke and from himself) bears a direct relation to his final act of atonement and offering. Understanding this relation will also allow us to better apprehend the kind of trace that Hauke's sacrificial drowning leaves behind. These specific issues surrounding secrecy, sacrifice, and intelligibility can be fruitfully approached via a detour into Søren Kierkegaard's thinking about them.

Sacrifice Conceived

The 1843 book (or "Dialectical Lyric," according to its subtitle) *Fear and Trembling* is first and foremost a sustained meditation upon the scene of Abraham's near sacrifice of Isaac in Genesis 22.[33] On a more essential level, though, it is an experimental foray into the imagined psychological interior of Abraham, from the moment of God's command that he sacrifice Isaac, to the three-day journey to Mount Moriah, to the instant in which he wholly commits, knife raised, to kill his son. Though there is much to be said about this text, the aspect of it that will be most immediately helpful for my reading of Hauke's drowning is Kierkegaard's linked assessments of sacrificial register, on the one hand, and the hiding of truth, on the other.

Throughout *Fear and Trembling*, the primary scale upon which Kierkegaard measures the gradation of Abraham's sacrificial will is his concealment from Isaac of what is about to happen. For Kierkegaard, the various registers within which Abraham's silence might be read—the aesthetic, the ethical, and the religious (a signature delineation that runs through most of Kierkegaard's work)—bear directly upon the sacrificial status of Abraham's (intended) act. Within the "aesthetic" sphere, one individual's decision to hide a certain truth

---

33. Søren Kierkegaard, *Fear and Trembling / The Sickness unto Death*, trans. Walter Lowrie (Princeton, NJ: Princeton University Press, 1968), 21–132.

from another individual might correspond to what is right if the concealed information had been deemed potentially traumatizing or otherwise painful for the latter. Within the ethical or "universal" sphere, by contrast, moral imperative mandates that the truth *always* be revealed, and thus designates any concealment of truth (regardless of the emotional or "aesthetic" effect it might have upon those who learn it) as being in opposition to what is right. However, within the so-called "religious" sphere, it becomes impossible either to reveal *or* to conceal truth (in this case, divinely imparted truth) because any semantic content it might contain would transcend human understanding in the first place; a message from God can never be fully enunciated or kept silent.[34] The implications of this classic apophatic stance extend beyond the domain of signification and language, however, for Kierkegaard maintains that any such act of faith necessarily occurs outside—and at times via an outright suspension of—the ethical. This is because faith places the human individual in a *direct* relation to the Absolute (the divine), whereas ethics *integrates* the individual into a universal (human) context.[35]

Having established these categories for judging human action in connection with the specific example of deciding to reveal (or not to reveal) the truth, Kierkegaard turns to the explicit issue of sacrifice. Like Erich Auerbach after him, Kierkegaard contrasts the ancient Greek paradigm with the biblical, taking the example of Agamemnon's sacrifice of his daughter Iphigenia.[36] Agamemnon, as a tragic hero, commits an unethical act of filicide (that is, an individuated transgression) in the service of a higher (collective or universal) ethical end. In this way Agamemnon "finds repose in the universal" and so is freed from having "only himself alone," which, as Kierkegaard notes, is what "constitutes the dreadfulness of the situation" that befalls Abraham.[37] That is, Agamemnon exchanges

---

34. Kierkegaard, *Fear and Trembling*, 94, 122.
35. Kierkegaard, *Fear and Trembling*, 64, 67.
36. Erich Auerbach, "Die Narbe des Odysseus," in *Mimesis: Dargestellte Wirklichkeit in der abendländischen Literatur* (Tübingen: Francke, 2001), 5–27, esp. 9–14.
37. Kierkegaard, *Fear and Trembling*, 89.

one level of the ethical for another, replacing his solitary anguish over having to kill his daughter with the acknowledgment and fulfillment of his royal duty to his troops and kingdom. By contrast, a "hero of faith" such as Abraham must suspend the universal altogether—according to which his acts of concealment and his intended act of slaughter have no intelligible correspondence with the ethical—through his acknowledgment and fulfillment of a direct relation to the divine.[38]

Ethics and reason are not the only things at stake in Abraham's sacrifice, though. Jacques Derrida notes how this scene (like many of the later Gospels) presents an annulment of the traditional sacrificial logic rooted in an economy of exchange and anticipated return. Ironically, he suggests, a sacrifice carried out in the register of faith as Kierkegaard conceives it is one in which there *can be no faith* in a symmetrical return on what is expended; here it is not an economy of sacrifice that is at issue, but the "sacrifice of economy." This is the paradoxical "commerce" of Christian sacrifice prefigured by Abraham's decision to offer up Isaac: it is "an economic calculation [that] integrates absolute loss," and yet in this very same "instant in which the sacrifice is at it were consummated ... God returns his son to him and decides by sovereign decision, by an absolute gift, to reinscribe sacrifice within an economy by means of what thenceforth comes to resemble a reward."[39]

Here it is necessary to consult the Jewish hermeneutic tradition, specifically the midrashic reading of this story in the *Bereshit Rabbah* (ca. 300–500 CE), according to which Isaac's age can be calculated to be anywhere between twenty-six and thirty-seven years,

---

38. Kierkegaard, *Fear and Trembling*, 69–70. Stanley Cavell suggests that the "pain" and "danger" of Abraham's silence derives not so much from a torsion between this acknowledgment and his ethical horror over "the inevitability of his silence," but more from his "fear of the false word, and the deep wish that the right word be found for doing what one must." Cavell, "Kierkegaard's *On Authority and Revelation*," in *Must We Mean What We Say?* (Cambridge: Cambridge University Press, 2002), 165.

39. Jacques Derrida, *The Gift of Death*, trans. David Wills (Chicago: University of Chicago Press, 1996), 95–96, 102.

thus implying that he is not only fully able to comprehend the unfolding situation, but also in a position to physically resist Abraham. Consequently, the reading goes, Isaac willingly allowed himself to be bound (LVI:VIII).[40] The midrashic understanding of this scene thus leaves room for a very different view than that of the philosophical tradition represented by Kierkegaard and Derrida: firstly, Abraham's actions would not technically constitute sacrifice within a Judaic liturgical context, because his son's life is not extinguished—hence the scene's designation within Rabbinic literature as the "binding [*akedah*]," rather than the sacrifice, of Isaac; and secondly, up to the instant of the sacrifice's deferral Isaac presents himself as a cognizant and willing offering (in the sense that would lead subsequent Christian writers to regard him as a typological foreshadowing of Jesus), as opposed to an unknowing, compelled, and therefore in a very different sense "innocent" victim.[41]

In other words, if we juxtapose the midrashic, Christian, and modern philosophical interpretations of Genesis 22, we can identify two different models of sacrificial impetus in both of the biblical characters. On the one hand, Isaac's consciously voluntary submission of himself to both a paternal and a divine will discloses the sacrificial paradigm of *self*-offering that would come to be associated with kenosis in Christianity. On the other, Abraham's submission of his will to God's in offering up a beloved *other* underscores the theme of expenditure that Kierkegaard and Derrida both highlight in their analyses not just of his sacrificial act but also of how

---

40. According to Jon D. Levenson, this is the groundwork for both the Christian and the medieval Jewish idea that the Akedah is as much a test for Isaac as it is for Abraham. Levenson, *The Death and Resurrection of the Beloved Son: The Transformation of Child Sacrifice in Judaism and Christianity* (New Haven, CT: Yale University Press, 1993), 134–135. Also see Steven Stern, "The Unbinding of Isaac," in *Sacrifice, Scripture, and Substitution: Readings in Ancient Judaism and Christianity*, ed. Ann W. Astell and Sandor Goodhart (Notre Dame, IN: University of Notre Dame Press, 2011), 272.

41. For a philological account of the relationship between these ritual and semantic paradigms of "offering" (as either distinct from or tantamount to formal sacrifice) and innocence, see Moshe Halbertal, *On Sacrifice* (Princeton, NJ: Princeton University Press, 2012), 9–10, 33–34.

the imbrication of this act with his "test of faith" ultimately bears upon the terrible question of the offering's return.[42] In the section that follows, I suggest that the climax of Storm's novella stages an intertwining of these two models: in his forceful submission of *nature* to his own will, Hauke both unwillingly offers up others (including his own loved ones) and creates the conditions for his final, willing offering of himself—ostensibly in the hope that his life might be exchanged for the lives of others. The issue of whether or not his sacrificial act is concomitant with the genuine hope, let alone faith, that such an exchange will occur is where Kierkegaard's reading, supplemented on either end by those of the Midrash and Derrida, has the most to offer us. Let's now return to Hauke's drowning in order to see exactly how.

Sacrifice Fulfilled

Having been momentarily immobilized by the sight of the breach in the old wall, Hauke races toward it on his horse: "The sea foamed all around the reclaimed area, but within it lay the peace of nightfall. Suddenly an unwilled joy of pride leaped up within Hauke, alone on his white horse. 'The Hauke Haien Dike! It will stand for more than a hundred years!'" (280–281).

In the very same instant, almost in response to his hubristic swell of triumph, the dike wall directly in front of him crumbles into the sea and the water redoubles its surging progress inland—"It was the Deluge [*Sündflut*] come back to devour the earth and its creatures" (281). Then, Hauke sees something that fills him with horror: a small horse-drawn cart descending the hill from his home and making its way toward him, a woman and child inside, unwittingly seconds away from meeting the onrushing torrent:

---

42. It bears noting that Kierkegaard's focus upon the matter of faith bespeaks the Christian (and, even more specifically, Lutheran) orientation of his reading, though there are some midrashic interpretations that also go in this direction. See, for example, Jacob Neusner, *Confronting Creation: How Judaism Reads Genesis: An Anthology of Genesis Rabbah* (Columbia: University of South Carolina Press, 1991), 205–216.

> And the whole sea thundered in. . . . Hauke saw the cart's wheels rise up from the confused horror and then quickly vanish into a whirlpool. He stood there alone on his dike, and his fixed eyes saw nothing further. "Ended," he murmured softly to himself. Then he rode to the edge of the abyss. . . . He stood up high in the saddle and drove his spurs into the flanks of the white horse. The animal reared up in pain and nearly fell backward; but the rider forced it to its feet again. . . . "Here, God, take me; but spare the others!" (282)

Hauke's plea invokes a system in which the divine and the human not only stand in relation to each other, but do so with respect to a shared framework of value. In other words, by articulating a wish for God to spare the lives of the villagers in exchange for his own death in the sea, Hauke seems to imply an economy of both human *and* divine deprivation and rectification in which sacrifice performs a decisive function; through self-offering, a debt (*Schuld*) is supposedly repaid in the same instant that guilt (*Schuld*) is acknowledged and atoned for.

Yet the question of what precisely this doubled *Schuld* consists in warrants further reflection. It is clear, on the one hand, that Hauke's initial deferral of sacrifice in the scene where he prevents his workers from burying the dog is ironically reversed through his own self-sacrifice at the end; in this instant, from the vantage point of the villagers' beliefs, a necessary and previously neglected oblation has finally been fulfilled.[43] On the other hand, in order to arrive at a satisfactory conclusion about the nature of sacrifice and atonement in Storm's late work we must attend to how Hauke's drowning stands in relation to his sense of having transgressed against his *own* laws and not merely those of his community's traditions. From this perspective, Hauke's silence about the compro-

---

43. Derek Hillard, "Violence, Ritual, and Community: On Sacrifice in Keller's *Romeo und Julia auf dem Dorfe* and Storm's *Der Schimmelreiter*," *Monatshefte* 101, no. 3 (2009): 373; Wolfgang Palaver, "Hauke Haien—ein Sündenbock? Theodor Storms *Der Schimmelreiter* aus der Perspektive der Theorie René Girards," in *Religion—Literatur—Künste: Aspekte eines Vergleichs*, ed. Peter Tschuggnall (Salzburg: Müller-Speiser, 1998), 221–236; Christoph Daniel Weber, "Deichbau und Selbstopfer: Der Katastrophendiskurs in Theodor Storms *Der Schimmelreiter*," *DVjs* 90, no. 1 (2016): 129.

mised integrity of the old dike wall is at the core of all the other forms of guilt surrounding the "Deluge" that impel him to offer up his life in exchange for the lives of others. After all, he not only allowed his pride to intervene in the workers' attempt to puncture his newly constructed dike in order to spare the old one, but he had also kept secret his recognition of the "*unheimliche* spot" and its (ultimately fatal) exposure to the sea. These very thoughts course through Hauke's mind shortly before his death:

> Just what was the fault that he would have to answer for at God's throne? The break through the new dike? No, the old dike was the broken one—but in ten more minutes the fools would have breached the new dike too! But there was something else, and he knew it only too well as it burned in his heart. . . . he alone had recognized the weakness in the old wall. He ought to have forced the repair-work through in spite of everything: "Lord God, I confess!" he yelled suddenly into the storm wind. "I failed my responsibility!" (280)

Moments after Hauke's repentant declaration, however, the waves burst through the old wall. This invites us to interpret Hauke's leap into the sea—which he himself articulates as an offering to substitute the lives of his neighbors—not as a pure "leap of faith" by which he abandons reason to divine will, nor merely as a suicidal act of desperation and guilt couched in the religious apparatus of his time and place.[44] Instead we must read it as a sacrificial gesture of atonement, though of a very particular kind and in a very particular sense. In this regard Kierkegaard's thoughts about concealment and sacrifice are helpful as a frame of reference, given that the penitential character of Hauke's drowning pertains directly to his prideful silence. There are several forms of sacrifice at work here, and even though Hauke's presentation of his own death as an exchange for the lives of others is the most immediate one, we must not forget that this situation was itself precipitated by another sacrifice altogether: namely, his decision to protect his legacy in place of his community by keeping the "*unheimliche* spot" a secret. The drowning is therefore not so much a sacrifice of the self for the sake

---

44. Jackson, *Theodor Storm*, 250.

of others as a penitential attempt to counterbalance a *prior* sacrifice of others for the sake of the self.

Moreover, a significant yet often unacknowledged victim of Hauke's actions is the land itself and its resident network of organic relationships; Kate Rigby proposes an "ecocritical Faustian" understanding of Hauke as not simply being overcome by the elements of nature (as Faust is in part 2 of Goethe's drama), but specifically as having fallen "prey . . . to the characteristically modern antroparchal illusion of unidirectional self-determined human agency" that causes him to fail to recognize the interpenetration of human technological activity and the nonhuman elements of the coast that have been endangered (in the case of animal and plant life) and made more destructive (in the case of the sea) by this activity.[45] Ecologically minded analyses such as this shed a relevant new light on the dynamics of Hauke's various sacrifices (both prior to and during the flood), which have often been seen to anticipate Horkheimer and Adorno's sweeping critique of the "myth" of rational modernity. Their *Dialectic of Enlightenment* (1944) traces this myth in connection, not primarily with class struggle, but instead with the elemental relationship between human society and nature, whereby the bad seed of sacrificiality turns out to be its very *internalization* by human beings in a rationalistic denial of our coextension with nature:

> In class society, the self's hostility to sacrifice included a sacrifice of the self, since it was paid for by a denial of nature in the human being for the sake of mastery of extrahuman nature . . . with the denial of nature in human beings, not only the *telos* of the external mastery of nature but also the *telos* of one's own life becomes confused and opaque. At the moment when human beings cut themselves off from the consciousness of themselves as nature, all the purposes for which they keep themselves alive—social progress, the heightening of material and intellectual

---

45. Kate Rigby, *Dancing with Disaster: Environmental Histories, Narratives, and Ethics for Perilous Times* (Charlottesville: University of Virginia Press, 2015), 96. Also see Katie K. Ritson, "Engineering the Anthropocene: Technology, Ambition, and Enlightenment in Theodor Storm's *Der Schimmelreiter*," in *Readings in the Anthropocene*, ed. Sabine Wilke and Japhet Johnstone (New York: Bloomsbury, 2017), 222–242.

forces, indeed, consciousness itself—become void . . . self-preservation destroys the very thing which is to be preserved.[46]

The logic of internalized sacrifice thus instigates a process by which the modern individual's conscious placement of the self in opposition to nature (usually with deleterious consequences for the latter) ultimately becomes an *un*conscious relinquishment of the self *to* nature. If read in this light, Storm's protagonist could be said to have carried out an initial "introversion" of sacrifice that ends up taking an "extroverted" form in which living victims of multiple kinds are claimed by the sea.[47] However, this process consists not so much in Hauke's renunciation of his personal nature as in, more significantly, his choice to remain silent about the "*unheimliche* spot" in full knowledge of its calamitous potential. This choice constitutes a calculated revision of his own moral coordinates, which had previously impelled him to rescue an innocent creature from being killed in the name of beliefs that he designated as "sacrilege" and "heathen nonsense," but that in their altered configuration now permit him to subordinate the safety of his coastal co-inhabitants.

So, what could possibly qualify as a symmetrical offering to atone for all of these human and nonhuman deaths in the flood and its aftermath? Hauke settles upon himself, the person who built the dike; and at first glance this seems fitting enough: a life in return for lost lives. Upon more careful reflection, however, it does not entirely balance out. The flood occurs not so much as a result of Hauke valuing his *life* over his neighbors' lives, but as a result of him valuing the dike—with which the *memory* of his life has been invested—over the safety of the village. We learn that this initial sacrificial exchange

---

46. Max Horkheimer and Theodor W. Adorno, *The Dialectic of Enlightenment: Philosophical Fragments*, trans. Edmund Jephcott (Stanford, CA: Stanford University Press, 2002), 42–43. Martin Jay proposes that for Horkheimer and Adorno, this denial both of one's inner nature *and* of one's intertwinement with external nature was not only "the price of subjective rationality" but also "at the root of all subsequent inadequacies of civilization." Jay, *The Dialectical Imagination: A History of the Frankfurt School and the Institute of Social Research, 1923–1950* (Berkeley: University of California Press, 1996), 263–264. Compare Ian Cooper, "Theodor Storm and Disenchantment," *German Life and Letters* 68, no. 4 (2015): 584–597.

47. Rigby, *Dancing with Disaster*, 106–110.

is successfully performed, for the schoolmaster notes after finishing his tale, "It has been a hundred years, and the Hauke Haien Dike is still standing," embedded in the local landscape and imagination (283). Yet by the same token, Hauke's drowning, insofar as it is intended as an *expiatory* offering, remains sacrificially incommensurate; that is to say, the material cause of the flood, which is also the physical monument to Hauke's memory, does not disappear under the water.

This, then, is the true nature of haunting that his specter evinces: if the original penitential intent had been to extinguish his *person*—but not his memorial—then the Dante-esque *contrapasso* for this only partial sacrifice is precisely the impossibility of being forgotten. The schoolmaster frames this vividly: "It is the way this world is built: men gave Socrates poison to drink, and then proceeded to nail Our Lord to the cross! During recent years, proceedings of that kind have become inconvenient. But we can still make an official saint out of a cruel brute or a vicious bull-necked priest—or we can make a proficient, gifted man into a ghoulish phantom, simply because he had more of a head on his shoulders than we do. That will always happen" (283). Crucially, it is not Hauke's actual death that the schoolmaster phrases in sacrificial terms, but the status of his memory in the collective imagination of the community. If, as I have suggested, Hauke's decision to drown himself is a gesture of atonement for his earlier, transgressive sacrifice, then the schoolmaster implies in turn that his preservation within local legend constitutes an additional sacrifice as well: by being remembered not as a heroic and enlightened ancestor but as a *pharmakós*—a curse upon the community that, in being destroyed, is also its own cure—he assumes this very role in the form of a "ghoulish phantom" that haunts his physical memorial (the dike wall). And ironically, this sentence to an "afterlife"—to be remembered for his death rather than for his life—retroactively fulfills the expiatory motivation behind his suicide. Storm's final drowning scene thus points to a fascinating variation on one of his signature themes: while so many of his tales are about the fragility of memory, his last work communicates the inverse dread, not only that certain memories will not fade, but that they may in fact change their form altogether over time by virtue of belonging to the jurisdiction of the living rather than the dead.

Hauke's sacrifice marks the end of his life (and of the innermost frame narrative), but it also returns us to the beginning of the novella and the ghostly spectacle witnessed by the frame narrator. This confluence of both temporal and diegetic frameworks adds one final layer to the drowning: if Hauke's final act is an ethical sacrifice made necessary by past transgression, and expresses a wish for the lives of others to be spared, then we can understand the instant of sacrifice, the *Augenblick* of drowning, as precisely that—as a "perilous moment," to borrow Benjamin's description of dialectical images once again, that is suspended between the past and the future. We have already observed this facet of the drowning motif in Storm's work, where it has likewise functioned as a singular moment that both opposes the movement of law from the past into the present and becomes integral to subsequent acts and objects of memorialization. Indeed, this precise instant replays before the eyes of the narrator and is later recapitulated by the schoolmaster. There are therefore two distinct figures of repetition and narrativity associated with Hauke's sacrifice: (1) the spectral trace of his drowning that will be given context retrospectively by the schoolmaster's narration; and (2) the physical sites of the dike, which still stands as Hauke had predicted, and of the sea, which continues to swallow his shadowy form whenever floods threaten the community.

This duality of spectral trace and material *sema* ultimately points to a duality of memory and memorial that was also at the center of *Aquis Submersus*. The spatial sites of the dike and the sea remain, but the phantoms of human lives and subjectivities to which these markers silently allude ceaselessly vanish and reemerge within the consciousness of those who come along after them. Hauke's transgressions of concealment and pride, as well as his sacrificial act of atonement for them, may well live on within a collective memory of lore and legend. However, the ghostly materialization of *him*— like the painted image of Johannes's son—remains a trace in search of memory. As the middle-frame narrator remarks at the beginning, had he not seen Hauke's "shadow" disappear into the sea, he would have no way of knowing that it had been there at all, for the water was "conspicuously unruffled. The rider could not have troubled it" (186). In other words, the subjective instance of Hauke's final moments, and the objective shadow of their having been, ultimately come to rest, respectively, beneath and above the water's surface.

If Adorno was right in saying that the flat line of "Storm's solemn hyphen" is one of the most ubiquitous features of his fiction on the level of form, then it would be just as fair to say that the line-like imagery of watery surfaces boasts this same degree of ubiquity on the level of content, accompanied by the recurrent thematic frameworks of memory, law, and sacrifice that have been my focus in this chapter. That seems more than merely fitting, as each of these themes shares in the figural as well as the figurative character of water—and specifically, *submergence*—with which they are so closely associated in Storm's corpus. Indeed, the recurrent act of remembrance that reaches "backward" in *erzählter Zeit* and thereby moves the *Erzählzeit* of the story "forward" could be conceived of as a sort of "horizontal submergence" that cooperates with the more literal, vertical depths inherent to the bodies of water that permeate so many of these narratives.[48] Again and again, the water's surface appropriately serves as the topological nexus of these literal and lateral depths. Relatedly, within Storm's work, drowning in general seems to evince anxiety over whether one will or will not leave behind a trace for others to find, as well as over the question of what the ethical status of this trace would be. Most significant, though, is the thought that just as memory itself relies upon traces that have been left behind, traces also in some sense rely upon memory. What seems to occupy Storm's late writing is the intuition that neither can succeed fully, and that while they hold together, they do so only as fragments of one another.

Among the many ghosts that populate Storm's remarkable contributions to literary realism, what seems to most consistently haunt

---

48. I borrow this helpful figure of mnemonic, horizontal submergence from Vera Bachmann's analysis of Storm's novella *Immensee* in *Stille Wasser—tiefe Texte? Zur Ästhetik der Oberfläche in der Literatur des 19. Jahrhunderts* (Bielefeld: Transcript, 2013), 218–244.

his writing is the awareness of time, for each text discussed in this chapter closes in upon the subjective burden of remembrance—a burden not merely of preserving the dead within one's own memory but also of considering how one will be remembered by others. (There is nothing new in this, of course, but it rings no less true as a consequence; Theodor Fontane, writing in 1853 of the then middle-aged Storm, observes that "he does not lay paths that are absolutely new, but the old ones that he wanders along are authentic and true.")[49] The urgency behind acts of atonement in the last of Storm's fiction arises from his characters' thoughts of what will be left behind rather than what is still to come, but such acts attain substance only if they are inscribed into space, molded into material traces that can be read and reread by those who later happen upon them, and not merely "writ in water," as Keats's famous epitaph intones. By contrast, it is the subjective interiors of the individuals who actually perform these acts that gradually shed their contours and dissipate—left to merge with the markers that have been forged into language, images, and nature, with memory trailing in their wake.

---

49. Theodor Fontane, "Unsere lyrische und epische Poesie seit 1848," in *Sämtliche Werke*, vol. 21.1, ed. Kurt Schreinert (Munich: Nymphenburger Verlagshandlung, 1963), 31.

Epilogue

Ophelia and the Boatman

> And if the earthly should forget you,
> say to the silent loam: I flow.
> To the rushing water speak: I am.
> —Rainer Maria Rilke, *Sonnets to Orpheus* II.29

On January 17, 1778, Christel von Laßberg, a young actress from Goethe's *Hoftheater* in Weimar, was found drowned on the banks of the Ilm. It was reported that a copy of Goethe's 1774 novel *Die Leiden des jungen Werther* (*The Sufferings of Young Werther*) had been discovered among her belongings nearby, adding to subsequent speculation that she had taken her life out of romantic despair.[1]

Epigraph: Rainer Maria Rilke, *Sonnets to Orpheus*, trans. Edward Snow (New York: North Point Press, 2004), 117 (lines 12–14).

1. Effi Biedrzynski, *Goethes Weimar: Das Lexikon der Personen und Schauplätze* (Zurich: Artemis und Winkler, 1993), 267.

Werther too had been tempted to jump into a river as he stood "with my arms wide open . . . facing the abyss and breathed down! down! and was lost in the bliss of hurling my torments, my suffering raging down! roaring away like the waves!" Here, as throughout the text, Werther's reaction to the external landscape is reflective of the particular emotional significance with which he has invested it. However, he resists the pull, even "as I looked down in my melancholy at a spot [*Plätzchen*] where I had rested with Lotte under a willow tree."[2] Christel's inverse fate is hauntingly reflected in Goethe's own account of constructing "a strange spot [*Plätzgen*] where poor Christel's memory will stand concealed."[3] There is a dark irony in the fact that Christel worked in the theater, for both the setting and the manner of her final, unwitnessed moments on the riverbank evoke the offstage death of Shakespeare's Ophelia, which would become one of the defining topoi of European culture in the nineteenth and twentieth centuries.

Just as Goethe's fictional character Ottilie served as a point of entry for this book's exploration of the thematic associations (that is, law and sacrifice) as well as narratological features (such as the *Augenblick*) of drowning scenes in realist narrative, the biographical and tragic event of Laßberg's death brings into focus the purpose of these last pages, which is to cast a brief glance on the ways Ophelia performed a role similar to Ottilie's for the works of prose and poetry that followed the epoch of German Realism. More broadly, I will explore how, in numerous important works of early modernism, the symbolism of water—in many cases including the figure of Ophelia—is used to convey an intriguing tension, standing both for the projection of the subjective interior onto nature as well as for the experience of alienation from that interior. This tension is one of the things that the inherent "boundary" of water—the

---

2. Johann Wolfgang Goethe, *The Sufferings of Young Werther*, trans. Stanley Corngold (New York: W. W. Norton, 2013), 72, 77. / Goethe, *Die Leiden des jungen Werther*, in *Werke: Hamburger Ausgabe in 14 Bänden*, vol. 6: *Romane und Novellen I*, ed. Erich Trunz (Munich: C. H. Beck, 1996), 99.

3. Johann Wolfgang Goethe, *Briefe: Historisch-kritische Ausgabe*, vol. 3.1, ed. Georg Kurscheidt and Elke Richter (Berlin: De Gruyter, 2014), 191 (no. 324, to Charlotte von Stein, January 19, 1778).

division between the world above the surface and the unseen domain beneath it—will come to mean in modernist literature, no longer merely *symbolizing* an intrinsic component of social and ethical existence, as in realism, but *embodying* a certain limit of human experience itself.

I.

Much attention has been paid to the reception and influence of Shakespeare's Ophelia in nineteenth-century art and literature, and more specifically in German Expressionism. Though the figure of Ophelia became a truly popular trope in the German sphere only toward the end of the nineteenth century, the intrinsic qualities of her character were long recognized for their strong resonances with Romantic lyric, particularly her inwardness, reverie, and close association with nature. Before getting to this, however, let us first turn to the *Quelle* (in every sense): namely, the standard instance of drowning in modern literature, as narrated by Gertrude in act 4, scene 7, of Shakespeare's *Hamlet*.[4]

The sequence begins with Gertrude's description of a willow tree growing "askant the brook" such that its leaves can be seen reflected in the water (line 165). This simple detail establishes the pulse of the drowning's symbolic significance by drawing attention to the theme of reflection; in this case, of one natural element functioning as the "mirror" for another. This image becomes more elaborate when Gertrude describes how Ophelia appears, drawing near the willow with garlands of flowers and nettles that she intends to hang from the branches, thus reiterating the motif of one facet of the natural world being reflected within another (here it is the quality of the willow's branches that the hand-fashioned garlands imitate, whereas in the previous lines it had been the very image of the tree itself that was repeated in the water's surface). However, as Ophelia is attempting to

---

4. William Shakespeare, *Hamlet Prince of Denmark* (1603/1605), in *The Complete Works of Shakespeare*, ed. Alfred Harbage and Willard Farnham (Baltimore: Penguin, 1969), 966.

weave "her weedy trophies" into the willow, an "envious sliver" breaks and Ophelia falls into the "weeping brook."

It is now no longer another element of nature that the tree and the water reflect, but instead human characteristics—the boughs are "envious," and the brook is "weeping" (lines 172, 174). This anthropomorphism precedes the crucial moment of Gertrude's monologue, in which Ophelia, while "clamb'ring" among "the pendent boughs" that she is trying to adorn with her "crownet weeds," is suddenly escorted by gravity from the willow's branches into her assigned domain; once in the water, she is briefly carried along by the brook's currents, "Which time she chanted snatches of old lauds, / As one incapable of her own distress, / Or like a creature native and indued / Unto that element" (lines 176–179). The dreaminess and supposed madness with which Ophelia's singing has been associated throughout the play are here echoed a final time, and together with her woven flowers evoke the traditional linkage between reverie and artistic activity. However, Ophelia's last moments are remarkable not solely for the fact that her song makes her seem "incapable of her own distress" but also for the sudden coalescence of her character with the water's characteristics. Just as nature had previously mirrored *itself* before taking on human features, now the human figure of Ophelia reciprocates this pattern by becoming a "creature native and indued" to water by way of her reflexive inwardness. (Or, as Laertes puts it with laconic double sense a few lines later: "Too much of water hast thou, poor Ophelia" [line 184].)

Ophelia's drowning thus communicates something particular about the characteristics of poeticity, dreaminess, and madness that she would come to embody in European culture, for it shows these themes to be tied not simply to her introversion but also to her participation in the metamorphic processes of *reflection* and *becoming* that had first appeared in the natural sphere. In reflecting and becoming "native" to water by the same poetic authority that allows the water to be said to weep, Ophelia's death is a culminative instance of the human figure and the natural landscape seeming to trade places. It is this mutual transformation that Ophelia's leitmotifs of poetic creation and introspective reverie ultimately convey, and it was this combination of aspects that consistently inspired German writers from different artistic epochs to explore and adapt her as a trope.

"A Creature Native and Indued / Unto That Element"

In the context both of Romanticism and Expressionism (along with several important moments in between), the association between women and the element of water typically signaled the conjoined themes of transition and escape. This is an ancient motif, going back to Ovid's *Metamorphoses*, in which the death of Canens is likened to that of a swan, when "At last, attenuated so by grief / that in her bones the marrow turned to water, / she melted down and vanished on the breezes" (Book 14), while Arethusa is literally transformed into water by Diana so that she might elude her pursuer (Book 5).[5] Similarly, Cyane (Book 5) and Egeria (Book 15) first perform watery qualities with their bodies (weeping, lugubriousness, and so forth) before actually turning into bodies of water. These female figures of Ovid's are not simply compared to water, nor does water itself assume their emotional and physical qualities in the mode of allegory. Instead they coalesce with each other: the natural environment becomes human in the same instant and degree that the human is literally incorporated into the natural environment. Gertrude's description of Ophelia's drowning can therefore be read as participating to a certain degree in the Ovidian trope of actual, hylo- (or perhaps hydro-) morphic convergence: first, a series of reflections—of nature within nature (lines 165–166), then of human qualities in nature (lines 172, 174), then of natural qualities in the human (lines 172, 178, 184)—followed by a unification of Ophelia's human form with the "element" of water to which it is "native and indued." This basic pattern would continue to play an important role in literary scenes of drowning throughout subsequent centuries, including several of the examples from German

---

5. Ovid, *Metamorphoses*, trans. Charles Martin (New York: W. W. Norton, 2004), 499 (XIV.606–608). Compare Simone Kindler, *Ophelia: Der Wandel von Frauenbild und Bildmotiv* (Berlin: Reimer, 2004), 55.

Realism that we have observed. What changes, however, is what *kind* of escape the imagery of drowning is used to evoke.

The Romantics frequently reached for the figure of the *Wasserfrau* (mermaid, siren, nymph, and so on) in order to underline a certain oneiric core to quotidian reality and experience, especially in lyric poetry. An idiomatic scene of this sort involves a (typically male) protagonist's surprise at witnessing a *Wasserfrau* of some denomination emerge from the water, suddenly transfiguring the realm of nature from within. In tandem with this external transformation, the poet-protagonist's inner world dissolves into reverie and fantasy, drawing his consciousness further *in* as his body is likewise lured further *on*, toward the water and its resident object of desire that now together form the fulcrum of the psychic and physical dimensions of poetic (read: subjective) experience. The symbolic message is fairly consistent: in moments of poetic encounter between the subject and the world, the dreamy and erotic domain of the unconscious can suddenly suffuse everyday life, more often than not with fatal consequences for those involved. *Wasserfrauen* either come out to claim mortals (as in Goethe's "The Fisherman" [1779] and Heine's "Loreley" [1824]) or—and the distinction is often pointedly ambiguous—the poet actively enters the underwater space, allegorizing the act of entering his own subjective interior (a number of Eichendorff's and Goethe's lyrics fall into this category, as does Friedrich Schlegel's "The Sunken Castle" [1807]).

The sequences from Droste-Hülshoff's *Ledwina* (1824) discussed in the introduction are certainly exceptional in this regard. There we do not find the stereotypically Romantic young man who is captivated by a nymphic *Wasserfrau* to whom he gives himself over (almost in sacrificial exchange for the poem that chronicles the fatal encounter with the muse, but one that has only *inspired* him in order to drown him, replacing the "inbreathed spirit"—the *inspiratio*—of his poetic genius just as quickly with water in his lungs). Instead, Droste-Hülshoff showed us the eponymous, female protagonist who is similarly submerged within her own poetic and imaginative depths by way of a watery encounter—not with a fantastical third-party *Wasserfrau*, however, but instead with third-person visions of *herself* as a *Wasserleiche*, drowned and decaying in the river that flows through the surrounding landscape. Yet in addition to their strikingly proto-modernist features, these passages from Droste-Hülshoff's novel fragment also stand out for their compelling demonstration of how the German literary inheritance of Ophelian tropes arguably begins in the early decades of the nineteenth century without explicitly invoking Shakespeare's character, and instead implicitly evoking her as part of a tropologically sui generis subgenre.

If Ophelia's name remains largely unspoken in the German literary sphere prior to the latter part of the century (before resounding clearly in the first decades of the twentieth), then its relatively late appearance mirrors that of German Realism itself vis-à-vis the British and French contexts, in which both realist narrative and widespread fascination with Ophelia had comparatively earlier starts. In her important essay on the representational history of Ophelia, Elaine Showalter notes the irony of the fact that in spite of the general neglect of Ophelia in textual criticism of *Hamlet*, the cultural representations of her far outnumber those of any other of Shakespeare's female characters.[6] From seventeenth-century appropriations of her as an emblem of erotomania (love-melancholy), to eighteenth-century stagings of the tragedy in which her dramaturgical function was reconstrued to be primarily musical and blankly decorative, to the sudden emergence of an almost iconographic fixation upon her within nineteenth-century literature and art (and also even within Victorian illustrated medical manuals on hysteria), Ophelia's aesthetic legacy was as multifaceted as it was proliferous.[7] For Showalter, an additional important aspect of this legacy pertains to the challenge it presents to feminist scholarship: How should the complex aesthetic history of Ophelia "after Hamlet" be engaged vis-à-vis the fact of her comparatively sparse presence in Shakespeare's

---

6. Elaine Showalter, "Representing Ophelia: Women, Madness, and the Responsibilities of Feminist Criticism," in *Shakespeare and the Question of Theory*, ed. Patricia Parker and Geoffrey Hartman (New York: Methuen, 1985), 78.

7. Showalter, "Representing Ophelia," 84, 86. Also see Kimberly Rhodes, *Ophelia and Victorian Visual Culture: Representing Body Politics in the Nineteenth Century* (London: Routledge, 2008), 17–84.

Figure 3. *Ophelia*, 1851–1852, Sir John Everett Millais. Tate, Presented by Sir Henry Tate 1894. © Tate, Photo: Tate.

actual text, and of her standard critical reception as a mere symbol of absence, speechlessness, female sexuality, and madness?[8]

Interestingly, though perhaps not surprisingly, Ophelia's representation in the arts during the long nineteenth century coincided with a broader cultural association of femininity with water, where the interwoven themes of beauty and death were emphasized to a pervasive degree. Scholars have noted connections between the fascination with Ophelia in specific cultural and artistic contexts and the broader phenomenon of libidinal aestheticization of the female corpse.[9] As Barbara Gates puts it, "The contrast between loveliness in death and guilt in life, between will-lessness and willingness, was what Victorians wanted to see in art about suicidal women. It amounted to a kind of necrophilia."[10]

Arguably one of the most iconic visual representations along nearly all of these lines is John Everett Millais's *Ophelia*. Completed slowly and painstakingly (not least for its live model, Elizabeth

---

8. Showalter, "Representing Ophelia," 91–92.
9. For a psychoanalytic account of the latter, see Elisabeth Bronfen's *Over Her Dead Body: Death, Femininity, and the Aesthetic* (New York: Routledge, 1992), esp. 205–219. Also see Magda Romanska, "Ontology and Eroticism: Two Bodies of Ophelia," *Women's Studies* 34 (2005): 485–513.
10. Barbara Gates, *Victorian Suicide: Mad Crimes and Sad Histories* (Princeton, NJ: Princeton University Press, 1988), 138.

Siddal)¹¹ during 1851 and 1852, the painting depicts Ophelia after she has exited the intradiegetic (off)stage space of Gertrude's speech from act 4, scene 7, of *Hamlet,* and in the moments (possibly even seconds) before she slips beneath the surface of the river. Dramaturgically speaking, then, the image is, like many of the other "offstage" drowning scenes examined in this book, "obscene" (*obskené*) at the same time that it makes its pastoral beauty available to our gaze. One of the aspects of that beauty most remarked upon in secondary literature is how Ophelia's features symmetrically mirror (or are mirrored by) those of her surroundings. We soon notice a dialectic of constriction and openness that is on display in her floating form: the fitted bodice of her dress is almost overlayed by the woven, circular garland, both of which communicate a sense of boundedness and enclosure that contrasts with the dilated, flowing freedom of her submerged hair and dress, her supinated hands, and her parted lips (perhaps in the midst of the "melodious lay" from which she will shortly be "pull'd" by "her garments, heavy with their drink").¹²

Staying with the metaphor of song, one finds that all of these physical details rhyme with the dense, almost curtain-like verdancy of the plants that grow thickly along the bank, but that seem almost unanimously to open out onto the placid water. The contrapuntal manifestations of boundedness and unboundedness that were present in Ophelia herself are likewise present here in her nonhuman counterparts, the two most prominent of which occupy the left-hand section of the painting. Parallel with each other, one in the foreground and one in the background on either side of Ophelia's body, stand the robin and the reflected blade of grass. Both communicate fixity as well as freedom, imbrication and extension, belonging and longing.

---

11. See Rhodes, *Ophelia,* 99–101.

12. Simonetta Falchi focuses on this detail while recounting the negative contemporary reception of Millais's painting, which disrupted the widespread Victorian vision of Ophelia as a delicate, chaste, and passively suffering innocent victim: "Her open arms suggest mature sexuality, and so does the mermaid-like spreading of her robes. Moreover, the association of death by water, and suicide, was at the time a prerogative of the representation of fallen women." Falchi, "Re-Mediating Ophelia with Pre-Raphaelite Eyes," *Interlitteraria* 2 (2015): 177. Compare Rhodes, *Ophelia,* 89–94.

The grass stalk "downstage" of Ophelia has its root beneath the surface, out of sight, while its tip stretches upward and outward in a similar elusion of complete view by resting just beyond the painting's framed edge. The robin, meanwhile, is embedded deep within the botanical weave of plant life "upstage" of Shakespeare's heroine, so integrated with its environment that it might at first be mistaken for another of the two crimson blossoms that punctuate the lower and right-hand zones of the image (one woven into the garland near Ophelia's abdomen and one floating just above the splayed hem of her dress near the riverbank), to which its red-feathered breast forms a triangular third. And yet, we know that sooner or later the bird will fly out of the frame.[13] Both the blade of grass and the bird also convey escape from their painted dwelling places in an additional way—namely, by mediation *through* the viewer: it is we, facing the robin, who can anticipate it singing like Ophelia is singing, and it is within our gaze that the blade of grass and the water beneath it cohere as a reflection. The river, then, becomes the nodal gathering point for all of the painting's binary pairings: the geometric as well as conceptual hinge of Ophelia and her environment, drawing together between its surface and depths their shared diastolic and systolic rhythms of restriction and release. Like the water itself, much of Ophelia's visual significance is linked to her interstitial status as something *between* the surface and the depths, as throughout Shakespeare's play she is in the midst of being hidden. Here, having already left the stage, she provides a last glimpse of herself as a figure of thresholds, partially underwater and partially above it, becoming incorporated into her natural surroundings and yet not wholly of them, in transit between life and death and, ultimately, between beauty and decay.

---

13. Peter Brix Søndergaard observes a similar tension in the painting between enclosure and escape that is conveyed by Ophelia (in paradigmatic embodiment of the *femme fragile*) and her environment, the naturalistic realism of which could "indicate a scientific wish to control the world.... The figure of Ophelia, in relation to her surroundings, can be seen to be both in conformity and in conflict with this controlling intention." Showalter, by contrast, says that the mimetic precision of the flora and fauna has the effect of reducing Ophelia's body to another mere object. Søndergaard, "'Something Strangely Perverse': Nature and Gender in J. E. Millais's *Ophelia*," *Romantik* 7, no. 1 (2018): 122; Showalter, "Representing Ophelia," 85.

During the course of the nineteenth century, the image of a woman in water ceased to stand for either the poetic potentiality of the subjective interior or the hazards of its irrational powers, and gradually came to symbolize a new sense of alienation from the subjective interior altogether. Moreover, this sense of self-alienation began to hint at a complex psychological relationship between the potentially deadly consequences of desire and the presence of an ambivalent desire *for* the mortification of a longed-for object.[14] This shift is connected to much broader developments in how modern European culture conceptualized and represented femininity in relation to death. Much as Romanticism had inherited and reinvented the antique mythos of the siren, undine, and naiad at the beginning of the nineteenth century, Symbolist and early Expressionist writers seized upon Ophelia as an object of fascination toward its end. To a substantial degree, the German modernist interest in Ophelia from roughly 1900 onward mimics that of English Victorianism as well as of French poets and artists like Delacroix, Hugo, Mallarmé, Musset, and Laforgue, to name but a few.

Rimbaud's poem "Ophélie" appeared in 1870, and many critics cite this literary event as one of the chief sources of modernist interest in Ophelia, particularly within the German-speaking world. This is because, in several documented ways, "Ophélie" set a course that German Expressionism would follow closely.[15] Like Millais's painting, Rimbaud's poem begins where Gertrude's speech leaves off, tracing the voyage of Ophelia's remains. This watery journey would gradually come to constitute the central scenography of Ex-

---

14. The thesis of a "Paradigm-shift from the undine to Ophelia" forms the cornerstone of Anna Maria Stuby's useful study *Liebe, Tod und Wasserfrau: Mythen des Weiblichen in der Literatur* (Opladen: Westdeutscher, 1992), here 165. For a more general overview of the nineteenth-century *Wasserfrau* motif that managed to circumvent the "Ophelia cult," see Matthias Vogel, *"Melusine . . . das lässt aber tief blicken": Studien zur Gestalt der Wasserfrau in dichterischen und künstlerischen Zeugnissen des 19. Jahrhunderts* (Bern: Peter Lang, 1989).

15. Bernhard Blume, "Das ertrunkene Mädchen: Rimbauds Ophélie und die deutsche Literatur," *Germanisch-Romanische Monatschrift* 4 (1955): 108–119; Jürg Peter Rüesch, *Ophelia: Zum Wandel des lyrischen Bildes im Motiv der "navigatio vitae" bei Arthur Rimbaud und im deutschen Expressionismus* (Zurich: Juris, 1964).

pressionist poems devoted to her. In an important sense, this particular focus also anticipates Naturalism's (somewhat like Millais's own) interest in unobscured access to the narrated event (as we shall see shortly). That is, in contrast to German Realism's more theatrical employment of the drowning scene as an "offstage" occurrence (in the vein of Hebbel's *Maria Magdalena*), Rimbaud's "Ophélie" accompanies the corpse's passage through a nocturnal landscape, with the reader in tow. Critics have underscored various dimensions of Rimbaud's poem that they consider to be most significant. Stefan Bodo Würffel, for instance, homes in on the text's intimation of a demythologized "beyond" (figured here as the human subject's reintegration into the natural environment), as well as its final invocation of Ophelia in opposition to the speaker, which establishes her as a poetological as well as a poetic figure (more about this later).[16] Others have attended to the poem's new emphasis on materiality and decay in contrast to the idealizing tendencies of other epochal adaptations of Ophelia's death scene.[17] Ulrike Weinhold extends this focus to the specific question of Ophelia's passivity as a female object of fascination for a male poetic voice.[18] Nearly all of these facets of Rimbaud's poem assume central positions in what one could justly call the iconography of Ophelia in German modernism, to which we will now turn.

---

16. Stefan Bodo Würffel, *Ophelia: Figur und Entfremdung* (Bern: Francke, 1985), 44–51. Compare Frauke Bayer, *Mythos Ophelia: Zur Literatur- und Bild-Geschichte einer Weiblichkeitsimagination zwischen Romantik und Gegenwart* (Würzburg: Ergon, 2009), 169–174, 217–223.

17. Jean-Louis Bandet, "Von Ophélie zu Ophelia: Wege eines Bildes von Arthur Rimbaud zu Georg Heym," in *Gallo-Germanica: Wechselwirkung und Parallelen deutscher und französischer Literatur (18.–20. Jahrhundert)*, ed. Eckhard Heftrich and Jean-Marie Valentin (Nancy: Presses universitaires de Nancy, 1986), 249–262; Rainer Nägele, "Phantom of a Corpse: Ophelia from Rimbaud to Brecht," *MLN* 117, no. 5 (2002): 1069–1082.

18. Ulrike Weinhold, "Bemerkungen zu Ophelia," in *Grenzgänge: Literatur und Kultur im Kontext*, ed. Guillaume van Gemert and Hans Ester (Amsterdam: Rodopi, 1990), 297–310; Würffel, *Ophelia*, 303.

II.

"Where with Stirring Steps Ophelia Once Trod"

How best to go about tracing the course taken by motifs of death in water after German Realism? One possible place to begin would be a point near the movement's end; namely, the conclusion of Fontane's 1891 novel *Irretrievable*, just after Christine Holk's drowned remains have been found by the sea. As her friend Julie Dobschütz recounts in a letter to the family's pastor: "We all went down. Her face that for so long had borne the expression of silent suffering had given way to one of almost cheerful transfiguration: so eagerly had her heart been longing for peace."[19] It would be possible to regard the vignette of Christine's retrieval from the sea as a point of convergence between the ancient and modern associations of death with water that would take center stage in literary epochs after Realism.[20] The fishermen who bring her body to shore might allude subtly to Charon, the boatman of the dead, whereas Dobschütz's description of Christine's features as having taken on a quality of "almost joyful transfiguration" anticipates the iconic visage of *L'Inconnue de la Seine*. Rainer Maria Rilke's 1910 novel *Die Aufzeichnungen des Malte Laurids Brigge* (*The Notebooks of Malte Laurids Brigge*), one of the paradigmatic texts of European modernism, would refer to a similar "face of the young drowned woman, which they took a cast of in the morgue, because it was beautiful, because it smiled, because it smiled so deceptively, as if it knew."[21]

---

19. Theodor Fontane, *Irretrievable*, trans. Douglas Parmée (New York: NYRB Classics, 2011), 254 (translation modified). / Fontane, *Unwiederbringlich: Große Brandenburger Ausgabe; Das erzählerische Werk*, vol. 13, ed. Christine Hehle (Berlin: Aufbau, 2003), 293.

20. The intertextual presence of classical antiquity in particular makes itself felt in this novel, especially the motif of conflated funeral and wedding processions as found in Euripides's tragedy *Alcestis*. See Alexander Sorenson, *Trials by Water: Law, Sacrifice and Submergence in German Realism*, (PhD diss., University of Chicago, 2019), 168–212.

21. Rainer Maria Rilke, *The Notebooks of Malte Laurids Brigge*, trans. Stephen Mitchell (New York: Random House, 1982), 76.

Maurice Blanchot's description of this same death mask (a copy hung in a room he once occupied) has even more in common with Dobschütz's vision of Christine, however. He remarks upon the drowned woman's face, "with closed eyes, but alive with such a fine, blissful (but veiled) smile, that one might have thought she had drowned in an instant of extreme happiness."[22] This is but one of numerous instances of "an entirely different conception of all things" that Rilke's eponymous narrator describes as having gradually "developed in me" since arriving in Paris, which has involved orientating himself not just to a new city but to "a different world. A new world filled with new meanings."[23] In Joachim Pfeiffer's reading of the novel, Malte's trajectory reveals a central component of the world's transformation to be the burgeoning of mass society, in which death ceases to be a "form-giver" of life and becomes instead an "allegory of alienation," which in Rilke's novel appears as a "loss of experience, memory, and of one's 'own' [*eigentlichen*] death."[24] (A loss, that is, of what Heidegger in the subsequent decade would call the "authenticity" [*Eigentlichkeit*] of one's *own* Being as a Being-unto-death.)

Speaking of Paris, the scenario of an untimely death in the Seine had already established itself as a familiar trope in French letters by the time of Balzac.[25] For example, in the opening pages of his 1831

---

22. Maurice Blanchot, *A Voice from Elsewhere*, trans. Charlotte Mandell (Albany: SUNY Press, 2007), 5. Blanchot and Malte's fascination with the death mask are representative of a widespread fixation upon *L'Inconnue* during the early twentieth century. Anne-Gaëlle Saliot suggests, for instance, that Rilke's Malte is struck by the death mask because it taps into his (Malte's) leitmotivic "fear of anonymous death ... death as an anonymous product, as an object without value." Malte finds the smile of the mask "deceitful precisely because it conceals the materiality of death" that has replaced the older conception of death that rested upon assumptions of individualization and the singularity of the human personality. Saliot, *The Drowned Muse: Casting the Unknown Woman of the Seine across the Tides of Modernity* (Oxford: Oxford University Press, 2015), 130. Compare Bayer, *Mythos Ophelia*, 197–205.

23. Rilke, *Notebooks of Malte Laurids Brigge*, 72.

24. Joachim Pfeiffer, *Tod und Erzählen: Wege der literarischen Moderne um 1900* (Tübingen: Max Niemeyer, 1997), 154ff.

25. Compare Lucette Besson, "L'eau de mort ou le thème de la noyade chez Balzac," *L'Année balzacienne* 1, no. 4 (2003): 307–329.

novel *La Peau de chagrin* (*The Wild Ass's Skin*), a young man—notably referred to at one point as "L'Inconnu" (the stranger)—strolls matter-of-factly toward the river in order to drown himself after losing all of his money at a gambling house. At the moment of his ruin, a fellow player frankly observes that "he is a young fool who'll throw himself in the river," and indeed, he seems to make his way to the Pont Royal almost out of a sense of custom, "thinking about the final fantasies of those who had gone before," even picturing a recent newspaper notice about a young woman who had taken her life in the same fashion.[26] Given this strikingly ubiquitous precedent, it is perhaps no accident that one of the more focused analyses of drowning from an aesthetic standpoint was written by a fellow countryman of Balzac, Rimbaud, and Blanchot.

Gaston Bachelard's essay on the "Charon Complex" and the "Ophelia Complex" begins by proposing two different spatial frameworks for the association between death and water: one of navigation (symbolized by the mythic figure of Charon) and the other of materialization (embodied by Ophelia). Like the binary images of water and the shore, these two spatial frameworks are also divided between "cultural dreams" of death in terms of metaphysical departure and in terms of physical (mortal) remains. Bachelard presents the Charon complex as a crystallization of the ancient notion of death as traversal or passage, the most widespread and ancient expression of which is the image of a boatman conveying the souls of the dead *away* from the realm of life and into Hades. The perspectival emphasis here falls on the vanishing point of life's horizon, seen, as it were, "from the shore." Water stands for the threshold between the living and the dead, with death being conceived as a "journey" or departure, and as such water constitutes the medium not only of conveyance into the afterlife but also of the survivors' (culture's) visualization of this conveyance.

By contrast, the Ophelia complex signals a concretization of death in *this* realm, as felt and understood by those still alive and left standing on the "shore." This perspectival shift from passage to

---

26. Honoré de Balzac, *The Wild Ass's Skin*, trans. Patrick Coleman (Oxford: Oxford University Press, 2012), 8, 10.

stasis—from the topos of the boat to that of the water beneath it—is at the heart of drowning's significance for Bachelard. Unlike the Charon complex, death in the Ophelian mode is not conceptualized as a journey to some other realm. Instead Ophelia's drowning materializes what Bachelard terms the "dream" of death per se, whereby "the imagination of misfortune and death finds in the matter of water a particularly powerful and natural material image. . . . Water makes death elemental. Water dies with the dead in its substance. Water is then a *substantial nothingness*."[27] This pertains to the modern representation of death from the vantage point of the living; that is, to the representation of death not as the cessation of life (from the perspective of the dead), but as the process of being restricted to *this* side of the boundary from the perspective of the living, who are left merely with the remains (rather than the testimony or explications) of those who have "departed." Ophelia's water contains death within it and is radically *here* and *individualized*, whereas Charon's water is a means of passage into the universal phenomenon of death as an imagined other place.

Not coincidentally, Bachelard speaks to a different degree of gendering in this specific domain of water's "material imagination" than in the Charon complex. There we encounter a certain "maternality" in the image of water as something that "carries" and "rocks" us into the antipode of our birth; in the Ophelia complex, meanwhile, we are alerted to water as "the true matter for a very feminine death," a death that is "for the sins of others . . . quietly, without fanfare."[28] Yet at the same time, Bachelard makes it clear that Ophelia is also to be understood as an emblem of that which is least "material" within the human individual: inwardness, imagination, and reverie. Interestingly, Bachelard notes that Shakespeare's description of the drowning is devoid of "realism," insofar as it is presented, not as something directly witnessed, but instead as something retrospectively and imaginatively recounted. Poetic Realists

---

27. Gaston Bachelard, "The Charon Complex: The Ophelia Complex," in *Water and Dreams: An Essay on the Imagination of Matter*, trans. Edith R. Farrell (Dallas: Pegasus Foundation, 1983), 89, 92 (emphasis in the original).

28. Bachelard, "The Charon Complex," 81.

such as Julian Schmidt would likely reply that such objectivity is precisely what their literary project is *not* reducible to.[29] But the key thing to note here is that for Bachelard the figure of Ophelia, as in Millais's painting, combines the final, exterior materiality of the body with the complex interiority of this body's former self. German literary movements after the epoch of Realism tend to emphasize precisely these two elements not just in actual scenes of drowning, but in the representation of place as such; the written and lived world of modernist subjectivity will reveal itself to be the same one "where with stirring steps Ophelia once trod," haunted as much by the present as the past.[30]

When German Naturalism emerged as a movement in the 1880s, it understood itself (and largely continues to be understood today) as a reaction against Poetic Realism, which it saw as being idyllic and false. Naturalism sought to be a perfectly accurate recording of reality as it *really* is, rather than as it can or should be in *truth* (hence Arno Holz's famous dictum that the movement's aesthetic objective should be "Nature minus x," with x standing for all traces of authorial artifice).[31] Consequently, when drowning occurs in naturalist texts, it often ceases to perform the central symbolic function we have observed in realism, instead becoming incidental to the event of death and the effect that this event has within the larger narrative economy. In other words, if water is nearby, it is only natural (or naturalist) to expect that someone might drown in it, but this becomes secondary to the circumstances surrounding the death itself.

All of these characteristics of German Naturalism are on display in Gerhart Hauptmann's 1891 drama *Einsame Menschen* (*Lonely*

---

29. And, in fact, Bachelard is not necessarily in disagreement, for he too notes that "such realism, far from evoking images, would rather block the poetic flight [*l'essor poétique*]" (Bachelard, "The Charon Complex," 81). / Bachelard, "Le complexe de Caron: Le complexe d'Ophélie," in *L'eau et les rêves: Essai sur l'imagination et de la matière* (Paris: Librairie genérale française, 2012), 98.

30. Georg Trakl, "Wind, weiße Stimme . . ." (ca. 1912), line 6.

31. For in-depth examinations of naturalist techniques of narration vis-à-vis this sociocultural context, see Roy Pascal, *From Naturalism to Expressionism: German Literature and Society, 1880–1918* (London: Wiedenfeld and Nicholson, 1973); Ingo Stöckmann, *Der Wille zum Willen: Der Naturalismus und die Gründung der literarischen Moderne, 1880–1900* (Berlin: De Gruyter, 2009).

People), which culminates in the offstage drowning of the protagonist, Johannes. In a sort of contrapuntal response to the death of Hebbel's Klara in *Maria Magdalena* some four decades earlier, with all of her concern for moral necessity and the reputation of her family members in the eyes of the community, the death of Hauptmann's Johannes comes as a final act of self-centeredness. Far from sacrificing his own life and reputation for the sake of others, Johannes commits suicide out of despair over the loss of his own happiness (his extramarital passion), which is grounded precisely in the betrayal of others (above all his wife). By comparison, in Hauptmann's slightly earlier novella of 1887, *Fasching* (*Carnival*), the drowning scene is framed as a result not of decision but instead of the protagonist's failure to recognize his vulnerability both to the natural environment and to the consequences of his own actions. In both of Hauptmann's texts, drowning is not the telos of decisions that are made "facing outward," as it were. Instead, death in water seems to underscore the relatively ignoble course of choices that either "turn inward" or are undertaken without substantial reflection.

In the first decade of the twentieth century, the short-lived literary movement of Impressionism sought to push back against the exacting criteria of Naturalism in order to delve into the sensuous and subjective dimensions of human experience. As such, the theme of drowning once again assumed the symbolic function that Hauptmann's Naturalism had deemphasized, particularly in the work of Eduard von Keyserling. In narratives such as the 1911 novel *Wellen* (*Waves*), for instance, the sea is used to reflect the ever-changing and uncontrollable inner landscape of the individual, consistently giving figural expression to the characters' desires, fears, and thoughts. Additionally, the eponymous waves of the sea are portrayed throughout the story in terms redolent of Schopenhauer's concept of the Will, manifesting a pre-rational, pre-subjective, and incomprehensible force that seems to govern and condition the natural world as much as it does the human subject. Therefore, whenever characters drown—and they do, or try to, quite often—it comes across as an attempted negation of the Will (but thereby ultimately a surrender to it) within the element that symbolizes the Will itself.

It was neither Naturalism nor Impressionism, however, but Expressionism that moved Ophelia onto the cultural stage as a truly central figure, where she bridged either end of the Great War with her concatenation of the Expressionists' characteristically grim preoccupations, including the absurdity of existence, psychological trauma, violence, and madness. Within the German canon, Georg Heym stands out as the Expressionist who most committedly worked in an Ophelian idiom, penning poems on subjects such as "Der Tod der Liebenden im Meer" ("The Lovers' Death in the Sea"), "Ophelia," and "Die Tote im Wasser" ("The Dead Woman in the Water"). (In a morbid echo of his own writings, Heym himself drowned in 1912 after falling through a patch of ice on the wintry river Havel, only several years after the first of these poems appeared.) As in Rimbaud's "Ophélie," in Heym's poems death is figured as a transition and transformation, but rather than emphasizing Ophelia's reintegration into nature in an image of unification between subject and object, here we discover death as a collaborator in the "disenchantment" of nature and myth diagnosed by Max Weber. Death is no longer a metamorphosis or journey, but instead an unveiling of the cold material to which all human life is eventually reduced.[32] In Heym's "drowning poems," the process of death delivers up remains for the living and the reader to find, and for nature to reclaim in decidedly unlyrical and de-idealized ways.

As two cases in point, in Heym's "Ophelia" and "The Dead Woman in the Water" (from 1910 and 1911, respectively), the drowned human figure that crosses paths with the lyric eye has been radically reduced to even less than a body, for we hear it described not in terms of *who* the unknown woman in the water had been in life, but instead in terms of the different ways in which her corpse now serves as a vessel and a means of survival for other living things (particularly rats, a grisly theme that Gottfried Benn would also play upon in his somewhat better-known poem of 1912, "Schöne Jugend" ["Beautiful Youth"]). As these brief examples illustrate, and as Bachelard's essay would later suggest, the trope of death-in-water

---

32. Weinhold, "Bemerkungen zu Ophelia," 305; Würffel, *Ophelia*, 61–83.

alters its message in modernism. It no longer communicates the mysterious departure and journey of the dead away from us, the living, which we can only watch and wonder about from the shore. In the modernist paradigm, our position on the shore has not changed, but death is now *in* the water in a different way; it rests there before us just as plainly as the water itself does, and it leaves its traces there for us to find. Insofar as the dead now seem reducible to their remains in a way that is newly raw and resistant to romanticization, they are suddenly and terribly still *here* in spite of seeming to be gone in a way that is equally sudden and terrible.

The contemporary English writer Roger Deakin was well acquainted with this experience. Himself an avid swimmer of Britain's rivers, lakes, and streams, in his later years he also took up the peculiar hobby of investigating instances of water deaths that occurred in the marshy countryside of his native Suffolk. After his own death, handwritten notes were found among his effects in which he had recorded and reflected upon these cases. One entry in particular speaks to his own encounters with the multivalent significance presented by the boundary between water and shore. It offers a fragmentary account of Deakin's conversation with a local inspector in which he was told that cases of suicide by drowning had once been quite prevalent, given the ubiquity of water on the East Anglian fens, but that in recent years incidents of this had become rarer. However, Deakin's notes indicate, "Old people still do it . . . it was a classic way to die. Old people have gone off and taken their glasses and teeth and left them in a pile and waded in."[33]

This vignette recounted by Deakin in many ways embodies the existential message of the drowning motif in modernist German literature, centering as it does upon our ability only to happen upon and perhaps catalog the traces that get left behind on this side of water. The shore represents a deeper boundary line of our knowledge, however, underscoring our *Diesseitigkeit*—our condition of being always on "this side" of ontological and epistemic horizons—which

---

33. Roger Deakin, "Drowning (Coroners), 1998," [RD/WLOG/2/24] (University of East Anglia Library, Norwich, UK), 4.

concomitantly stokes a desire to encounter the "other side."[34] The "this-sidedness" in which we are all embedded as living beings that are also conscious of our own Being mandates by its own token that we cannot directly access or experience anything that lies beyond the boundaries of this frame. However, even though these boundaries are typically thought of as being impenetrable, in the course of our lives we do encounter phenomena and undergo experiences that are thought somehow to correspond to this otherwise inaccessible domain, even if we cannot understand exactly how.

"Spread Out and Open in This Endless Becoming"

The institutions of religion, philosophy, and poetry have tended to be the most at ease with this notion of boundaries (the most at ease, that is, with "being in uncertainties, Mysteries, doubts, without any irritable reaching after fact and reason," as John Keats memorably defined negative capability).[35] Hence the liturgical potency of a sacrament for Augustine, as a visible sign within which "divine" and "invisible things" are "honored."[36] Or the true substance of all phenomena for Kant, who writes that "if we view the objects of the senses as mere appearances, as is fitting, then we thereby admit at the very same time that a thing in itself underlies them."[37] A main point of this duality is that objects that are present and appear to us are signifi*cant* insofar as they are signifi*catory*, referring to some-

---

34. As a parenthetical item of interest, Freud remarks in passing that the very terms *Diesseits* and *Jenseits* originated in reference to riverbanks, as older customs held that the dead should be kept separate from the living community by being interred on the opposite side of a body of water. Sigmund Freud, *Totem und Tabu: Einige Übereinstimmungen im Seelenleben der Wilden und der Neurotiker*, in *Gesammelte Werke*, vol. 9, ed. Anna Freud, Edward Bibring, and Ernst Kris (Frankfurt am Main: Fischer, 1986), 74–75.

35. Letter of December 21, 1817 to George and Tom Keats, in John Keats, *Selected Letters* (revised edition), ed. Grant F. Scott (Cambridge, MA: Harvard University Press, 2002), 60.

36. Augustine, *De catechizandis rudibus*, ed. William Yorke Fausset (London: Methuen, 1912), 75 (XXVI.50).

37. Immanuel Kant, *Prolegomena to Any Future Metaphysics*, trans. Gary Hatfield (Cambridge: Cambridge University Press, 2004), 66 (§32).

thing that is not present and does not appear to us, and that thereby furnishes the rest with meaning. This signification of the thing necessarily points to a dimension of meaning beyond itself, allowing meaning to become immanent after first manifesting itself in the limits of an encountered object. And sometimes (especially in modern poetry) the limit of the object *is* its meaning; thus, it is a conjunction of beauty and sadness that Rilke finds in

> . . . the flowers, those true to the earthly,
> to whom we lend fate from the edge of fate,—
> yet who can say? If they regret their fading,
> it is for us to *be* their regret.[38]

This basic structure is also at work in those scenes of modern German literature in which characters unexpectedly find themselves confronted by human remains in water—characters such as Malte Brigge as he looks at the face of an *inconnue* that seems to be smiling "as if it knew."

Just what kind of knowledge does this smile intimate? It is a question that has drawn numerous philosophers as well as poets to the water's edge. Heraclitus and Thales are two well-known such cases from among the Presocratics, for whom the distinguishing line between philosophy and poetry was generally waterlike to begin with. Yet the examples also continue well after Plato draws cleaner distinctions between the two. Even Aristotle was attracted to the imagery of drowning; while discussing the topic of decision in the *Nicomachean Ethics*, for example, he argues that in order for people to attain the Good, which is ultimately reached by acting in accordance with reason, they must first act in accordance with virtue, which comes forth in decisions made using practical wisdom (*phronesis*).[39] For Aristotle, famously, virtue is always to be found within the mean, within a middle point between extremes, and it is in illustrating the sense of this virtuous *via media* that he cites the

---

38. Rilke, *Sonnets to Orpheus*, 87 (II, 14, lines 1–4, emphasis in the original).
39. Aristotle, *Nicomachean Ethics*, trans. Robert Crisp (Cambridge: Cambridge University Press, 2000), Bks. I, II, VI.

advice given to Odysseus about steering his ship between Scylla and Charybdis in order to preserve himself and his crew from the sea's depths (1109b).[40]

Philosophy's affinity for oceanic imagery is by no means unique to the ancient world. Indeed, a key work of twentieth-century feminist thought by Luce Irigaray gives voice to a specifically feminine imaginary by way of the sea, and in doing so returns to Greek antiquity and the Homeric idiom alluded to by Aristotle in the *Ethics* while at the same time charting a thoroughly modern course. Irigaray's assumed interlocuter is Nietzsche and the various avatars that populate his works and through whom he articulates a philosophy of life and truth with which Irigaray's "marine lover" juxtaposes herself. Thus, it is implicitly to Zarathustra "whispering of eternal things" with the dwarf beneath the gateway of "Moment" (*Augenblick*) or to the hypothetical demon describing the Eternal Return in *The Gay Science* that she says:[41] "I have no need to turn round and round to come back to the same or to enter into eternity. For same have I been from all eternity, and, at the same time, ever different. And thus I come and go, change and stay, go on and come back, without any circle. Spread out and open in this endless becoming."[42] Or she may be addressing herself to the boat adrift on the open sea elsewhere in that same book of Nietzsche's, all land having been demolished as if to symbolically presage the death of God (which the Madman will announce in the subsequent aphorism), just after the solitary vessel is informed by the text's speaker that "there will be hours when you will realize that [the ocean] is infinite and that there is nothing more awesome than infinity."[43] To that boat floating alone on its surface, Irigaray's sea might add:

---

40. Aristotle, *Nicomachean Ethics*, 35–36 (Bk. II, chap. 9).
41. Friedrich Nietzsche, *Thus Spake Zarathustra*, trans. Adrian Del Caro (Cambridge: Cambridge University Press, 2006), 126. The latter allusion is to §341 in *Die fröhliche Wissenschaft* (see below).
42. Luce Irigaray, *Marine Lover of Friedrich Nietzsche*, trans. Gillian C. Gill (New York: Columbia University Press, 1991), 14.
43. Friedrich Nietzsche, *The Gay Science*, trans. Josefine Nauckhoff (Cambridge: Cambridge University Press, 2001), 126 (§124).

And the sea can shed shimmering scales indefinitely. Her depths peel off into innumerable thin, shining layers. And each one is the equal of the other as it catches a reflection and lets it go. As it preserves and blurs. As it captures the glinting play of light. As it sustains mirages. Multiple and still far too numerous for the pleasure of the eye, which is lost in that host of sparkling surfaces. And with no end in sight.... And whoever looks upon her from the overhanging bank finds there a call to somewhere farther than his farthest far. Toward an other ever more other. Beyond any anchorage yet imaginable.[44]

On a number of levels, Irigaray's aqueous female speaker echoes Malwida von Meysenbug's prefiguration of Romain Rolland's "oceanic feeling" in her *Memoirs of an Idealist* (1876), as well as their common prefiguration by Karoline von Günderrode's *Apocalyptical Fragment* (1801/1804), both of which I examined in the introduction. Why, ever since antiquity, have thinkers such as the few briefly surveyed above settled upon water—and specifically the space between its surface and its depths—as an image for meditating on topics from ethics to metaphysics to phenomenology?[45]

Perhaps one reason is that both the surface and the depths at heart involve the potential for either movement or stasis between different spheres.[46] Whatever relevance this may have for the history of philosophy, it certainly bears directly upon this book's central question of why German Realist authors return again and again to water, and so often structure their narratives around drowning; and in those narratives, as we have seen, the specific figural characteristics of drowning illustrate a certain "middle-space" of ethical action and temporal perception. That literary facet invites us to wonder what kind of middle space drowning might represent within

---

44. Irigaray, *Marine Lover*, 46–47.
45. See Edmund Husserl, *Ideas for a Pure Phenomenology and Phenomenological Philosophy*, trans. Daniel O. Dahlstrom (Indianapolis: Hackett, 2014), 79–80 (§44); Hans Blumenberg, *Quellen, Ströme, Eisberge*, ed. Ulrich von Bülow and Dorit Krusche (Berlin: Suhrkamp, 2012), 108, 118–120.
46. Compare Bernhard Blume, "Lebendiger Quell und Flut des Todes: Ein Beitrag zu einer Literaturgeschichte des Wassers," *Arcadia* 1, no. 2 (1966): 19–20; Hartmut Böhme, "Umriß einer Kulturgeschichte des Wassers: Eine Einleitung," in *Kulturgeschichte des Wassers*, ed. Hartmut Böhme (Frankfurt am Main: Suhrkamp, 1988), 1–42.

the broader epistemic and aesthetic context of the German nineteenth century. It is a large question, and one possible though ultimately unsatisfactory answer is that drowning illuminates a zone of experience in which we press up against the border with that which is not part of us; and whatever is not part of us always implicitly communicates its ability to outlast us (whether or not that ends up being the case). Similarly, when the basic opposition between the subjective experience of nature—here metonymically represented by water—and the vast, uninhabitable position of nature itself becomes a topic of concern in modernist literature and art, nature at once seems to be no longer anthropomorphized or "embodied," no longer capable of hosting an imagined vantage point that might return humanity's gaze, wonder, and concern; instead, nature is now simply *there*, and at once foreboding as a consequence. To get both Genettian and Kantian about it, in nineteenth-century German literature and in Poetic Realism especially, water operates as a *boundary* on two levels: first and foremost, it does so as a "diegetic phenomenon" in the stories themselves by virtue of being a liminal space on the edge of "nature" and "culture" that characters disappear into. And yet, due to precisely this, it also functions as a "narratological noumenon," as a boundary that gives form to these narrative instants but that cannot be directly experienced "in itself" by (living) characters—or, consequently, by the reader. Drowning scenes manifest that antinomy: they are scenes in which someone disappears from view, while the water into which they disappear exists as a constitutive part of the narrative landscape. The unseeable is intrinsic to what German Realism tells stories about seeing and losing sight of.

As we have observed throughout this book, realist writers again and again seem compelled to linger over this space of opposition between the surface and the depths; and furthermore, as I have tried to show in this concluding chapter, what had been a subtle implication in realist literature from the latter half of the nineteenth century would become concrete and vivid by the first decades of the twentieth. Within that span of time Ophelia emerged as a salient trope, not only as the explicit subject of numerous poems but also as a poetological figure in her own right.⁴⁷ In the former case, the character of Ophelia is often cast as a melancholy bearer of the news that the de-idealized, pure materiality of the body is the only stable truth of human existence to have outlived the horrors of the Great War. In the latter case, we encounter the antipode of the Romantic *Wasserfrau*: in reflecting on the poetic process itself, writers no longer seem to conceptualize their craft as an entrance into the "hidden depths" of the subjective interior (and thereby also into communion with the unifying substance of nature, spirit, and imagination). Rather, the emphasis begins increasingly to fall upon the act of retrieving, in order to become reconciled with, those things that "come back to the surface" in their insistent materiality.

This poetological development was by no means restricted to German-speaking lands (as is only natural, given the importance of figures like Shakespeare and Rimbaud for the German modernists). A powerful illustration of this fact can be found in the work of T. S. Eliot. Water, and particularly the imagery of seafaring and its hazards, appears with remarkable consistency throughout his oeuvre, from relatively early points such as part 4 of *The Waste Land* (1922), in which we are told of how the drowned sailor Phlebas at last "Forgot the cry of gulls, and the deep sea swell / And the profit and loss" of the world above the surface.⁴⁸ A similar note is sounded by the dying father in "Marina" (1930), who likens his own fading presence to a battered ship, and most clearly by the speaker of "The Dry Salvages" in *Four Quartets* (1941), who conjures a nocturnal moment at sea in which "The tolling bell / Measures time not our time, rung by the unhurried / Ground swell."⁴⁹ It is a moment of

---

47. This is the view of critics such as Hanspeter Zürcher, who proposes that water motifs function within modernist lyric and painting according to either a "Narcissan" or an "Ophelian" structure, which reflect the artwork's creator and hermeneutic potentialities, respectively. Zürcher, *Stilles Wasser: Narziß und Ophelia in der Dichtung und Malerei um 1900* (Bonn: Bouvier, 1975).

48. T. S. Eliot, "Death by Water," in *The Poems of T. S. Eliot*, vol. 1, *The Collected and Uncollected Poems*, ed. Christopher Ricks and Jim McCue (Baltimore: Johns Hopkins University Press, 2015), 67 (lines 313–314).

49. Eliot, *The Poems of T. S. Eliot*, 194 (lines 35–37)

internal awareness that everything we have ever experienced time to consist in has never had bearing upon anything beyond the narrow edges of our inhabited vantage point and will come to an end along with us, once we can no longer continue

> Trying to unweave, unwind, unravel
> And piece together the past and the future,
> Between midnight and dawn, . . .
> . . . .
> . . . before the morning watch
> When time stops and time is never ending;
> And the ground swell, that is and was from the beginning,
> Clangs
> The bell.[50]

Eliot not only suffused his poems with water imagery but invoked the specific theme of submergence as an illustration of how the creative process itself functions. In his concluding Norton Lecture (March 31, 1933), Eliot remarks how often poems address the scenario of their own composition as one of "mystical inspiration." He goes on to say, however, that poetry of this sort should be understood, not so much as a *positive* event of inspiration being visited upon the poet by a muse or other external agent, but instead as a *negative* instance of the poet's quotidian, internal barriers being dismantled in order to reveal what lies beneath them—and has lain there all along. Moreover, what lends a poem its particular quality is not the conditions of its enunciation (whether "mystical" or not), but instead an image that has been incubated within the poet after entering her or his psyche—consciously or unconsciously, through intertextual influence or personal experience—and then "sinking" to the depths of the subjective interior, beyond the reaches of memory and cognition, before eventually "resurfacing."

Eliot takes Coleridge's "Kubla Khan" (1816) as an example, writing that "the imagery of that fragment . . . sank to the depths of Coleridge's feeling, was saturated, transformed there . . . and

---

50. T. S. Eliot, *The Poems of T. S. Eliot*, 194 (lines 41–48).

brought up into daylight again."⁵¹ The heart of *poeisis* for him is this species of image that has been "saturated while it lay in the depths of . . . memory" and that "will rise like Anadyomene from the sea" as a "reborn image": "I suggest that what gives [this imagery] such intensity as it has in each case is its saturation . . . with feelings too obscure for the authors to know quite what they were. . . . The song of one bird, the leap of one fish, at a particular place and time, the scent of one flower . . . such memories may have a symbolic value, but of what we cannot tell, for they represent the depths of feeling into which we cannot peer."⁵²

Care, Earth, and the Drowning World

Eliot's poetology of submergence and resurfacing provides us with a fitting place to begin drawing this book to a close, because its dialectic illustrates precisely the two essential "movements" that the drowning motif performs in German literature of the late nineteenth and early twentieth centuries. In the narratives of German Realism, as we have seen, when characters vanish beneath the water's surface following an *Augenblick* of sacrificial decision, it symbolically highlights the fluid threshold between the realms of order and communal existence and the realm of subjective experience. However, by having begun with Goethe's Ottilie and ended with Ophelia, it has been possible to catch a glimpse of how German writers after 1900 become concerned less with the instant of submergence than with the implications of "resurfacing." In this they are of a piece with a general literary trend of their day, which was becoming increasingly interested in the issue of "temporal experience" because it was in the midst of undergoing cultural as well as phenomenological transformations. Yet as Pfeiffer notes, during this period "the changed structures of perception and consciousness are not merely

---

51. T. S. Eliot, *The Use of Poetry and the Use of Criticism (The Charles Eliot Norton Lectures, 1932–1933)* (Cambridge, MA: Harvard University Press, 1996), 139.
52. Eliot, *The Use of Poetry*, 140–141.

taken up as literary themes, but in fact determine the very form of narrativity itself."[53]

One of the core facets of the Ophelia topos in modernist German literature is its refocusing of the narrative gaze upon the remains that return to us and thereby reinforce how simultaneously close yet immoveable the boundary with them is. The weight of emphasis here falls on the meeting point of earth and water, though, which is where these remains appear (and increasingly so in the twentieth century). That makes good sense in its own way, as the earth has been recognized over many centuries as the "ground" not just of our physical lives but also of our *world* in a Heideggerian sense: of our collective as well as individual memories, present existences, and eventual resting places. "For what can we bequeath, / save our deposèd bodies to the ground?" asks Shakespeare's Richard II before going on to exclaim, "And nothing can we call our own but death / and that small model of the barren earth / which serves as paste and cover to our bones."[54]

Yet it is not just our *own* end that over time we come to localize in the ground beneath our feet, but also the end of those who have gone before and will go after us; the whole earth becomes their *sema*, a memorializing sign that, like the grave itself, conjugates their current as well as future absence with its physical presence in the world. Robert Pogue Harrison neatly sketches these phenomenological and hermeneutic applications of the classical *sema* as follows: "For the Greeks the grave marker was not just one sign among others. It was a sign that signified the source of signification itself, since it 'stood for' what it stood in—the ground of burial as such. In its pointing to itself, or to its own mark in the ground, the *sema* effectively opens up the place of the 'here,' giving it that human foundation without which there would be no places in nature."[55] In a similar spirit, the lyric voice of one of Wendell Berry's "Sab-

---

53. Pfeiffer, *Tod und Erzählen*, 220.

54. William Shakespeare, *The Tragedy of King Richard the Second* (1595), in *Complete Works of Shakespeare*, 633–667 (653), act 3, scene 2, lines 149–150, 152–154.

55. Robert Pogue Harrison, *The Dominion of the Dead* (Chicago: University of Chicago Press, 2003), 20.

bath poems" registers that the earth in a way becomes part of the self well before one's own body goes into the ground:

> Less and less you are
> That possibility you were.
> More and more you have become those lives and deaths
> That have belonged to you.
> You have become a sort of grave
> Containing much that was
> And is no more in time, beloved
> Then, now, and always.
> And so you have become a sort of tree
> Standing over a grave.[56]

Here the human speaker realizes that, as "a sort of tree," his own roots are housed and nourished by a *humus* that comprises countless other past presences that have since joined the soil, and thus illuminates a foundational facet of the earth we stand on when water meets it with its own genre of remains in tow.

However often the keynote of care and all of its ingredient melodies and modes of mortal finitude has rightly been associated with the earth, particularly from Greek antiquity onward, a remarkable figure from the Latin tradition is just as right to locate it along the riverbank. In his *Fabulae*, the Roman writer Hyginus takes this meeting point of earth and water as the setting for one of the briefest yet most haunting myths of human origins:

> When Cura [care] was crossing a certain river, she saw some clayey mud [*cretosum lutum*]. She took it up thoughtfully and began to fashion a man. While she was pondering on what she had done, Jove came up; Cura asked him to give the image life, and Jove readily granted this. When Cura wanted to give it her name, Jove forbade, and said that his name should be given it. But while they were disputing about the name, Tellus [earth, land] arose and said that it should have her name, since she had given her own body. They took Saturn for a judge; he seems to have decided for them: "Jove, since you gave him life, take his soul after

---

56. Wendell Berry, *A Timbered Choir: The Sabbath Poems, 1979–1997* (Berkeley: Counterpoint, 1998), 167 (I [1993], lines 2–12).

death; since Tellus offered her body, let her receive his body; since Cura first fashioned him, let her possess him as long as he lives, but since there is controversy about his name, let him be called *homo*, since he seems to be made from *humus* [soil, dirt]." (220)[57]

This fable has had no shortage of German interpreters (Heidegger being among the best-known of them), but one of the most consequential insights about it, at least for our present purposes, has come relatively recently. Hans Blumenberg provides it in posing a seemingly basic question: Why, after crossing the river, does Care think to mold the clay at her feet in the way that she does? "Where does the shape come from that lets Care ponder what it is? Is it only playful experimentation followed by a capricious outcome and a belated sanctioning?"[58] Blumenberg's thought is that the "core element" of the story, "the element that could explain how Care arrives at precisely this shape," is to be found on its innermost edge (or bank). What would otherwise appear as arbitrary chance suddenly obtains explanatory clarity when we remember that the fable begins with Care as she is in the process of *crossing* the river, as opposed to walking alongside it: "Cura crosses the river so that she can see herself mirrored in the river," Blumenberg proposes. The conclusion drawn from this is elegantly simple: "Therefore, Care may possess the human for its entire life, not, as in Saturn's judgment, because she invented humanity, but rather because the human was made in her image and likeness, and thus partakes in her being."[59]

In many ways, the theme of submergence in nineteenth-century German Realism illuminates Hyginus's mythic account of how earth *and* water co-determine humanity as an embodied, mortal consciousness made "in the image and likeness" of Care, born as it is *from* "clayey mud" (*cretosum lutum*) or soil ("*ex humo*") and not *by* the

---

57. Caius Iulius Hyginus, *The Myths of Hyginus*, trans. Mary Grant (Lawrence: University of Kansas Press, 1960), 157 (parenthetical translations mine). / Hyginus, *Hygini Fabulae*, ed. Peter K. Marshall (Leipzig: Teubner, 1993), 171–172.

58. Blumenberg, *Care Crosses the River*, trans. Paul Fleming (Stanford, CA: Stanford University Press, 2010), 140.

59. Blumenberg, *Care Crosses the River*, 141.

divine personification of Earth (Tellus).⁶⁰ After all, the poetics of drowning, along with its corollary themes of order and sacrifice, calls attention to the site of jointure between land and water as a place of encounter—not simply between human beings and the natural world, but also between life and death (the topological cradle of *cura*). If we turn to our present moment of ecological catastrophe, there is clearly much of value that a philosophical engagement with the question of the natural environment in the Anthropocene could draw from the littoral logic of the *cura* fable. After all, in Hyginus's text Care presents herself not merely as a core condition or etiological ingredient of human consciousness, but also precisely as an *imbrication* of this consciousness with natural elements, as a "shore" of sorts in which the human and the more-than-human coalesce in an originary way.

Such questions of extra-humic topography—not to say topology—become especially interesting when it comes to current trends in the environmental humanities, particularly work being done at the intersection of fields like eco-criticism and posthumanism. One thinks, for example, of Donna Haraway's and Marjolein Oele's recent attention to *humus* (soil) as a favored place for new directions of thinking about trans-species and even posthuman vitality.⁶¹ Comparatively, some of the more recent eco-criticism (at least of a literary bent) that

---

60. Tellus is the Roman equivalent of the Greek goddess Gaia; in this respect the distinction drawn in Hyginus's text seems to be that between a given material substance and its representative deity. See Harry Thurston Peck, "Gaea," in *Harper's Dictionary of Classical Antiquities*, vol. 1, ed. H. T. Peck (New York: Harper and Brothers, 1897), 702.

61. Haraway's account of multispecies "becoming-with," or sympoiesis, is especially pertinent to the existential valences of care outlined above, given that it does not shy away from, but in fact foregrounds, the intertwining of death with life. Haraway illustrates this with reference to the imagery and material actuality of "compost": various earthen settings in which the co-implication (*compositus*) of decay and growth (as in soil) might, by means of the *humus*, begin to reshape human relations to the nonhuman. Similar to Haraway, Oele thinks that *humus* is the best place to found (or ground) "e-co-affectivity" as a form of affectivity that is "focused on ontogenesis versus being ... it opens up to a temporality and a place beyond that of human temporality, thus drawing consolation and hope for a time and place beyond the anthropocene." Donna Haraway, *Staying with the Trouble: Making Kin in the Chthulucene* (Durham. NC: Duke University Press, 2016); Marjolein Oele, *E-Co-Affectivity: Exploring Pathos at Life's Material Interfaces* (Albany: SUNY Press, 2020), 142–143.

focuses upon water—particularly the sea—trains its gaze backward in literary history rather than beyond the horizon of the future of human history *tout court*.⁶² For instance, as part of an analysis of the English Elizabethan writer Walter Raleigh, Steven Swarbrick develops the thesis, *pace* Heidegger, that the faculty of "worlding" is not restricted to humans; instead, "indeed, oceans, rivers, and other sea-like bodies *have world* and are world-forming to the extent that they not only relate to the environment but also actively transform it."⁶³ In writings such as these, Swarbrick argues, one finds evidence of "the uncanny 'thereness' of the ocean" that plays a role in its "inhuman worlding," which nevertheless makes itself felt in Raleigh's conception of his relation to the environment as "a *scene of writing* enacted in and by the materials of the earth."⁶⁴

Such instances of "inhuman worlding" and "writing" certainly represent fertile ground for future eco-critical work in the sphere of German Studies, but the findings of this book oblige us, at least for the moment, to stay with the topic of writing *about* rather than *by* water, and of the specifically human confrontation with it. Throughout the realist narratives that we have explored in the preceding pages, the spatio-ontological setting for that confrontation has largely been the one that stretches vertically between water's surface and its depths. To an equal degree, though, and especially with an eye to the broader span of literary history, an even more charged zone of this sort is the one that extends laterally from the "home turf" of the shore to the *unheimlich* plane of open water. As Bachelard points out, water as it is known from the land is as much a boundary as a repository, and as Ophelia shows us, it is a boundary felt from *this* side of our lives that

---

62. This trend has begun to include the sphere of German Studies. See, for instance, Benjamin D. Schluter's recent remarks about several possibilities for future work on the age of Goethe from a "blue humanities" angle, in Schluter, "Unexpected Bodies of Water: On the 'Blue' *Goethezeit*," *Goethe Yearbook* 30 (2023): 147–154.

63. Steven Swarbrick, *The Environmental Unconscious: Ecological Poetics from Spenser to Milton* (Minneapolis: University of Minnesota Press, 2023), 274n73 (emphasis in the original). Swarbrick also notes the "oceanic turn" within early modern literary studies alluded to above, singling out the work of critics such as Dan Brayton, Lowell Duckert, and Steve Mentz (272n27).

64. Swarbrick, *The Environmental Unconscious*, 117, 134 (emphases in the original).

is replete with our dead, as well as the memories, fears, and hopes we attach to them; and as Charon shows us, it is a threshold that is as immovable as it is (in every sense) fluid, signifying the frontier that we have no ability to cross until we leave the land behind us—the land of the living, that is—in order to make the passage.

Shores can embody what Frank Kermode called the "sense of an ending" to the same degree that they can represent the idea of beginnings, since departure is proper to both. Hence the paradigmatic convergence of life and death on so many shores, horizons, and other watery boundaries throughout the literary tradition, as in the ancient Mesopotamian trope of land reached after a cosmic Deluge (as in *Gilgamesh* and Genesis) or in visits with the dead in epic poems of Greek and Latin antiquity as well as medieval Christian literature (such as *Odyssey* XI, *Aeneid* VI, and Dante's *Inferno* and *Purgatorio*). Of the many motifs and topoi associated with the dialectic of land and water, seafaring is arguably one of the most metaphorically and metaphysically rich as a symbol for the agon of ambition and limitation that characterizes so much of human existence; we are ever apart from the sea, and nevertheless we never tire in our attempts to traverse it, with all literal and literary means known to us. Perhaps it is no coincidence that it was this particular predilection of ours that Sophocles had his chorus of Thebes cite in their "ode on humanity" in *Antigone* as an illustration of what makes us so essentially *deinon*—both "wondrous and terrible" (*ungeheuer* is the German term that Hölderlin chose for his 1804 translation of the play, and that, five years later, Goethe would also have Ottilie choose to describe the notion of fate in *Elective Affinities*):[65]

Numberless wonders
Terrible wonders walk the world but none the match for man—

---

65. Hölderlin's rendering of the above quoted lines from Sophocles reads: "Ungeheuer ist viel. Doch nichts / Ungeheuerer als der Mensch. / Denn der, über die Nacht / Des Meers, wenn gegen den Winter wehet/ Der Südwind, fähret er aus / In geflügelten sausenden Häußern." Friedrich Hölderlin, *Die Trauerspiele des Sophokles: Antigonae*, in *Sämtliche Werke: Große Stuttgarter Ausgabe*, vol. 5, ed. Friedrich Beissner (Stuttgart: W. Kohlhammer, 1952), 219.

> That great wonder crossing the heaving gray sea,
> Driven on by the blasts of winter
> On through breakers crashing left and right,
> Holds his steady course
> . . . .
> ... ready, resourceful man!
> Never without resources
> Never an impasse as he marches on the future—
> Only Death, from Death alone he will find no rescue.⁶⁶

The "heaving" of that gray sea is conjured by the almost vertiginous rise and plunge of the chorus's words, swinging as they do across these few lines from mastery to vulnerability. Born aloft on the seaworthy crafts of their seemingly boundless "resources" of mind and *techne*, human beings find themselves as quickly in need of "rescue" from that very sea and *its* boundlessness.

Nowadays, things are the same and also different. It is our very commitment to horizonless mastery over the natural world, along with the ceaseless increase of this activity's consequences, that ironically has brought about our unprecedentedly radical abandonment to those very forces. A 2023 piece in the *New York Times* puts matters plainly: "Research shows that drownings rise with every degree on a thermometer"; in other words, as the planetary temperature increases, so do the instances of death in water.⁶⁷ One could hardly imagine a more concrete and urgent scenario of order, sacrifice, and submergence coming together: in refusing to acknowledge the biosphere's inbuilt boundaries, and obdurately continuing to stoke the flames of our collective home's hearth ever higher, we're consigning

---

66. Sophocles, *Antigone*, in *The Three Theban Plays: Antigone, Oedipus the King, Oedipus at Colonus*, trans. Robert Fagles (New York: Penguin Random House, 2000), 76–77 (lines 376–381, 401–404).

67. Emily Baumgaertner, "Drowning Is No. 1 Killer of Young Children—U.S. Efforts to Fix It Are Lagging," *New York Times*, July 8, 2023, https://www.nytimes.com/2023/07/08/health/children-drowning-deaths.html?smid=url-share. See the following corroborating studies: Deborah Girasek et al., "Patterns of Behaviour That Pose Potential Drowning Risk to Hikers at Yosemite National Park," *Journal of Travel Medicine* 23, no. 1 (2016): 1–7; Rebecca Sindall et al., "Drowning Risk and Climate Change: A State-of-the-Art Review," *Injury Prevention* 28, no. 2 (2022): 185–191.

to ever-rising waters not just our planet but each other as well. Unlike the ancient subjects of Sophocles's ode, we have made it possible in the intervening centuries to slowly but surely strip ourselves of fear before the elements; more like Ophelia, we are "singing snatches of old lauds" without even realizing that we're halfway to submergence; that our ontic earth is already drowning, with our ontological world soon to follow. By disinheriting ourselves of hereditary *cura* by means (and for the sake) of "resource," we have left ourselves room only for terror born of the need for rescue, which we have both necessitated and banished from reach in a single, centuries-long gesture.

Nonetheless, poets may well serve as our best guides for these uncharted waters, not because they can "save" us or are in a better position than climate experts in the natural and social sciences to identify risks and outline responsive courses of action—quite the contrary. Rather, they are guides because they are the ones best equipped to articulate in existential, psychic, and even spiritual terms our need for saving in the first place. One such poet, to whom I'll give the last word, is one who has also, fittingly, offered his own rendition of Sophocles's tragedy. In his retelling of the choral ode quoted above, Seamus Heaney inserts a sustained *basso continuo* of vestigial care, if not outright fearfulness, that only comes as a grace note at the end of Sophocles's original lines, and that tends to be expressed by too many in our own historical moment merely as intermittent pauses and silence:

> Among the many wonders of the world
> Where is the equal of this creature, man?
> First he was shivering on the shore in skins,
> Or paddling a dug-out, terrified of drowning.
> Then he took up oars, put tackle on a mast
> And steered himself by the stars through the gales.[68]

Perhaps the great lesson is to feel this care purposively and in advance, while we are still in transit between shores. In that respect

---

68. Seamus Heaney, *The Burial at Thebes: A Version of Sophocles' Antigone* (New York: Farrar, Straus and Giroux, 2004), 24.

Heaney's poetry leads by example, and arguably nowhere more so than in the 1991 collection *Seeing Things*. Coincidence probably plays little to no role in the fact that water is nearly omnipresent in these poems; it seeps up from bogs in order to be crossed by causeways, it draws the eye to itself on the outer edges of the visible horizon and close by in the harbor, "every stone / clarified and dormant" in it. It is present figuratively in thought and language as "the very currents memory is composed of," and throughout the discrete memories that many of the poems themselves are composed of, such as the river Heaney's "undrowned father" returns home from following a narrowly averted tragedy, or the one into whose "steady purchase and thrum" a fishing line had been cast in youth. Incidentally, it is in passages of remembered childhood that water in these poems of Heaney's most closely resembles what we have seen it convey in this book, magnifying the faint line separating chance from fate, choice from decision, and mere loss from sacrifice. This becomes especially clear in the titular, triptychal poem of Heaney's cycle, the first section of which charts its course through the very same thematic currents that so many narratives of German Realism traverse: the fragility of innocence, the contingency of order, and—above all—the waiting water:

> ...All the time
> As we went sailing evenly across
> The deep, still, seeable-down-into water,
> It was as if I looked from another boat
> Sailing through air, far up, and could see
> How riskily we fared into the morning,
> And loved in vain our bare, bowed, numbered heads.[69]

---

69. Seamus Heaney, "Seeing Things" (I), in *Seeing Things* (New York: Farrar, Straus and Giroux, 1991), 18. The other poems alluded to above are found on pages 78, 95, 20, and 13, respectively.

BIBLIOGRAPHY

Abram, David. *The Spell of the Sensuous: Perception and Language in a More-Than Human World*. New York: Pantheon Books, 1996.

Adorno, Theodor. "Satzzeichen." In *Noten zur Literatur: Gesammelte Schriften*, vol. 11, edited by Rolf Tiedemann, 106–113. Frankfurt am Main: Suhrkamp, 1974.

Agamben, Giorgio. *Homo Sacer: Sovereign Power and Bare Life*. Translated by Daniel Heller-Roazen. Stanford, CA: Stanford University Press, 1998.

———. *State of Exception*. Translated by Kevin Attell. Chicago: University of Chicago Press, 2005.

———. *The Use of Bodies*. Translated by Adam Kotsko. Stanford, CA: Stanford University Press, 2015.

Aichinger, Ingrid. "Harmonisierung oder Skepsis? Zum Prosawerk der Marie von Ebner-Eschenbach." *Österreich in Geschichte und Literatur* 16 (1971): 483–495.

Alighieri, Dante. *The Divine Comedy of Dante Alighieri*. Vol. 2, *Purgatorio*. Edited and translated by Robert M. Durling. Oxford: Oxford University Press, 2000.

Ambrose, Kathryn. "Women in Theodor Storm: The Opposition of Conformity and 'Otherness.'" In *The Woman Question in Nineteenth-Century*

English, German and Russian Literature, 93–116. Leiden: Brill Rodopi, 2016.

Aquinas, Thomas. *On Law, Morality, and Politics*. Translated by Richard J. Regan. Indianapolis: Hackett, 2002.

Arendt, Hannah. *The Human Condition*. Chicago: University of Chicago Press, 1998.

Argast, Regula. *Staatsbürgerschaft und Nation: Ausschliessung und Integration in der Schweiz, 1848–1933*. Göttingen: Vandenhoeck und Ruprecht, 2007.

Aristotle. *De Anima: Books I and II*. Translated by D. W. Hamlyn. Oxford: Oxford University Press, 1993.

———. *Nicomachean Ethics*. Translated by Robert Crisp. Cambridge: Cambridge University Press, 2000.

———. *Rhetoric*. Translated by C. D. C Reeve. Indianapolis: Hackett, 2018.

Arndt, Christiane. *Abschied von der Wirklichkeit: Probleme bei der Darstellung von der Realität im deutschsprachigen literarischen Realismus*. Freiburg im Breisgau: Rombach, 2009.

Auden, W. H. *Selected Poems: Expanded Edition*. Edited by Edward Mendelson. New York: Vintage International, 2007.

Auerbach, Erich. *Mimesis: Dargestellte Wirklichkeit in der abendländischen Literatur*. Tubingen: Francke Verlag, 2001.

———. "Philology and *Weltliteratur*," translated by Maire and Edward Said. *The Centennial Review* 13, no. 1 (1969): 1–17

Augustin, Hermann. *Adalbert Stifters Krankheit und Tod: Eine biographische Quellenstudie*. Basel: Schwabe, 1964.

Augustine. *Confessiones: Bibliotheca Sanctorum Patrum et Scriptorum ecclesiasticorum Theologiae et christianarum Litterarum cultoribus accommodata*, ser. 6, vol. 2. Edited by Felice Ramorino. Rome: Bibliotheca Ss. Patrum, 1909.

———. *Confessions*. Translated by Henry Chadwick. Oxford: Oxford University Press, 2008.

———. *De catechizandis rudibus*. Edited by William Yorke Fausset. London: Methuen, 1912.

———. *On Christian Doctrine*. Translated by J. F. Shaw. In *A Select Library of Nicene and Post-Nicene Fathers of the Christian Church*, vol. 2, edited by Philip Schaff, 515–597. New York: Scribner, 1907.

Baade, Hans W. "Springs, Creeks and Groundwater in Nineteenth-Century German Roman Law Jurisprudence with a Twentieth-Century Postscript." In *Comparative and Private International Law: Essays in Honor of John Henry Merryman on his Seventieth Birthday*, edited by David S. Clark, 61–91. Berlin: Duncker und Humblot, 1990.

Bachelard, Gaston. *L'eau et les rêves: Essai sur l'imagination et de la matière*. Paris: Librairie genérale française, 2012.

———. *Water and Dreams: An Essay on the Imagination of Matter*. Translated by Edith R. Farrell. Dallas: Pegasus Foundation, 1983.

Bachmann, Vera. *Stille Wasser—tiefe Texte? Zur Ästhetik der Oberfläche in der Literatur des 19. Jahrhunderts*. Bielefeld: Transcript Verlag, 2013.
Balzac, Honoré de. *The Wild Ass's Skin*. Translated by Patrick Coleman. Oxford: Oxford University Press, 2012.
Bandet, Jean-Louis. "Von Ophélie zu Ophelia: Wege eines Bildes von Arthur Rimbaud zu Georg Heym." In *Gallo-Germanica: Wechselwirkung und Parallelen deutscher und französischer Literatur (18.–20. Jahrhundert)*, edited by Eckhard Heftrich and Jean-Marie Valentin. Nancy: Presses universitaires de Nancy, 1986.
Bärtschi, Hans-Peter. *Industrialisierung, Eisenbahnschlachten und Städtebau: Die Entwicklung des Zürcher Industrie- und Arbeiterstadtteils Aussersihl; Ein vergleichender Beitrag zur Architektur- und Technikgeschichte*. Basel: Birkhäuser, 1983.
Bataille, Georges. *The Accursed Share: An Essay on General Economy*. Vol. 1. Translated by Robert Hurley. New York: Zone Books, 1993.
Baumann, Walter. *Gottfried Keller: Leben, Werk, Zeit*. Zurich: Artemis, 1986.
Baumgaertner, Emily. "Drowning Is No. 1 Killer of Young Children—U.S. Efforts to Fix It Are Lagging." *New York Times*, July 8, 2023.
Bayer, Frauke. *Mythos Ophelia: Zur Literatur- und Bild-Geschichte einer Weiblichkeitsimagination zwischen Romantik und Gegenwart*. Würzburg: Ergon Verlag, 2009.
Beckmann, Martin. "Stifters 'sanftes Gesetz': Selbstwiederholung in der Wirklichkeit." *Neophilologus* 80, no. 3 (1996): 435–459.
Beebee, Thomas Oliver. *Citation and Precedent: Conjunctions and Disjunctions of German Law and Literature*. New York: Continuum, 2012.
Begemann, Christian. "Figuren der Wiederkehr: Erinnerung, Tradition, Vererbung und andere Gespenster der Vergangenheit bei Theodor Storm." In *Wirklichkeit und Wahrnehmung: Neue Perspektive auf Theodor Storm*, edited by Elisabeth Strowick and Ulrike Vedder, 13–37. Bern: Peter Lang, 2013.
Beiser, Frederick C. *After Hegel: German Philosophy, 1840–1900*. Princeton, NJ: Princeton University Press, 2014.
Benjamin, Walter. *The Arcades Project*. Translated by Howard Eiland and Kevin McLaughlin. Cambridge, MA: Harvard University Press, 2002.
———. "Critique of Violence." In *Selected Writings*, vol. 1, *1913–1926*, edited by Marcus Bullock and Michael W. Jennings, translated by Edmund Jephcott, 236–252. Cambridge, MA: Harvard University Press, 1996.
———. *Das Passagen-Werk*. In *Gesammelte Schriften*, vol. 5.1, edited by Rolf Tiedemann. Frankfurt am Main: Suhrkamp, 1982.
———. "Goethe's *Elective Affinities*." In *Selected Writings*, vol. 1, *1913–1926*, translated by Stanley Corngold, 297–360. Cambridge, MA: Harvard University Press, 1996.
———. "Goethes *Wahlverwandtschaften*." In *Gesammelte Schriften*, vol. 1.1, edited by Rolf Tiedemann and Hermann Schweppenhäuser, 125–201. Frankfurt am Main: Suhrkamp, 1974.

———. "Gottfried Keller: Zu Ehren einer kritischen Ausgabe seiner Werke." In *Gesammelte Schriften*, vol. 2.1, *Aufsätze, Essays, Vorträge*, edited by Rolf Tiedemann and Hermann Schweppenhäuser, 283–295. Frankfurt am Main: Suhrkamp, 1977.

———. "Stifter." In *Gesammelte Schriften*, vol. 2.2, *Aufsätze, Essays, Vorträge*, edited by Rolf Tiedemann and Hermann Schweppenhäuser, 608–610. Frankfurt am Main: Suhrkamp, 1977.

———. "Zur Kritik der Gewalt." In *Gesammelte Schriften*, vol. 2.1, edited by Rolf Tiedemann and Hermann Schweppenhäuser, 179–204. Frankfurt am Main: Suhrkamp, 1977.

Bennett, Jane. *Vibrant Matter: A Political Ecology of Things*. Durham, NC: Duke University Press, 2010.

Berlin, Isaiah. *The Roots of Romanticism*. Edited by Henry Hardy. Princeton, NJ: Princeton University Press, 1999.

Bernd, Clifford A. *German Poetic Realism*. Boston: Twayne, 1981.

———. *Poetic Realism in Scandinavia and Central Europe, 1820–1895*. Columbia, SC: Camden House, 1995.

Berry, Wendell. *A Timbered Choir: The Sabbath Poems, 1979–1997*. Berkeley: Counterpoint, 1998.

Besson, Lucette. "L'eau de mort ou le thème de la noyade chez Balzac." *L'Année balzacienne* 1, no. 4 (2003): 307–329.

Biedrzynski, Effi. *Goethes Weimar: Das Lexikon der Personen und Schauplätze*. Zurich: Artemis und Winkler, 1993.

Blackbourn, David. *The Conquest of Nature: Water, Landscape and the Making of Modern Germany*. London: Jonathan Cape, 2006.

Blanchot, Maurice. *A Voice from Elsewhere*. Translated by Charlotte Mandell. Albany: SUNY Press, 2007.

Bleckwenn, Helga. "Aquis Submersus: das Motiv des ertrinkenden Kindes in Storms Novelle und in Goethes *Die Wahlverwandtschaften*." *Schriften der Theodor-Storm-Gesellschaft* 52 (2003): 75–83.

Blume, Bernhard. "Das ertrunkene Mädchen: Rimbauds Ophélie und die deutsche Literatur." *Germanisch-Romanische Monatschrift* 4 (1955): 108–119.

———. "Lebendiger Quell und Flut des Todes: Ein Beitrag zu einer Literaturgeschichte des Wassers." *Arcadia* 1, no. 2 (1966): 19–20.

Blumenberg, Hans. *Care Crosses the River*. Translated by Paul Fleming. Stanford, CA: Stanford University Press, 2010.

———. *Quellen, Ströme, Eisberge*. Edited by Ulrich von Bülow and Dorit Krusche. Berlin: Suhrkamp, 2012.

———. *Schiffbruch mit Zuschauer: Paradigma einer Daseinsmetapher*. Frankfurt am Main: Suhrkamp, 1979.

———. "Wirklichkeitsbegriff und Möglichkeit des Romans." In *Nachahmung und Illusion: Kolloquium Gießen Juni 1963; Vorlagen und Verhandlungen*, edited by Hans Robert Jauß, 9–27. Munich: Eidos Verlag, 1964.

Böhme, Gernot. *Für eine ökologische Naturästhethik*. Frankfurt am Main: Suhrkamp, 1989.

———. *Leib: Die Natur, die wir selbst sind*. Frankfurt am Main: Suhrkamp, 2019.
Böhme, Hartmut, ed. *Kulturgeschichte des Wassers*. Frankfurt am Main: Suhrkamp, 1988.
Boll, Karl Friedrich. "Das Bonnixsche Epitaph in Drelsdorf und die Kirchenbilder in Theodor Storms Erzählung *Aquis Submersus*." *Schriften der Theodor-Storm-Gesellschaft* 14 (1965): 24–38.
Bolterauer, Alice. *Ritual und Ritualität bei Adalbert Stifter*. Vienna: Edition Praesens, 2005.
Bolz, Norbert. "Ästhetisches Opfer: Die Formen der Wünsche in Goethes *Wahlverwandtschaften*." In *Goethes "Wahlverwandtschaften": Kritische Modellen und Diskursanalysen zum Mythos Literatur*, edited by Norbert Bolz, 64–87. Hildesheim: Gerstenberg, 1981.
Bovenschen, Silvia. *Die imaginierte Weiblichkeit: Exemplarische Untersuchungen zu kulturgeschichtlichen und literarischen Präsentationsformen des Weiblichen*. Frankfurt am Main: Suhrkamp, 1979.
Braidotti, Rosi. *The Posthuman*. Cambridge: Polity Press, 2013.
Bramkamp, Agatha C. *Marie von Ebner-Eschenbach: The Author, Her Time, and Her Critics*. Bonn: Bouvier Verlag, 1990.
Breyer, Till. *Chiffren des Sozialen: Politische Ökonomie und die Literatur des Realismus*. Göttingen: Wallstein, 2019.
Brinkmann, Richard. *Wirklichkeit und Illusion: Studien über Gehalt und Grenzen des Begriffs Realismus für die erzählende Dichtung des 19. Jahrhunderts*. Tübingen: Niemeyer, 1957.
Bronfen, Elisabeth. "Leichenhafte Bilder—bildhafte Leichen: Zu dem Verhältnis von Bild und Referenz in Theodor Storms Novelle *Aquis Submersus*." In *Die Trauben des Zeuxis: Formen künstlerischen Wirklichkeitsaneignung*, edited by Hans Körner et al., 305–334. Hildesheim: G. Olms, 1990.
———. *Over Her Dead Body: Death, Femininity, and the Aesthetic*. New York: Routledge, 1992.
Bubbio, Paulo Diego. *Sacrifice in the Post-Kantian Tradition: Perspectivism, Intersubjectivity and Recognition*. Albany: SUNY Press, 2014.
Bullock, Marcus. "Goethe versus Benjamin: *Elective Affinities* and Marriage Equality." *Monatshefte* 112, no. 1 (2020): 76–101.
Burkert, Walter. *Homo Necans: Interpretationen altgriechischer Opferriten und Mythen*. Berlin: De Gruyter, 1972.
Byrd, Vance. *A Pedagogy of Observation: Nineteenth-Century Panoramas, German Literature, and Reading Culture*. Lewisburg, PA: Bucknell University Press, 2017.
Carlen, Louis. *Rechtsgeschichte der Schweiz: Eine Einführung*. Bern: Francke Verlag, 1978.
Cassian, John. *The Institutes*. Translated by Boniface Ramsey. New York: Newman Press, 2000.
Cavell, Stanley. "Kierkegaard's *On Authority and Revelation*." In *Must We Mean What We Say? A Book of Essays*, 151–166. Cambridge: Cambridge University Press, 2002.

Conklin, William E. *Hegel's Laws: The Legitimacy of a Modern Legal Order.* Stanford, CA: Stanford University Press, 2008.
Cooper, Ian. "Theodor Storm and Disenchantment." *German Life and Letters* 68, no. 4 (2015): 584–597.
Cunningham, William L. "Wassersymbolik in *Aquis Submersus*," *Schriften der Theodor Storm-Gesellschaft* 27 (1978): 40–49.
Dangel-Pelloquin, Elsbeth. "Weiße Wäsche: Zur Synthese von Reinheit und Erotik bei Keller und Stifter." In *Die Dinge und die Zeichen: Dimensionen des Realistischen in der Erzählliteratur des 19. Jahrhunderts*, edited by Sabine Schneider and Barbara Hunfeld, 143–156. Würzburg: Königshausen und Neumann, 2008.
Deakin, Roger. "Drowning (Coroners), 1998." [RD/WLOG/2/24]. University of East Anglia Library, Norwich, UK.
De Certeau, Michel. *The Practice of Everyday Life.* Translated by Steven Rendall. Berkeley: University of California Press, 1988.
Deleuze, Gilles. *Difference and Repetition.* Translated by Paul Patton. New York: Columbia University Press, 1994.
Demetz, Peter. "Walter Benjamin als Leser Adalbert Stifters." *Neue Rundschau* 91, no. 1 (1980): 148–162.
Derrida, Jacques. *The Gift of Death.* Translated by David Wills. Chicago: University of Chicago Press, 1996.
Dooren, Thom van. *Flight Ways: Life and Loss at the Edge of Extinction.* New York: Columbia University Press, 2014.
Downing, Eric. *Double Exposures: Repetition and Realism in Nineteenth-Century German Fiction.* Stanford, CA: Stanford University Press, 2000.
Droste-Hülshoff, Annette von. *Ledwina.* In *Historisch-kritische Ausgabe: Werke, Briefwechsel*, vol. 5.1, edited by Winfried Woesler and Walter Huge, 77–121. Tübingen: Max Niemeyer Verlag, 1978.
Eagleton, Terry. *Radical Sacrifice.* New Haven, CT: Yale University Press, 2018.
Ebner-Eschenbach, Marie von. *Aus einem zeitlosen Tagebuch.* Berlin: Paetel, 1916.
———. *Beyond Atonement.* Translated by Vanessa Van Ornam. Columbia, SC: Camden House, 1997.
———. *Unsühnbar.* Edited by Burkhard Bittrich. In *Kritische Texte und Deutungen*, vol. 1, edited by Karl Konrad Polheim. Bonn: Bouvier Verlag, 1978.
Eisele, Ulf. "Realismus-Theorie." In *Deutsche Literatur: Eine Sozialgeschichte*, vol. 7, *Vom Nachmärz zur Gründerzeit: Realismus, 1848–1880*, edited by Horst Albert Glaser, 36–46. Reinbek bei Hamburg: Rowohlt, 1982.
Eliot, T. S. "Hamlet and His Problems." In *The Sacred Wood: Essays on Poetry and Criticism*, 95–103. London: Methuen, 1960.
———. *The Poems of T.S. Eliot.* Vol. 1, *The Collected and Uncollected Poems.* Edited by Christopher Ricks and Jim McCue. Baltimore: Johns Hopkins University Press, 2015.
———. *The Use of Poetry and the Use of Criticism (The Charles Eliot Norton Lectures, 1932–1933).* Cambridge, MA: Harvard University Press, 1996.

Emison, Patricia. "The *Paysage Moralisé*." *Artibus et Historiae* 16, no. 31 (1995): 125–137.
Ermatinger, Emil. *Gottfried Kellers Leben, Briefe und Tagebücher*. Vol. 1. Stuttgart: J. G. Cotta, 1924.
Eversberg, Gerd. *Der echte Schimmelreiter: So (er)fand Storm seinen Hauke Haien*. Heide: Boyens Verlag, 2010.
Falchi, Simonetta. "Re-Mediating Ophelia with Pre-Raphaelite Eyes." *Interlitteraria* 2 (2015): 171–183.
Fontane, Theodor. *Fragmente: Erzählungen, Impressionen, Essays*. Vol. 1. Edited by Christine Hehle and Hanna Delf von Wolzogen. Berlin: De Gruyter, 2016.
———. *Irretrievable*. Translated by Douglas Parmée. New York: NYRB Classics, 2011.
———. "Unsere lyrische und epische Poesie seit 1848." In *Sämtliche Werke*, vol. 21.1, edited by Kurt Schreinert, 7–33. Munich: Nymphenburger Verlagshandlung, 1963.
———. *Unwiederbringlich: Große Brandenburger Ausgabe; Das erzählerische Werk*. Vol. 13. Edited by Christine Hehle. Berlin: Aufbau Verlag, 2003.
Foucault, Michel. *On the Government of the Living (Lectures at the Collège de France, 1979–1980)*. Edited by Michel Senellart. Translated by Graham Burchell. New York: Palgrave Macmillan, 2014.
Frederick, Samuel. *The Redemption of Things: Collecting and Dispersal in German Realism and Modernism*. Ithaca, NY: Cornell University Press, 2022.
Freud, Sigmund. *Totem und Tabu: Einige Übereinstimmungen im Seelenleben der Wilden und der Neurotiker*. In *Gesammelte Werke*, vol. 9, edited by Anna Freud, Edward Bibring, and Ernst Kris. Frankfurt am Main: Fischer, 1986.
———. *Werke aus den Jahren 1892–1899*. In *Gesammelte Werke*, vol. 1, edited by Anna Freud, Edward Bibring, and Ernst Kris. Frankfurt am Main: Fischer, 1977.
Gaius, *Institutes*. Translated by W. M. Gordon and O. F. Robinson. Ithaca, NY: Cornell University Press, 1988.
Gates, Barbara. *Victorian Suicide: Mad Crimes and Sad Histories*. Princeton, NJ: Princeton University Press, 1988.
Gese, Hartmut. *Zur biblischen Theologie: Alttestamentliche Vorträge*. Munich: Kaiser, 1977.
Geulen, Eva. "Toward a Genealogy of Gender in Walter Benjamin's Writing." *German Quarterly* 69, no. 2 (1996): 161–180.
Girard, René. "Mimesis and Violence: Perspectives in Cultural Criticism." *Berkshire Review* 14 (1979): 9–19.
———. *Things Hidden since the Foundation of the World*. Translated by Stephen Bann and Michael Metteer. Stanford, CA: Stanford University Press, 1987.
———. *Violence and the Sacred*. Translated by Patrick Gregory. Baltimore: Johns Hopkins University Press, 1977.
Girasek, Deborah et al. "Patterns of Behaviour That Pose Potential Drowning Risk to Hikers at Yosemite National Park." *Journal of Travel Medicine* 23, no. 1 (2016): 1–7.

Godau, Michèle. *Wirkliche Wirklichkeit: Mythos und Ritual bei Adalbert Stifter und Hans Henny Jahnn*. Würzburg: Königshausen und Neumann, 2005.
Goethe, Johann Wolfgang. *Briefe: Historisch-kritische Ausgabe*. Vol. 3.1. Edited by Georg Kurscheidt and Elke Richter. Berlin: De Gruyter, 2014.
———. *Elective Affinities: A Novel*. Translated by David Constantine. Oxford: Oxford University Press, 2008.
———. *The Sufferings of Young Werther*. Translated by Stanley Corngold. New York: W. W. Norton, 2013.
———. *Werke: Hamburger Ausgabe in 14 Bänden*. Edited by Erich Trunz and Benno von Wiese. Munich: C. H. Beck, 1996.
Grätz, Katharina. "Erzählte Rituale—ritualisiertes Erzählen: Literarische Sinngebung bei Adalbert Stifter." In *Ordnung—Raum—Ritual: Adalbert Stifters artifizieller Realismus*, edited by Sabine Becker, 147–174. Heidelberg: Universitätsverlag Winter, 2007.
Günderrode, Karoline von. *Correspondence of Fräulein Günderode [sic] and Bettine von Arnim*. Translated by Margaret Fuller. Boston: Burnham, 1860.
Günter, Manuela. "'Ermanne dich, oder vielmehr erweibe dich einmal!': Gender Trouble in der Literatur nach der Kunstperiode." *Internationales Archiv für Sozialgeschichte der deutschen Literatur* 30, no. 2 (2005): 38–61.
Hadot, Pierre. *The Veil of Isis: An Essay on the History of the Idea of Nature*. Translated by Michael Chase. Cambridge, MA: Harvard University Press, 2006.
Hahn, Barbara. *Unter falschem Namen: Von der schwierigen Autorschaft der Frauen*. Frankfurt am Main: Suhrkamp, 1991.
Halbertal, Moshe. *On Sacrifice*. Princeton, NJ: Princeton University Press, 2012.
Haraway, Donna. *Staying with the Trouble: Making Kin in the Chthulucene*. Durham, NC: Duke University Press, 2016.
Harnisch, Antje. *Keller, Raabe, Fontane: Geschlecht, Sexualität und Familie im bürgerlichen Realismus*. Frankfurt am Main: Peter Lang, 1994.
Harrison, Robert Pogue. *The Dominion of the Dead*. Chicago: University of Chicago Press, 2003.
Heaney, Seamus. *The Burial at Thebes: A Version of Sophocles' Antigone*. New York: Farrar, Straus and Giroux, 2004.
———. "The Makings of a Music: Reflections on Wordsworth and Yeats." In *Preoccupations: Selected Prose, 1968–1978*, 61–78. New York: Farrar, Straus and Giroux, 1980.
———. *Seeing Things*. New York: Farrar, Straus and Giroux, 1991.
Hegel, G. W. F. *Aesthetics: Lectures on Fine Art*. Vol. 2. Translated by T. M. Knox. Oxford: Oxford University Press, 1975.
———. *Elements of the Philosophy of Right*. Translated by H. B. Nisbet. Cambridge: Cambridge University Press, 1991.
———. *Enzyklopädie der philosophischen Wissenschaft im Grundriss III*. In *Werke*, vol. 10, edited by Eva Moldenhauer and Karl Markus Michel. Frankfurt am Main: Suhrkamp, 1979.

———. *Grundlinien der Philosophie des Rechts*. In *Werke*, vol. 7, edited by Eva Moldenhauer and Karl Markus Michel. Frankfurt am Main: Suhrkamp, 1979.
———. *Phänomenologie des Geistes*. In *Werke*, vol. 3, edited by Eva Moldenhauer and Karl Markus Michel. Frankfurt am Main: Suhrkamp, 1976.
———. *The Phenomenology of Spirit*. Edited and translated by Terry Pinkard. Cambridge: Cambridge University Press, 2018.
———. *Vorlesungen über die Ästhetik*. In *Werke*, vol. 14, edited by Eva Moldenhauer and Karl Markus Michel. Frankfurt am Main: Suhrkamp, 1986.
Heidegger, Martin. *Einführung in die Metaphysik*. Tübingen: Niemeyer, 1987.
———. *Sein und Zeit*. Edited by Friedrich-Wilhelm von Herrmann. Frankfurt am Main: Klostermann, 1977.
Hein, Edgar. *Gottfried Keller: "Romeo und Julia auf dem Dorfe"—Interpretation*. Munich: Oldenbourg, 1988.
Hein, Jürgen. *"Romeo und Julia auf dem Dorfe": Erläuterungen und Dokumente*. Stuttgart: Reclam, 1971.
Heise, Ursula K. *Imagining Extinction: The Cultural Meanings of Endangered Species*. Chicago: University of Chicago Press, 2016.
Herbermann, Charles George, ed. *The Catholic Encyclopedia*, vol. 13. New York: Appleton, 1913.
Herminghouse, Patricia. "Women and the Literary Enterprise in Nineteenth-Century Germany." In *German Women in the Eighteenth and Nineteenth Centuries: A Social and Literary History*, edited by Ruth-Ellen B. Joeres and Mary Jo Maynes, 78–93. Bloomington: Indiana University Press, 1986.
Herrmann, Elisabeth. *Die Todesproblematik in Goethes Roman "Die Wahlverwandtschaften."* Berlin: Erich Schmidt Verlag, 1998.
Heusler, Andreas. *Schweizerische Verfassungsgeschichte*. Aalen: Scientia-Verlag, 1968.
Hillard, Derek. "Violence, Ritual, and Community: On Sacrifice in Keller's *Romeo und Julia auf dem Dorfe* and Storm's *Der Schimmelreiter*." *Monatshefte* 101, no. 3 (2009): 361–381.
Holmes, Tove. "Literary Images: Viewing and Visuality in German Realism." PhD diss., Johns Hopkins University, 2011.
Holub, Robert C. *Reflections of Realism: Paradox, Norm, and Ideology in Nineteenth Century German Prose*. Detroit: Wayne State University Press, 1991.
Honneth, Axel. *Der Kampf um Anerkennung: Zur moralischen Grammatik sozialer Konflikte*. Frankfurt am Main: Suhrkamp, 1994.
Honold, Alexander. "Vermittlung und Verwilderung: Gottfried Kellers 'Romeo und Julia auf dem Dorfe.'" *DVjs* 78, no. 3 (2004): 459–481.
Horkheimer, Max, and Theodor W. Adorno. *The Dialectic of Enlightenment: Philosophical Fragments*. Translated by Edmund Jephcott. Stanford, CA: Stanford University Press, 2002.
Hölderlin, Friedrich. *Die Trauerspiele des Sophokles: Antigonae*. In *Sämtliche Werke: Große Stuttgarter Ausgabe*, vol. 5, edited by Friedrich Beissner, 203–262. Stuttgart: W. Kohlhammer, 1952.

Höller, Hans. "Die Sozialgeschichtliche Bedeutung der ästhetischen Wahrnehmung bei Adalbert Stifter." *Wirkendes Wort* 4 (1982): 255–267.
Hubert, Henri, and Marcel Mauss. *Sacrifice: Its Nature and Function.* Translated by W. D. Halls. Chicago: University of Chicago Press, 1981.
Hughes, Derek. *Culture and Sacrifice: Ritual Death in Literature and Opera.* Cambridge: Cambridge University Press, 2007.
Husserl, Edmund. *Ideas for a Pure Phenomenology and Phenomenological Philosophy.* Translated by Daniel O. Dahlstrom. Indianapolis: Hackett, 2014.
Hyginus, Caius Iulius. *Hygini Fabulae.* Edited by Peter K. Marshall. Leipzig: Teubner, 1993.
———. *The Myths of Hyginus.* Translated by Mary Grant. Lawrence: University of Kansas Press, 1960.
Irigaray, Luce. *Marine Lover of Friedrich Nietzsche.* Translated by Gillian C. Gill. New York: Columbia University Press, 1991.
Irmscher, Hans Dietrich. *Adalbert Stifter: Wirklichkeitserfahrung und gegenständliche Darstellung.* Munich: Winkler Verlag, 1971.
———. "Konfiguration und Spiegelung in Gottfried Kellers Erzählungen." *Euphorion* 65 (1971): 319–333.
Irsigler, Franziska A. *Beschriebene Gesichter: Ekphrastische Porträts in der Erzählkunst des Poetischen Realismus.* Bielefeld: Aisthesis-Verlag, 2012.
Jackson, David A. *Theodor Storm: The Life and Works of a Democratic Humanitarian.* New York: Berg, 1992.
Jakobson, Roman. "On Realism in Art." In *Readings in Russian Poetics: Formalist and Structuralist Views*, edited by Ladislav Matejka and Krystyna Pomorska, 38–46. Normal, IL: Dalkey Archive Press, 2002.
Jameson, Fredric. "The Realist Floor Plan." In *On Signs*, edited by Marshall Blonsky, 373–384. Baltimore: Johns Hopkins University Press, 1985.
Jay, Martin. *The Dialectical Imagination: A History of the Frankfurt School and the Institute of Social Research, 1923–1950.* Berkeley: University of California Press, 1996.
Jørgensen, Sven-Aage. "Vergangenheit und Vergänglichkeit: Zur Funktion des Erinnerns in Theodor Storms Novellen." *Schriften der Theodor-Storm-Gesellschaft* 35 (1986): 9–15.
Justinian. *Institutes.* In *Corpus Iuris Civili*, vol. 1, edited by Paul Krueger. Hildesheim: Weidmann, 1993.
Kaiser, Gerhard. "Aquis Submersus—versunkene Kindheit: Ein Literaturpsychologischer Versuch über Theodor Storm." *Euphorion* 73 (1979): 410–434.
Kant, Immanuel. *Prolegomena to Any Future Metaphysics.* Translated by Gary Hatfield. Cambridge: Cambridge University Press, 2004.
Keats, John. *Selected Letters.* Revised edition. Edited by Grant F. Scott. Cambridge, MA: Harvard University Press, 2002.
Keller, Gottfried. *Gesammelte Briefe.* Vol. 4. Edited by Carl Helbling. Bern: Benteli, 1954.

———. *Sämtliche Werke: Historisch-kritische Ausgabe.* Vol. 4. Edited by Walter Morgenthaler. Frankfurt am Main: Stroemfeld, 1996.
———. *A Village Romeo and Juliet.* Translated by Paul Bernard Thomas. New York: Frederick Ungar, 1955.
———. *A Village Romeo and Juliet.* Translated by Ronald Taylor. Richmond, VA: Alma Classics, 2015.
Kelsen, Hans. *Reine Rechtslehre.* Vienna: Deuticke, 1960.
Kenworthy, B. J. "Ethical Realism: Marie von Ebner-Eschenbach's *Unsühnbar.*" *German Life and Letters* 41, no. 4 (1988): 479–487.
Kierkegaard, Søren. *Fear and Trembling / The Sickness unto Death.* Translated by Walter Lowrie. Princeton, NJ: Princeton University Press, 1968.
———. *Repetition / Fear and Trembling.* Edited and translated by Howard V. Hong and Edna H. Hong. Princeton, NJ: Princeton University Press, 1983.
———. *Works of Love.* Edited and translated by Howard V. Hong and Edna H. Hong. Princeton, NJ: Princeton University Press, 1998.
Kindler, Simone. *Ophelia: Der Wandel von Frauenbild und Bildmotiv.* Berlin: Reimer, 2004.
Kinnell, Galway. *A New Selected Poems.* New York: Mariner Books, 2001.
Koerner, Joseph Leo. *Caspar David Friedrich and the Subject of Landscape.* London: Reaktion, 1990.
———. *Reformation of the Image.* Chicago: University of Chicago Press, 2004.
Korff, Friedrich Wilhelm. *Diastole und Systole: Zum Thema Jean Paul und Adalbert Stifter.* Bern: Francke Verlag, 1969.
Kristeva, Julia. *Black Sun: Depression and Melancholia.* Translated by Leon S. Roudiez. New York: Columbia University Press, 1989.
Kuiken, Kir. "On the Delineation of Choice and Decision in Benjamin's 'Goethe's *Elective Affinities,*'" *Canadian Review of Comparative Literature* 31, no. 3 (2004): 286–308.
Lacan, Jacques. *The Ethics of Psychoanalysis: The Seminar of Jacques Lacan, Book VII.* Edited by Jacques-Alain Miller. Translated by Dennis Porter. London: Routledge, 1992.
Lehmann, Christine. *Das Modell Clarissa: Liebe, Verführung, Sexualität und Tod der Romanheldinnen des 18. und 19. Jahrhunderts.* Stuttgart: Metzler, 1991.
Levenson, Jon D. *The Death and Resurrection of the Beloved Son: The Transformation of Child Sacrifice in Judaism and Christianity.* New Haven, CT: Yale University Press, 1993.
Levinas, Emmanuel. *Totality and Infinity. An Essay on Exteriority.* Translated by Alphonso Lingis. The Hague: Martinus Nijhoff, 1979.
Lorenz, Hildegard. *Varianz und Invarianz: Theodor Storms Erzählungen; Figurenkonstellationen und Handlungsmuster.* Bonn: Bouvier Verlag, 1985.
Lukács, Georg. *Deutsche Realisten des 19. Jahrhunderts.* Bern: Francke Verlag, 1951.
Lyon, John B. *Out of Place: German Realism, Displacement, and Modernity.* New York: Bloomsbury, 2013.

MacLeod, Catriona. *Fugitive Objects: Sculpture and Literature in the German Nineteenth Century*. Evanston, IL: Northwestern University Press, 2014.

Mann, Thomas. *Die Entstehung des Doktor Faustus: Roman eines Romans (1949)*. Frankfurt am Main: Suhrkamp, 1984.

Marion, Jean-Luc. "Sketch of a Phenomenological Concept of Sacrifice." In *The Reason of the Gift*, translated by Stephen E. Lewis, 69–90. Charlottesville: University of Virginia Press, 2011.

Marx, Alfred. *Les systèmes sacrificiels de l'Ancien Testament: Formes et fonctions du culte sacrificiel à Yhwh*. Leiden: Brill, 2005.

Matz, Wolfgang. *Adalbert Stifter oder "Diese fürchterliche Wendung der Dinge."* Munich: Hanser, 1995.

McClymond, Kathryn. *Beyond Sacred Violence: A Comparative Study of Sacrifice*. Baltimore: Johns Hopkins University Press, 2008.

Meier, Thomas Dominik, and Rolf Wolfensberger. *"Eine Heimat und doch keine": Heimatlose und Nicht-Sesshafte in der Schweiz (16.–19. Jahrhundert)*. Zurich: Chronos, 1998.

Menninghaus, Winfried. "*Romeo und Julia auf dem Dorfe*: Eine Interpretation im Anschluß an Walter Benjamin." In *Artistische Schrift: Studien zur Kompositionskunst Gottfried Kellers*, 91–159. Frankfurt am Main: Suhrkamp, 1982.

Meszaros, Julia, and Johannes Zachhuber, eds. *Sacrifice and Modern Thought*. Oxford: Oxford University Press, 2013.

Meysenbug, Malwida von. *Memoiren einer Idealisten*. Vol. 3. Stuttgart: Verlag Auerbach, 1876.

Müllenhoff, Karl, ed. *Sagen, Märchen und Lieder der Herzogthümer Schleswig, Holstein und Lauenburg*. Kiel: Schwersche Buchhandlung, 1845.

Müller-Tamm, Jutta. "Farben, Sonne, Finsternis: Von Goethe zu Adalbert Stifter." *Goethe-Jahrbuch* 125 (2008): 165–173.

Nagel, Barbara A. *Ambiguous Aggression in German Realism and Beyond: Flirtation, Passive Aggression, Domestic Violence*. New York: Bloomsbury, 2021.

Nägele, Rainer. "Phantom of a Corpse: Ophelia from Rimbaud to Brecht." *MLN* 117, no. 5 (2002): 1069–1082.

Nagy, Gregory. "Sêma and Nóēsis: The Hero's Tomb and the 'Reading' of Symbols in Homer and Hesiod." In *Greek Mythology and Poetics*, 202–222. Ithaca, NY: Cornell University Press, 1992.

Neimanis, Astrida. *Bodies of Water: Posthumanist Feminist Phenomenology*. London: Bloomsbury, 2017.

Neusner, Jacob. *Confronting Creation: How Judaism Reads Genesis: An Anthology of Genesis Rabbah*. Columbia: University of South Carolina Press, 1991.

Nietzsche, Friedrich. *Beyond Good and Evil*. Translated by Judith Norman. Cambridge: Cambridge University Press, 2002.

———. *The Gay Science*. Translated by Josefine Nauckhoff. Cambridge: Cambridge University Press, 2001.

———. *Thus Spake Zarathustra*. Translated by Adrian Del Caro. Cambridge: Cambridge University Press, 2006.
Nightingale, Andrea. *Once Out of Nature: Augustine on Time and the Body*. Chicago: University of Chicago Press, 2011.
Nitschke, Claudia. "Chaos und Form, Raum und Ethos in Stifters *Bunte Steine*." *German Life and Letters* 68, no. 4 (2015): 554–568.
Oele, Marjolein. *E-Co-Affectivity: Exploring Pathos at Life's Material Interfaces*. Albany: SUNY Press, 2020.
Ort, Claus-Michael. *Zeichen und Zeit: Probleme des literarischen Realismus*. Tübingen: Niemeyer, 1998.
Ovid. *Metamorphoses*. Translated by Charles Martin. New York: W. W. Norton, 2004.
Palaver, Wolfgang. "Hauke Haien—Ein Sündenbock? Theodor Storms *Der Schimmelreiter* aus der Perspektive der Theorie René Girards." In *Religion—Literatur—Künste: Aspekte eines Vergleichs*, edited by Peter Tschuggnall, 221–236. Salzburg: Müller-Speiser, 1998.
Panofsky, Erwin. *Meaning in the Visual Arts*. Chicago: University of Chicago Press, 1982.
———. *Studies in Iconology: Humanistic Themes in the Art of the Renaissance*. New York: Routledge, 2018.
Parry, Idris. *Speak Silence: Essays*. Manchester, UK: Carcanet, 1988.
Pascal, Roy. *From Naturalism to Expressionism: German Literature and Society, 1880–1918*. London: Wiedenfeld and Nicholson, 1973.
Peck, Harry Thurston, ed. *Harper's Dictionary of Classical Antiquities*. Vol. 1. New York: Harper and Brothers, 1897.
Peucker, Brigitte. "Droste-Hülshoff's Ophelia and the Recovery of Voice." *Journal of English and Germanic Philology* 82, no. 3 (1983): 374–391.
Pfeiffer, Joachim. *Tod und Erzählen: Wege der literarischen Moderne um 1900*. Tübingen: Max Niemeyer Verlag, 1997.
Pfeiffer, Peter C. "'Den Tod aus dem Bereich des Romans fernhalten': Zur ästhetischen Funktion des Todes in der Literatur des bürgerlichen Realismus." *Germanic Review* 70 (1995): 15–23.
———. "Genre, Gender, and Aesthetic Evaluation of Novels of Adultery: Theodor Fontane's *Effi Briest* and Marie von Ebner-Eschenbach's *Unsühnbar*." *Colloquia Germanica* 52, no. 1–2 (2021): 131–148.
Plato. *Minos*. In *Plato in Twelve Volumes*, vol. 12, translated by W. R. M. Lamb. Cambridge, MA: Harvard University Press, 1955.
Potthast, Barbara. "'Ein lastend unheimliches Entfremden unserer Natur': Adalbert Stifters 'Die Sonnenfinsterniß am 8. Juli 1842' als Dokument einer anderen Moderne." *Scientia Poetica* 12 (2008): 114–140.
Preisendanz, Wolfgang. "Voraussetzungen des poetischen Realismus in der deutschen Erzählkunst des 19. Jahrhunderts." In *Wege des Realismus: Zur Poetik und Erzählkunst im 19. Jahrhundert*, 68–91. Munich: Wilhelm Fink Verlag, 1977.

Reddick, John. "Tiger und Tugend in Stifters 'Kalkstein': Eine Polemik." *Zeitschrift für deutsche Philologie* 95 (1976): 235–255.
Rhodes, Kimberly. *Ophelia and Victorian Visual Culture: Representing Body Politics in the Nineteenth Century*. London: Routledge, 2008.
Richter, Simon. "Goethe's *Faust* and the Ecolinguistics of <Here>." In *German Ecocriticism in the Anthropocene*, edited by Caroline Schaumann and Heather I. Sullivan, 45–64. New York: Palgrave Macmillan, 2017.
Ricoeur, Paul. *Memory, History, Forgetting*. Translated by Kathleen Blamey and David Pellauer. Chicago: University of Chicago Press, 2004.
Rigby, Kate. *Dancing with Disaster: Environmental Histories, Narratives, and Ethics for Perilous Times*. Charlottesville: University of Virginia Press, 2015.
———. *Topographies of the Sacred: The Poetics of Place in European Romanticism*. Charlottesville: University of Virginia Press, 2004.
Rilke, Rainer Maria. *The Notebooks of Malte Laurids Brigge*. Translated by Stephen Mitchell. New York: Random House, 1982.
———. *Sonnets to Orpheus*. Translated by Edward Snow. New York: North Point Press, 2004.
Ritson, Katie K. "Engineering the Anthropocene: Technology, Ambition, and Enlightenment in Theodor Storm's *Der Schimmelreiter*." In *Readings in the Anthropocene: The Environmental Humanities, German Studies, and Beyond*, edited by Sabine Wilke and Japhet Johnstone, 222–242. New York: Bloomsbury, 2017.
Roebling, Irmgard. "Wasserfrauen zwischen Fließen und Festschreibung: Storms Darstellung von Geschlechterverhältnissen am Beispiel seiner Novelle *Psyche*." In *Theodor Storms ästhetische Heimat: Studien zur Lyrik und zum Erzählwerk Storms*, 275–310. Würzburg: Königshausen und Neumann, 2012.
Romanska, Magda. "Ontology and Eroticism: Two Bodies of Ophelia." *Women's Studies* 34 (2005): 485–513.
Roochnik, David. "What is *Theoria*? *Nichomachean Ethics* Book 10.7–8." *Classical Philology* 104, no. 1 (2009): 69–82.
Rothenberg, Jürgen. *Gottfried Keller: Symbolgehalt und Realitätserfassung seines Erzählens*. Heidelberg: Universitätsverlag Winter, 1976.
Rüesch, Jürg Peter. *Ophelia: Zum Wandel des lyrischen Bildes im Motiv der "navigatio vitae" bei Arthur Rimbaud und im deutschen Expressionismus*. Zurich: Juris-Verlag, 1964.
Saliot, Anne-Gaëlle. *The Drowned Muse: Casting the Unknown Woman of the Seine across the Tides of Modernity*. Oxford: Oxford University Press, 2015.
Santner, Eric L. *The Royal Remains: The People's Two Bodies and the Endgames of Sovereignty*. Chicago: University of Chicago Press, 2011.
———. *The Weight of All Flesh: On the Subject-Matter of Political Economy*. Oxford: Oxford University Press, 2015.
Savigny, Friedrich Karl von. *Das Recht des Besitzes: Eine Civilistische Abhandlung*. Gießen: Heyer, 1803.
Schiffermüller, Isolde. *Buchstäblichkeit und Bildlichkeit bei Adalbert Stifter: Dekonstruktive Lektüren*. Vienna: Studien-Verlag, 1996.

——. "'Jenes Ding... das Licht': Zum Glanz in der Prosa von Adalbert Stifter." In *Fleck, Glanz, Finsternis: Zur Poetik der Oberfläche bei Adalbert Stifter*, edited by Thomas Gann and Marianne Schuller, 15–33. Paderborn: Fink Verlag, 2014.
Schiller, Friedrich. "Über den Gebrauch des Chors in der Tragödie." In *Sämtliche Werke: Historisch-kritische Ausgabe in zwanzig Bänden*, vol. 20, edited by Otto Güntter and Georg Witkowski, 251–258. Leipzig: Hesse und Becker, 1910.
Schilling, Diana. *Kellers Prosa*. Frankfurt am Main: Peter Lang, 1998.
Schlegel, Friedrich. "Ideas." In *The Early Political Writings of the German Romantics*, edited by Frederick C. Beiser, 123–140. Cambridge: Cambridge University Press, 1996.
Schluter, Benjamin D. "Unexpected Bodies of Water: On the 'Blue' *Goethezeit*." *Goethe Yearbook* 30 (2023): 147–154.
Schmidt, Julian. "Die neue Generation." In *Bilder aus dem geistigen Leben unserer Zeit*, 1–41. Leipzig: Duncker und Humblot, 1870.
——. "Der neueste englische Roman und das Princip des Realismus." In *Realismus und Gründerzeit: Manifeste und Dokumente zur deutschen Literatur, 1848–1880*, vol. 2, edited by Max Bucher et al., 90–93. Stuttgart: J. B. Metzler, 1975.
Schmitt, Carl. *Political Theology. Four Chapters on the Concept of Sovereignty*. Translated by George Schwab. Chicago: University of Chicago Press, 1985.
——. *Politische Theologie: Vier Kapitel zur Lehre von der Souveränität*. Munich: Duncker und Humblot, 1922.
Schopenhauer, Arthur. *The World as Will and Representation*. Vol. 1. Translated by Judith Norman, Alistair Welchman, and Christopher Janaway. Cambridge: Cambridge University Press, 2010.
Schweizerischer Bundesrat. "Bericht des Bundesrathes an die Bundesversammlung über das Gesetz, betreffend die Heimathlosigkeit, vom 30. September 1850." *Schweizerisches Bundesblatt*, II. Jg., vol. 3, no. 46 (1850): 123–139.
Sebald, W. G. *Die Beschreibung des Unglücks: Zur österreichischen Literatur von Stifter bis Handke*. Frankfurt am Main: Fischer, 1994.
Selbmann, Rolf. *Gottfried Keller: Romane und Erzählungen*. Berlin: Erich Schmidt Verlag, 2001.
Selge, Martin. *Adalbert Stifter: Poesie aus dem Geist der Naturwissenschaft*. Stuttgart: W. Kohlhammer, 1976.
Sengle, Friedrich. *Biedermeierzeit: Deutsche Literatur im Spannungsfeld zwischen Restauration und Revolution, 1815–1848*. 3 vols. Stuttgart: J. B. Metzler, 1971.
Sengupta, Karl Shankar. *Otherwise, then Being: Kenosis in the Thought of Emmanuel Levinas*. PhD diss., University of Texas–Dallas, 2021.
Shakespeare, William. *The Complete Works of Shakespeare*. Edited by Alfred Harbage and Willard Farnham. Baltimore: Penguin, 1969.
Showalter, Elaine. "Representing Ophelia: Women, Madness, and the Responsibilities of Feminist Criticism." In *Shakespeare and the Question of Theory*,

edited by Patricia Parker and Geoffrey Hartman, 77–94. New York: Methuen, 1985.
Silz, Walter. *Realism and Reality: Studies in the German Novelle of Poetic Realism*. Chapel Hill: University of North Carolina Press, 1954.
Sindall, Rebecca et al. "Drowning Risk and Climate Change: A State-of-the-Art Review." *Injury Prevention* 28, no. 2 (2022): 185–191.
Søndergaard, Peter Brix. "'Something Strangely Perverse': Nature and Gender in J. E. Millais's *Ophelia*." *Romantik* 7, no. 1 (2018): 115–125.
Sophocles. *The Three Theban Plays: Antigone, Oedipus the King, Oedipus at Colonus*. Translated by Robert Fagles. New York: Penguin Random House, 2000.
Sorenson, Alexander. "The Bride by the Water: Duty, Procession, and Sacrifice in Theodor Fontane's *Unwiederbringlich*." *German Life and Letters* 72, no. 2 (2019): 151–167.
———. *Trials by Water: Law, Sacrifice and Submergence in German Realism*. PhD diss., University of Chicago, 2019.
Spinoza, Benedict de. *On the Improvement of the Understanding / The Ethics / Correspondence*. Translated by R. H. M Elwes. New York: Dover, 1955.
———. *A Theologico-Political Treatise and Political Treatise*. Translated by R. H. M Elwes. New York: Dover, 2004.
Staub, Werner. "Christina Luise Scheidegger (1843–1866): Die Braut von Gottfried Keller." *Jahrbuch des Oberaargaus* 25 (1982): 159–184.
Stein, Malte. "Grenzgänge: Zur Bedeutung des Wasserfrau-Motivs in Storms Erzählung *Auf der Universität* und *Der Schimmelreiter*." *Storm-Blätter aus Heiligenstadt* 11 (2005): 19–32.
———. *"Sein Geliebtestes zu töten": Literaturpsychologische Studien zum Geschlechter- und Generationskonflikt im erzählerischen Werk Theodor Storms*. Berlin: Erich Schmidt Verlag, 2006.
Stein, Peter. *Roman Law in European History*. Cambridge: Cambridge University Press, 1999.
Stern, Steven. "The Unbinding of Isaac." In *Sacrifice, Scripture, and Substitution: Readings in Ancient Judaism and Christianity*, edited by Ann W. Astell and Sandor Goodhart, 261–283. Notre Dame, IN: University of Notre Dame Press, 2011.
Stifter, Adalbert. *Abdias*. Translated by Helen Watanabe-O'Kelly. London: Angel Books, 1990.
———. *The Bachelors*. Translated by David Bryer. London: Pushkin Press, 2008.
———. *Gesammelte Werke in vierzehn Bänden*. Vol. 14. Edited by Konrad Steffen. Basel: Birkhäuser, 1972.
———. *Motley Stones*. Translated by Isabel Fargo Cole. New York: NYRB Classics, 2021.
———. *Sämtliche Werke*. Vol. 15, *Vermischte Schriften II*. Edited by Gustav Wilhelm. Reichenberg: Sudetendeutscher Verlag, 1935.
———. "The Solar Eclipse on July 8th, 1842." Translated by Jocelyn Holland. *Configurations* 23, no. 2 (2015): 253–258.

Stockinger, Claudia. *Das 19. Jahrhundert: Zeitalter des Realismus*. Berlin: Akademie Verlag, 2010.
Stöckmann, Ingo. *Der Wille zum Willen: Der Naturalismus und die Gründung der literarischen Moderne, 1880–1900*. Berlin: De Gruyter, 2009.
Storm, Theodor. *Der Briefwechsel zwischen Paul Heyse und Theodor Storm*. Vol. 1. Edited by Georg Plotke. Munich: J. F. Lehmann, 1917.
———. *A Doppelgänger—Aquis Submersus*. Translated by Denis Jackson. London: Angel Books, 2015.
———. *The Rider on the White Horse and Selected Stories*. Translated by James Wright. New York: NYRB Classics, 1964.
———. *Sämtliche Werke in vier Bänden*. Edited by Karl Ernst Laage and Dieter Lohmeier. Frankfurt am Main: Deutscher Klassiker Verlag, 1987–1988.
Stroumsa, Guy G. *The End of Sacrifice: Religious Transformations in Late Antiquity*. Translated by Susan Emanuel. Chicago: University of Chicago Press, 2009.
Strowick, Elisabeth. "'Eine andere Zeit': Storms Rahmentechnik des Zeitsprungs." In *Wirklichkeit und Wahrnehmung: Neue Perspektiven auf Theodor Storm*, edited by Elisabeth Strowick and Ulrike Vedder, 55–72. Bern: Peter Lang, 2013.
Stuby, Anna Maria. *Liebe, Tod und Wasserfrau: Mythen des Weiblichen in der Literatur*. Opladen: Westdeutscher Verlag, 1992.
Swales, Erika. *The Poetics of Skepticism: Gottfried Keller and "Die Leute von Seldwyla."* Oxford: Berg, 1994.
Swales, Martin, and Erika Swales. *Adalbert Stifter: A Critical Study*. Cambridge: Cambridge University Press, 1984.
Swarbrick, Steven. *The Environmental Unconscious: Ecological Poetics from Spenser to Milton*. Minneapolis: University of Minnesota Press, 2023.
Szondi, Peter. *Versuch über das Tragische*. Frankfurt am Main: Insel-Verlag, 1964.
Tanzer, Ulrike. *Frauenbilder im Werk Marie von Ebner-Eschenbachs*. Stuttgart: Akademischer Verlag, 1997.
Tebben, Karin. *Von der Unsterblichkeit des Eros und den Wirklichkeiten der Liebe: Geschlechterbeziehungen—Realismus—Erzählkunst*. Heidelberg: Universitätsverlag Winter, 2011.
———. "'Wo keine Göttinnen sind, da walten Gespenster': Dämoninnen und Philister im Werk Theodor Storms." *Germanic Review* 79, no. 1 (2004): 7–38.
Tielke, Martin. *Sanftes Gesetz und historische Notwendigkeit: Adalbert Stifter zwischen Restauration und Revolution*. Bern: Peter Lang, 1979.
Titzmann, Michael. *Zwischen Goethezeit und Realismus*. Tübingen: Niemeyer, 2002.
Toegel, Edith. "'Entsagungsmut' in Marie von Ebner-Eschenbach's Works. A Female-Male Perspective." *Forum for Modern Language Studies* 28 (1992): 140–149.
Tremblay, Jean-Thomas. *Breathing Aesthetics*. Durham, NC: Duke University Press, 2022.

Usener, Hermann, ed. *Scholia in Lucani bellum civile: Commenta Bernensia*. Hildesheim: Georg Olms Verlagsbuchhandlung, 1967.
Vico, Giambattista. *The New Science (Third Edition of 1744)*. Translated by Thomas Bergin and Max Fisch. Ithaca, NY: Cornell University Press, 1984.
Vismann, Cornelia. *Medien der Rechtsprechung*. Frankfurt am Main: Fischer, 2011.
Vogel, Matthias. "*Melusine . . . das lässt aber tief blicken*": Studien zur Gestalt der Wasserfrau in dichterischen und künstlerischen Zeugnissen des 19. Jahrhunderts. Bern: Peter Lang, 1989.
Voß, Stefan. *Männlichkeit und soziale Ordnung bei Gottfried Keller: Studien zu Geschlecht und Realismus*. Berlin: De Gruyter, 2019.
Weber, Christoph Daniel. "Deichbau und Selbstopfer: Der Katastrophendiskurs in Theodor Storms *Der Schimmelreiter*." *DVjs* 90, no. 1 (2016): 109–133.
Weinhold, Ulrike. "Bemerkungen zu Ophelia." In *Grenzgänge: Literatur und Kultur im Kontext*, edited by Guillaume van Gemert and Hans Ester, 297–310. Amsterdam: Rodopi, 1990.
Wellbery, David E. "Die Wahlverwandtschaften (1809)." In *Goethes Erzählwerk: Interpretationen*, edited by Paul Michael Lützeler and James W. McLeod, 291–318. Stuttgart: Reclam, 1985.
Wellek, René. "The Concept of Realism in Literary Scholarship." *Neophilologus* 45 (1961): 1–20.
Wels, Volkhard. "Opfer und Erlösung: Eine Auslegung von Goethes *Wahlverwandtschaften* nach ihrer theologischen Begrifflichkeit." *Euphorion* 88, no. 4 (1994): 406–417.
Whitman, James Q. *The Legacy of Roman Law in the German Romantic Era: Historical Vision and Legal Change*. Princeton, NJ: Princeton University Press, 1990.
Wilke, Sabine. *German Culture and the Modern Environment: Narrating and Depicting Nature*. Leiden: Brill Rodopi, 2015.
Woodford, Charlotte. "Realism and Sentimentalism in Marie von Ebner-Eschenbach's *Unsühnbar*." *Modern Language Review* 101 (2006): 151–166.
Wünsch, Marianne. "'Tod' in der Erzählliteratur des deutschen Realismus." *Jahrbuch der Raabe-Gesellschaft* 40 (1999): 1–14.
Würffel, Stefan Bodo. *Ophelia: Figur und Entfremdung*. Bern: Francke Verlag, 1985.
Wysling, Hans, ed. *Gottfried Keller, 1819–1890*. Zurich: Artemis, 1990.
Ziolkowski, Theodore. *The Mirror of Justice: Literary Reflections of Legal Crises*. Princeton, NJ: Princeton University Press, 1997.
Zürcher, Hanspeter. *Stilles Wasser: Narziß und Ophelia in der Dichtung und Malerei um 1900*. Bonn: Bouvier, 1975.

Index

Abdias (Stifter), 78, 87, 90, 96, 115, 118, 119n66
Abraham (Bible), 193–96, 195n38, 196n40
Adorno, Theodor, 188–89, 200–201, 204
Aeschylus, 127n11
Agamben, Giorgio, 20–22, 65–66, 86, 124
Agamemnon, 194–95
Aichinger, Ingrid, 52n34, 61n37, 68, 73n52
"Andenken" (Remembrance) (Hölderlin), 164
Antigone (Sophocles), 239
Apokalyptisches Fragment (Apocalyptical Fragment) (Günderrode), 29–30, 229
Aquinas, Thomas, 14–15, 15n24

Aquis Submersus (Storm), 25, 165, 171–86
Arendt, Hannah, 8, 99
Aristotle, 64n42, 101, 118n62, 227
"As I Walked Out One Evening" (Auden), 121
atonement
  in Ebner-Eschenbach, 40, 52, 55, 63, 67, 70–73
  in Goethe, 47, 49–50, 69
  in Stifter, 110, 114
  in Storm, 184–85
Auden, W. H., 121
Auerbach, Erich, 184n24, 194
Auf dem Staatshof (In the Great Hall) (Storm), 166–67
Auf der Universität (At the University) (Storm), 166–67

Aufzeichnungen des Malte Laurids Brigge, Die (The Notebooks of Malte Laurids Brigge) (Rilke), 218–19, 219n22
Augustine, 82, 116n59, 139n25, 158–60
Aus dem bairischen Walde (From the Bavarian Forest) (Stifter), 76

Bachelard, Gaston, 26–27, 55, 60, 220–22, 222n29, 238–39
Bachmann, Vera, 74n53, 204n48
Balzac, Honoré de, 219–20
baptism, 116n59, 183–84
Bataille, Georges, 18–19, 22
Baumann, Walter, 122n2
Benjamin, Walter, 37, 42–44, 47–49, 92–93, 120, 122n4, 185, 203
Benn, Gottfried, 224
Bereshit Rabbah, 195–96
Berry, Wendell, 234–35
Biedermeier period, 3, 11, 120
Bishop, Elizabeth, 1
Bittrich, Burkhard, 61
Blanchot, Maurice, 219, 219n22
Bleckwenn, Helga, 182n20
Blumenberg, Hans, 7n10, 106–7, 236
Böhme, Gernot, 32, 191–92
Breyer, Till, 17–18
Brinkmann, Richard, 8
Bubbio, Paolo Diego, 83
Bullock, Marcus, 45
Bunte Steine (Motley Stones) (Stifter), 78, 91–96, 98, 107n47
bürgerliches Trauerspiel (bourgeois mourning-play), 2
Burkert, Walter, 22–23
Byrd, Vance, 102n42

Cassian, John, 111n50
Cavell, Stanley, 195n38
Certeau, Michel de, 81
"Charon Complex," 220–21
Clarissa (Richardson), 41
climate change, 240–41
Coleridge, Samuel Taylor, 232–33

Commenta Bernensia, 86n14
Constantine, David, 45
contract, 137–38

Dante Alighieri, 157, 202
"Dead Woman in the Water, The" (Heym), 224
Deakin, Roger, 225
death, 11–12, 224–25. *See also* drowning
 in Bachelard, 220–21
 of Christ, 84–85
 in Ebner-Eschenbach, 56–57, 71
 female, 41
 in Rilke, 219n22
 in Stifter, 84–85, 87–88
 in Storm, 166n3, 167, 181, 186, 202
Deleuze, Gilles, 111, 118
Derrida, Jacques, 195–97
Donatists, 116n59
Dooren, Thom van, 33
Downing, Eric, 93n24
Draußen im Heidedorf (The Village on the Moor) (Storm), 166–68, 178
Droste-Hülshoff, Annette, 28–29, 211–12
drowning, 2–3
 in Aristotle, 227
 in Ebner-Eschenbach, 69–70, 72–73
 gendering of, 24–25, 24n41
 in Goethe, 50
 in Keller, 155–63
 as "middle space," 229–30
 narrative landscape and, 10–14
 as "offstage" occurrence, 217
 in Shakespeare, 208–10
 in Storm, 167, 171–85, 199–200, 202–3
 truth and, 74–75
"Dry Salvages, The" (Eliot), 231–32

Eagleton, Terry, 20–21
Ebner-Eschenbach, Marie von, 3, 25, 37–42, 49–62, 54n35, 61n37, 63–73, 68n48, 73n52
eclipse, solar, 77, 80–90, 98, 103, 117–20

eco-criticism, 237–38
Einsame Menschen (Lonely People) (Hauptmann), 222–23
Eisele, Ulf, 6n6
Eliot, T. S., 113n44, 231–33
Enlightenment, 11, 13
Eumenides (Aeschylus), 127n11

Fabula (Hyginus), 235–37
Falchi, Simonetta, 214n12
Fasching (Carnival) (Hauptmann), 223
Fear and Trembling (Kierkegaard), 193–94
femininity, 25, 27, 213, 216
floods, 77–79, 82, 192, 197–98, 239
Fontane, Theodor, 6–8, 11, 25, 218–19
Foucault, Michel, 183
French Realism, 4–5
Freud, Sigmund, 11, 22, 30, 33, 115, 133n18, 226n34
Freytag, Gustav, 5, 25
Friedrich, Caspar David, 13–14

Gaius, 128n12
Gates, Barbara, 24n41
gender
    drowning and, 24–25, 24n41
    in Ebner-Eschenbach, 51–52
    genealogy of, 48
    in Keller, 154–55
    in Storm, 168
    submergence and, 27
    water and, 168–69
German Expressionism, 208, 210, 224
German Naturalism, 222–23
German Realism
    emergence of, 2
    French Realism *vs.*, 4–5
    poeticism in, 9
    program of, 5–10
    reality in, 5
    Romanticism *vs.*, 12–13
Geulen, Eva, 48
Girard, René, 22–23, 124, 133–34, 150–51

Goethe, Johann Wolfgang von, 25, 39, 42–51, 49n29, 50–51, 56–59, 64–65, 71n50, 143, 182, 206–7
Gotthelf, Jeremias, 82
graves, 234–35
Grenzboten, Die (periodical), 5
Grimm, Jacob, 16
Günderrode, Karoline von, 29–30, 229

habit, 110–11, 111n52, 112–13
Hadot, Pierre, 13
Hagestolz, Der (The Bachelors) (Stifter), 114n56
Halbertal, Moshe, 23
Hamlet (Shakespeare), 208–10, 214. *See also* Ophelia (Shakespearean character)
Haraway, Donna, 237, 237n61
Harrison, Robert Pogue, 234
Hauptmann, Gerhart, 25n43, 222–23
Heaney, Seamus, 125, 241–42
Hebbel, Friedrich, 1–2, 223
Hegel, Georg, 22, 39, 111, 111n52, 116, 137–38, 138n23
Heidegger, Martin, 11, 15n25, 219, 236, 238
Hein, Edgar, 129n16
Heinrich von Ofterdingen (Novalis), 27
Heise, Ursula K., 32–33
Heraclitus, 87n15, 118, 120, 227
Hermann und Dorothea (Goethe), 143
Heym, Georg, 224
Heyse, Paul, 157n43
Hillard, Derek, 123n5
Hölderlin, Friedrich, 164, 239
Höller, Hans, 97
Holz, Arno, 222
Home Sacer (Agamben), 20
Horkheimer, Max, 200–201, 201n46
Hubert, Henri, 20
Hughes, Derek, 21
humus, 235–37, 237n61
Husserl, Edmund, 32n55
Hyginus, 235–37, 237n60

idealism, 6n6
Ideen (Schlegel), 21n37

Immensee (Storm), 204n48
Impressionism, 25n43, 223–24
Inconnue de la Seine, L', 218–19, 219n22
inheritance, 170–71
Institutes (Cassian), 111n50
Institutes (Gaius), 128n12
Institutes (Justinian), 141n28
"In the Village" (Bishop), 1
Iphigenia, 194–95
Irigaray, Luce, 30, 33, 228–29
Irretrievable (Fontane), 218–19
Isaac (Bible), 193–96, 196n40

Jakobson, Roman, 4
Jay, Martin, 201n46
Jenseits von Gut und Böse (Beyond Good and Evil) (Nietzsche), 62–63
Jesus Christ, 83–85, 100–101
Jung, Carl, 33
Justinian, 141n28

Kalkstein (Limestone) (Stifter), 25, 78–79, 99–117, 113n44
Kant, Immanuel, 226
Katzensilber (Cat-Silver) (Stifter), 107n47
Keats, John, 37, 205, 226
Keller, Gottfried, 3, 5–6, 25, 121–63, 123n5, 142n29
Kelsen, Hans, 86n15
kenosis, 83–84, 114, 116, 196
Kenworthy, B. J., 41
Kermode, Frank, 239
Keyserling, Eduard von, 25n43, 223
Kierkegaard, Søren, 22, 78, 100, 100n37, 108, 110, 110n49, 112, 114, 193–97, 195n38, 197n42
Koerner, Joseph Leo, 13–14
Korff, Friedrich Wilhelm, 80n3
Koselleck, Reinhart, 17
"Kubla Khan" (Coleridge), 232–33

Lacan, Jacques, 147, 147n32
Laßberg, Christel von, 206–7
law, 14–18, 20–21, 40, 43, 51–52, 77.
    See also contract

in Agamben, 86
in Deleuze, 111
in Goethe, 46–47
in Keller, 127, 129–30, 149n33, 150–51
in Kierkegaard, 100–101, 114
in Lacan, 147, 147n32
in Stifter, 77–79, 91–98, 113–17, 119
in Storm, 165–67, 177–78, 189–90
in Vico, 170
Ledwina (Droste-Hülshoff), 28–29, 211–12
Lehmann, Christine, 41
Leiden des jungen Werther, Die (The Sufferings of Young Werther) (Goethe), 206–7
Levenson, Jon D., 196n40
Lewis, C. S., 160
liberalism, 6n6
light
    in Stifter, 80–87, 103–4, 117–19
    water and, 77–78
Lorenz, Hildegard, 166n3
love, 78, 100–101, 110, 110n49, 114
Ludwig, Otto, 3, 5–6, 9
Lukács, Georg, 4
Luke, Gospel of, 100n37
Lyon, John B., 6n6

Mann, Thomas, 92
Maria Magdalena (Hebbel), 1–2, 223
"Marina" (Eliot), 231
Marion, Jean-Luc, 138, 140
Marxism, 18
masculinity, 25, 154. *See also* patriarchy
materialism, 5–6, 32, 97
Mauss, Marcel, 20
Mein Leben (My Life) (Stifter), 120
memory
    in Keller, 157–60
    in Stifter, 110–11, 120
    in Storm, 165, 171–74, 186–87, 202–5
Menninghaus, Winfried, 123n5
Metamorphoses (Ovid), 210
Meyer, Conrad Ferdinand, 6, 76
Meysenbug, Malwida von, 30–31, 37

Millais, John Everett, 213–14, 214n12
Milton, John, 80n7
mimesis, 7, 9–10, 124, 133, 140
Mügge, Theodor, 128, 129n16

Nagel, Barbara, 31
Naturalism, 25n43. *See also* German Naturalism
Neoplatonism, 66, 82, 139n25
New Science (Vico), 170
Nicomachean Ethics (Aristotle), 227
Nietzsche, Friedrich, 22, 62–63, 228
Nightingale, Andrea, 158–60
Novalis, 27

objectivity, 7–9, 222
Oele, Marjolein, 237, 237n61
oikonomia, 17–19
Ophelia (Millais), 213–14, 214n12
Ophelia (Shakespearean character), 24, 26–27, 207–10, 212–17, 214n12, 215n13, 224, 230–31
"Ophelia" (Heym), 224
"Ophelia Complex," 220–21
"Ophélie" (Rimbaud), 216–17
Ovid, 210

Part maudite, La (The Accursed Share) (Bataille), 18–19
patriarchy, 41, 51, 54n35, 61, 68, 72. *See also* masculinity
Peau de chagrin, La (The Wild Ass's Skin) (Balzac), 220
Pfeiffer, Joachim, 11–12, 12n19, 19, 54n35, 233–34
Pfeiffer, Peter C., 133n17
Plato, 64, 88, 151, 183, 227. *See also* Neoplatonism
Plotinus, 66
Poetic Realism, 3, 3n1. *See also* German Realism
posthumanism, 237–38
postmodernity, 74n53
Preisendanz, Wolfgang, 7, 9
property, 137–38

Psyche (Storm), 168
Purgatorio (Dante), 157

Raabe, Wilhelm, 6
Raleigh, Walter, 238
realism, 4n3, 5. *See also* French Realism; German Realism
reality, 5, 7n10, 222
   in Aristotle, 101
   in Benjamin, 43
   death and, 11–12
   in Plato, 64
   as subject, 8
   in Vico, 16
Regine (Keller), 155n41
repentance, 50, 113, 183–84
revelation, 64, 80–81, 83–85
Rhetoric (Aristotle), 64n42
Richardson, Samuel, 41
Rigby, Kate, 12–13, 200
Rilke, Rainer Maria, 206, 218–19, 219n22
Rimbaud, Arthur, 216–17, 231
Roebling, Irmgard, 168
Rolland, Romain, 30, 33, 229
Romanticism, 3, 11–14, 21, 210–11
Romeo und Julia auf dem Dorfe (A Village Romeo and Juliet) (Keller), 25, 122–63, 123n5, 142n29
Rothenberg, Jürgen, 141n27

Saar, Ferdinand von, 6
"Sabbath poems" (Berry), 234–35
sacrifice, 18–24, 40, 44, 49n29, 51, 233
   of Christ, 83
   in Ebner-Eschenbach, 59–60, 68–72
   in Girard, 133
   in Goethe, 47–50
   in Keller, 124, 131–34, 138–40, 152–53, 158
   in Kierkegaard, 110n49
   in Stifter, 79, 108–10, 111n52, 112–17
   in Storm, 165–66, 188–204
Saliot, Anne-Gaëlle, 219n22

Samson Agonistes (Milton), 80n7
Santner, Eric, 18–19, 70
Savigny, Friedrich Karl von, 16, 141n28
Schiffermüller, Isolde, 104n45
Schiller, Friedrich, 7, 9–10, 24, 74
Schilling, Diana, 141n27
Schimmelreiter, Der (The Rider on the White Horse) (Storm), 165, 186–204
Schlegel, Friedrich, 21–22, 21n37
Schluter, Benjamin D., 238n62
Schmidt, Julian, 5–9, 222
Schmitt, Carl, 85–86, 91
"Schöne Jugend" ("Beautiful Youth") (Benn), 224
Schopenhauer, Arthur, 61–62, 223
Sebald, W. G., 79
"Seeing Things" (Heaney), 242
sensemaking, 11
Shakespeare, William, 24, 26, 208–10, 212–13, 231. See also Ophelia (Shakespearean character)
shipwreck, 106–7
Showalter, Elaine, 212–13, 215n13
Siddal, Elizabeth, 213–14
Smith, William Robert, 20
solar eclipse, 77, 80–90, 98, 103, 117–20
Soll und Haben (Debit and Credit) (Freytag), 25
Søndergaard, Peter Brix, 215n13
Sonnenfinsterniß am 8. Juli 1842 (The Solar Eclipse of July 8, 1842) (Stifter), 77–90, 98, 103–4, 117, 119–20
Sonnets to Orpheus (Rilke), 206
Sophocles, 239
spectatorship, 127n11
Spinoza, Baruch, 90–91, 94
Stifter, Adalbert, 2–3, 6, 25, 76–79
  Abdias, 87, 90, 96, 115, 118, 119n66
  Limestone, 99–117, 113n44
  Motley Stones, 91–96, 98, 107n47
  Solar Eclipse, 80–90, 98, 103–4, 117, 119–20

Storm, Theodor, 3, 25
  Aquis Submersus, 165, 171–86
  Rider on the White Horse, 165, 186–204
subjectivity, 8, 222
submergence, 2, 27, 236–37
  in Droste-Hülshoff, 28–29, 211
  in Ebner-Eschenbach, 54
  in Keller, 140
  liminality and, 73–74
  in Stifter, 107
  in Storm, 168, 171–85, 204
Swarbrick, Steven, 33n59, 238, 238n63
sympoiesis, 237n61

Tanzer, Ulrike, 52n33, 61n38, 68
Tertullian, 183
Thales, 227
theatricality, 127n11
Thus Spake Zarathustra (Nietzsche), 228
Tielke, Martin, 97–98
Totem and Taboo (Freud), 22, 115, 133n18
Tractatus-Theologico-Politicus (Spinoza), 90–91
transfiguration, 9, 68, 72, 211, 218
transgression, 51–60
Tylor, Edward Burnett, 20

"Über den Gebrauch des Chors in der Tragödie" (On the use of the chorus in tragedy) (Schiller), 9
Unsühnbar (Beyond Atonement) (Ebner-Eschenbach), 25, 38–42, 49–62, 54n35, 63–73, 73n52
Unwiederbringlich (Irretrievable) (Fontane), 25

Verklärung, 9, 12. See also transfiguration
Vico, Giambattista, 15–16, 15n25, 170
Vismann, Cornelia, 127n11

Wahlverwandtschaften, Die (Elective Affinities) (Goethe), 39, 42–50, 49n29, 50–51, 56–59, 64–65, 71n50, 182, 239–40
Wasserfrau, 36, 168, 211–12, 231
Waste Land, The (Eliot), 231
water, 2, 10–11, 207–8, 224–25. *See also* drowning
 in Bachelard, 220–21
 breath and, 40
 dichotomy inherent to, 106–8
 in Ebner-Eschenbach, 52–53, 55–62
 in Eliot, 231
 as feminine, 27
 gender and, 168–69
 in Goethe, 44–45, 58–59
 in Keller, 140–43, 142n29
 light and, 77–78
 memory and, 173–74
 in Shakespeare, 209
 in Storm, 165, 167–68, 173–74, 176, 181, 183, 186, 188, 197–98
 in women writers, 28–31
Weber, Max, 12, 224
Weinhold, Ulrike, 217
Wellen (Waves) (von Keyserling), 223
Wirklichkeit und Illusion (Reality and illusion) (Brinkmann), 8
women. *See also* femininity; gender
 female death and, 41
 Wasserfrau, 211–12
 water in writing of, 28–31
Works of Love (Kierkegaard), 100–101, 100n37
Wünsch, Marianne, 11–12
Wysling, Hans, 122n2

Zürcher, Hanspeter, 231n47

www.ingramcontent.com/pod-product-compliance
Lightning Source LLC
Chambersburg PA
CBHW030822230426
43667CB00008B/1331